A GUIDE TO TREASURE

IN

COLORADO

by

H. GLENN CARSON

A GUIDE TO TREASURE IN COLORADO

H. Glenn Carson

PRINTED BY CARSON ENTERPRISES

PO Box 716, Dona Ana, NM 88032

(c) 1995 by H. Glenn Carson

978-0-941620-63-5

TABLE OF CONTENTS

COUNTY   **PAGE**

TREASURE TALES AROUND THE CAMPFIRE

So you want to hear about treasures in Colorado? Well, you've come to the right place. I see some of you've brought fold-down chairs, the rest of you can pull around that old log, or use that food chest there. Glad to see you brought the ladies, or they brought you, whichever.

There's plenty to tell. Things have been lost or hidden on purpose from the Kansas line to Utah, stashed from the border into New Mexico north to where Wyoming begins. There's tales of treasures up close to Nebraska down to where if you walk a ways you'll be in Arizona.

Colorado has all sorts of treasure stories, but I want to remind you that for every such tale you listen to here there are a hundred more that never offended a human ear. Don't ever forget it, folks don't talk about good things they've found, then lost. Nor do most people talk about stashes they've put down. The things they hid were meant to stay hidden, so don't worry about ever running out of treasures still lost and hidden away.

Yes, get settled down comfortable. Pull that end of the log up closer to the fire. I see you found a good stump. One of you pass around the rest of that coffee, if you will, and then be good enough to get another pot going. No use sitting here uncomfortable. Might better put on a jacket, too. It might have been almost hot today, but these high mountain evenings cool off fast enough.

You say you're all ready? Colorado treasures? Well, let's get on with it!

ADAMS COUNTY

Many of the streams in Adams County are gold bearing. A good rule of thumb is the farther from the mountains one gets the finer the gold is and the deeper in alluvial fill it is to be found, but there is gold there.

You folks will make a mistake to think of only the mountain counties in Colorado as having treasure potentials.

ALAMOSA COUNTY

Sure, get the best metal detector you can afford. Just don't forget to use your powers of thought and observation. You can see things on the other side of a canyon, but you'll not be able to use your detector until you get over there. And there's no reason to go over there unless you see something maybe worth checking out.

During the 1920's a group of thieves robbed shops and stores from Pueblo to Denver. Their loot supposedly is hidden behind the remains of a cabin located close to the junction of Alamosa Creek and the Rio Grande River.

***

The Lost Perkins Mine may well be located on the west side of Blanca Peak. (See Costilla County).

ARAPAHOE COUNTY

A person would never need to leave Denver to have more than enough treasure hunting to last a lifetime, if that's what they wanted. It's a little town grown big, and almost everyone who ever lived in or passed through Colorado has at least visited the city. Arapahoe and all the counties around Denver have a Siamese twin relationship with the city. We'd sure have problems if we tried to build a campfire like this one is down there in the Civic Center.

In 1863 a man named B. C. Hunt bought a lot in Denver and built a house on it. He didn't stay long, for went to Idaho and made a good living. Before he left he made arrangements with a Mr. Dunn to look after his house. Dunn was to rent it out, collect the rents, maintain the place, and send Hunt the money. After a time any such money or correspondence stopped coming to Hunt.

In 1871 Hunt made a trip back to Denver to see what had happened, for Dunn had begun his duties well enough. Mr. Dunn had died and the house had been torn down. It was then Hunt remembered he'd buried a buckskin bag containing $1,200 worth of gold dust in one corner of the house.

Hunt hired a man to help him dig through the foundations of the demolished house. A buckskin bag of gold dust was soon recovered. The bag contained almost 68 Troy ounces of gold dust and was worth about $1,200 at the time.

A thorough search of the site could be productive, once the actual site is determined, and access gained. Mr. Hunt may have done so well in Idaho he forgot a few other buckskin bags of gold dust.

***

Train robbers were shot to death a short distance from a bridge crossing the South Platte River near 47th and Downing Streets in the late 1800's. They had no loot on them.

Their stolen loot was not recovered then nor for many years. In 1914 a hypnotist named Pryor enlisted the help of some people, putting them into trances to gain some spiritualistic assistance. There were three bridges, though, any one of which could be the right one. Pryor and friends managed to get into all sorts of problems without recovering a single coin.

A cloudburst roared down the South Platte River on June 15, 1963. The waters of the Platte River poured up over the banks, wrecking havoc, moving untold cubic yards of sand and debris. After the waters subsided one Ray Andis, who knew the train robbery story, recovered some old coins on the mucky shore near the Washington Street Bridge. He and treasure hunting friend, Bill DeBaca then recovered 192 Civil War era coins from that same site. One of them was an 1865 two cent piece. They sold the coins to collectors for about $500.

Others arrived and also found coins. Exactly how many isn't known. They also found parts of a wooden chest, three guns, and several old rings. These finds very well may have been from the train robbery stash. If so, there are a good many more coins in that area awaiting future recovery.

Remember, metal detectors in 1963 were not as efficient as the metal detectors in the 1990's. Some intensive searching went on in 1963, but the sum recovered at the time does not begin to add up to what those thieves took off the train.

***

Three robbers in 1960 went into a Denver cigar store more into book-making than it was cigars. The thieves took some $34,000 in currency. Bookies don't report thefts, and there was no report turned in on this robbery. Part of this was stashed nearby a churchyard in Littleton. The remaining portion of the loot was cached on Lookout Mountain to the southwest of Golden. If either cache has been recovered it has not been reported.

***

The Denver mint was robbed of $80,000 in the late 1800's. Many of those who've studied the matter believe that loot was buried within the old Denver city limits.

***

William Boegel, had he been poor, would have been considered a fool. Having considerable wealth, everyone called him an eccentric miser. Evidence points to his possibly having cached money south of Denver.

***

Four boys were playing along the banks of a tributary near its entry into the South Platte River in 1972. This is close to right-down-town. On the muddy banks they found a metal box. Opening it, they found $29,000. Elderly George H. Mahoney, often forgetful, claimed it. Others backed his claim. He had been sitting beside a tree and simply gotten up and walked away, leaving the box where he'd been sitting. The boys did get small gifts from a business-man who thought their honesty should not go unrewarded. Mahoney, when asked, could not remember if he'd even thanked the boys.

***

The year was 1870. Two brothers, carrying some $10,000 in U. S. and Spanish gold coins, were ambushed not far from Beecher Island. Both wounded, they fled more or less south in their escape attempt. One brother died. His brother buried his body, and close by buried the gold coins. He marked the site by half driving a wagon rod into the soil. Wounded, the fellow made it into Cheyenne Wells. From there he was taken on into Denver in an effort to save his life. There in a hospital, realizing he was dying, the second brother wrote explanations of where he had buried his brother and the money.

Some time later the relatives hunted for the coins. Their search took them to the Shaal homestead, which is located thirteen miles north of Burlington, and some four miles west. Old Mr. Shaal told them he had once pulled an old wagon rod from the ground. He could no longer remember the exact location. The Shaals and others have for generations searched, but a recovery has never been reported. The coins may have had a face value of $10,000 then, that gold coin stash, but it's worth far more today!

ARCHULETA COUNTY

Are there any ghost stories in amongst the Colorado treasure tales? I mean to tell you there are! Somebody else will have to tell them, though. As for tommyknockers, apparitions, moaning and groaning, and something maybe lurking further down one dark drift or another, let's leave that to discuss around some other campfire.

Come to think about it, throw on a couple more logs. Pass me that coffee pot! I don't think ghosts care much for caffiene.

In the Wolf Creek Pass area of Archuleta County is the so-called Treasure Mountain. This mountain is to the south of the top of Wolf Creek Pass. The story need not be retold completely here, but sometime between 1770 and 1790 a Frenchman named Remi Ledoux took a group of approximately three hundred men on a mining expedition. The group was well-rounded. There were mechanics, skilled miners, geologists capable of doing smelting and other metallurgical work, and soldiers to defend the expedition. With four hundred fifty or so horses, the most modern mining equipment available at the time, they set out from a French outpost very near where Leavenworth, Kansas is today. Theirs is an epic tale.

The story is as sound as most treasure tales. Old French documents are said to verify the basic tale. Many of the various places and objects at the core of the story have been discovered. It all may have happened over two hundred years ago, and much is no longer known or understood, but much of it actually happened.

The large party worked down the South Platte River, small groups exploring as they went for good gold. They found some at what would become Cripple Creek and Summitville, and in other spots, but never in the amounts they desired. Not until they worked their way onto Treasure Mountain.

The group worked the area centered about four miles south of Wolf Creek Pass Summit for three years and recovered several tons of gold dust and nuggets. Much of this they smelted, casting ingots. There was plenty of game to supplement their provisions. They accumulated an amount of gold worth at the time from five to thirty-three million dollars in value, this dependant upon which version of the tale one reads.

Indian and Spanish interference forced them to shut down their operations. During the time before they finally decided they must leave, they carefully hid their gold. To keep track of the cache sites they blazed trees, made maps of their cache sites, and erected stone cairns as markers.

The group made certain their would be no easy, accidental recovery of their gold. They dug a 32 foot shaft, from which they ran several side tunnels. All this they lined with fitted rocks. Within these workings they stashed their gold. On the low side, at today's prices, there should be more than $100,000,000 worth of the yellow stuff.

The chamber was sealed and carefully buried and concealed. They placed markings on rocks and trees for five miles around, V's pointing to the shaft.

Indians had been friendly for a time, but towards the end were making life difficult. This may have been encouraged by the Spaniards, resentful of the French being in Spanish lands. It became obvious the group had remained in the region for too long. One at a time, in small groups, the party was cut down. Supplies ran out. It was no longer safe to hunt game because the Indians were a constant menace.

At least one report states that only seventeen members of the group at last got out of the mountains alive. The survivors fled, but the hardships continued. Somewhere along the Arkansas River they suffered another major Indian attack. It sounds as though after that battle there were only five men left. The endless miles were hard enough. There was little to eat, their footwear and clothing wore out. There is a story of at last suffering such huger the men drew lots, and the loser was eaten so the others could go on. According to some accounts only three ever reached the outpost near Leavenworth. It may be that only Lebreau ever got there, and it is certain only he ever got back to France. Terror, starvation, wounds, perhaps cannibalism, and unending long miles took a heavy toll.

Lebreau did bring back to France an oilskin packet containing maps, lists of the cached treasure, and other important notations. He gave a copy of this to both his family and the government who'd sent the group on the expedition.

France at that time had plenty of other problems to take care of. Napoleon was in charge and Europe was embroiled in war. A second expedition to recover the stashed gold was something to put off for the time, which was done.

In 1844 such an expedition, of some fifty men, was at last sent out under the leadership of a man named LeBlanc. According to Don Archuleta, land and cattle owner in Archuleta County, this group of frenchmen was guided into the area by one elderly Taos Mexican, Bernardo Sanchez.

This group was in the area for three years. Sanchez packed in supplies for them, but he swore there was never anything packed out. To haul what the original group had stashed would require at least six hundred mules, probably more. That sort of thing could scarcely happen without being noticed.

The second group was eventually attacked and entirely wiped out by Indians.

Bernardo Sanchez was the only survivor, and he returned to Taos. There were many who wondered how Sanchez alone survived.

One of the Frenchmen had told Sanchez a clue. A grave-like mound had been erected by the original group. If one stood on it on a September morning their shadow would fall upon where the buried gold lay buried. Sanchez and Don Archuleta both searched for the mound, but they never found it.

The loot is still there. For those who'd care to look, that shaft is some three or four miles from the top of Wolf Creek Pass in the direction of Summitville. The sealed shaft likely sits on the line between Mineral and Rio Grande Counties.

The grandson of Ledoux headed up a search for the cache in 1884. He found many clues but did not find the gold. His attempts seemed doomed from the start and he eventually was drowned in the San Juan River. No maps or records were found upon his body. He did, however, leave copies with a frenchman. This man for some reason gave the papers to an Archuleta County rancher, William Yule.

Others have looked over the years, many of them. In 1975 a group of treasure hunters found shreds of buckskin clothing, worn old mining tools, and some guns. Several of the workings have been found, but that rock-lined shaft and its gold-filled side tunnels is probably right where the Frenchmen left it.

Traces of very old mines have been found above Pagosa Springs. This is up from the Montroy Ranch, southeasterly from the Wolf Creek Summit, in the area where Ledoux and his ill-fated group hid their gold so well.

In the late 1870's one Asa Poor discovered a grave on Treasure Mountain, and felt that it possibly was that important marker for the Ledoux cache. It was empty, but Poor and Yule figured is was only put there as a marker. They believed they had the important clues to possibly find the treasure shaft. So great was their confidence they'd find the treasure they destroyed every marking they could find.

Their enthusiasm gradually died away. Look though they would, they could not find the filled-in shaft.

Asa Poor several years later hired men to do some digging. They did find several walled-shafts. Empty.

The Archuleta family spent $50,000 in a vain effort to locate the treasure, but found nothing.

Montroy, one of Poor's partners, had a copy of the map. It disappeared just after his death.

***

Look near the point where the Stollsteimer Creek runs into the Piedra River, southwest some five miles from the town of Chimney Rock. Five men, perhaps miners, perhaps thieves, returning from the California gold fields were killed by Utes there in the 1851 or 1852. Five of their seven mules were each loaded with two sacks of gold bullion, a total of 650 to 700 pounds of gold. How they obtained this is not known. It probably was not gained honestly, and that may have been their reason for traveling a little used route through hostile Indian lands.

How and where they got the gold, who they were, why they chose that particular route, these things may never be known. The fact was, they camped late one afternoon on the banks of the Piedra River, close to where it is joined by Stoltsteimer Creek. They needed to rest and eat a supper that turned out to be the last meal of all but one of them.

The passing group had accidentally ridden into a small Ute camp earlier that same day. Their sudden appearance, strange bearded white men, frightened the women and children into fleeing and hiding in the nearby woods. The men were hungry, so two of them took some food from the campsite. That was said by both the Utes and the sole survivor of what then took place. The taking of the food could have forgiven, according to old Utes long after the incident, but as the bearded white men rode out of camp, one of the teepees was knocked down by a horse. Shortly after the white men rode off the teepee was ignited by coals in the firepit and everything in camp went up in flames . The Utes had no idea it was accidental, they only thought this was a

-11-

mean, hateful thing for the bearded strangers to do.

An old Ute later related to Mexican friends a tale of what happened once the Indian men came back to camp. The Utes were not on speaking terms with any white people but did have many friends among the Mexican people. They never made friends with more than a handful of whites, and that was not until well after the turn of the century. They deeply resented being driven from their beautiful mountain lands, and who can blame them?

The story was therefore well known among the Mexican people, but there was little communication in the days before and after the turn of the century between the Anglo and Mexican peoples. Thus the story was unknown among white settlers.

The Indians, angry that strangers would act in such a mean way, attacked the traveling miners the following morning while they were still half asleep. Leaping from a nearby ravine, they killed four of the five men within a minute or two. The fifth man, who had no beard like the other four, was already up that morning. He had been rounding up the horses, and thus managed to escape. The Indians wanted to capture the horses far more than they wanted to chase the bare-faced man trying to get away.

After killing the white men, and securing their valued horses, the Indians dumped the six or seven hundred pounds of gold bullion carried by the mules beneath an overhanging bank in a narrow gulley. They then kicked the bank down upon it. The gold was in ten leather bags. The Utes well knew that the next rains would completely cover the sacks of gold.

One old Ute, who was only a young boy at the time, but who was there when the teepee was burned, gave as good directions as exist, to Mexican friends. He was called Old Washington, and the tough old man lived to be about 100 years of age. He died about the time the First World War was going on.

He would give no better directions, even to his Mexican friends, than the narrow ravine into which the sacks of gold were dropped was very close to where the Stolsteimer runs into the Piedra. He knew it was still where the warriors put it, undisturbed, because every once in a while he would go by just to check.

It was during the year of 1890, give or take a year either way, when a beardless man in his early sixties visited for a time one summer with a family named Cooper. His name seemed to be Carven, or something close to that. The Coopers were then farming land in the Pine River Valley, near Bayfield.

This Carven, it turns out, was the only survivor of a group passing through the area about forty years earlier. He was the beardless man the Utes had allowed to escape because they would rather round up his horses. Carven had never in his life had any facial hair. As he helped around the farm that summer his story came out.

He would never tell Cooper how he and his partners got that much gold, but he at last admitted he was only in the area to attempt to find it.

Carven did some looking by himself. He and Cooper eventually did go together to the site, and the two of them without knowing it may have stood within a short distance of where the gold lay buried. Carven noticed the prominent Chimney Rocks. They easily could be seen from that open stretch along the river. He told Cooper the rocks were one landmark he clearly remembered. He also thought he was on the camping place along the river, or awfully close to it. Everything looked right. After a time Carven left the area, and never returned.

It was ten or fifteen years after Carven's departure before this beardless man's story and the stories told by Indians to the Mexican people were compared. Suddenly there was what seemed to be a very real treasure in the area. But by then all the old Utes who knew where the gold was buried were gone, Carven was gone, and only the buried gold remained.

***

Of course there's another set of directions for the same story. This directs one to look from where Highway 160 crosses the Ignacios. About half a mile from the highway, along Stollstiemer Creek, then up Beaver Creek and down Yellowjacket Creek to the Piedra River. Trouble is, we know nothing much about the five miners' side of the story.

Many have looked for this gold, and if you do so you will probably encounter some more directions, possibly even more confusing than these. When that happens the search area begins to enlarge. The fact is, stream action could have either washed out that stash one or more times or buried it even deeper.

***

A treasure hunter in the mid 1970's recovered a ten ounce bar of gold and some very old items far downslope from Treasure Mountain. These items were in a ravine, in a stream at the base of some extremely steep cliffs.

***

In the 1920's a Mexican sheepherder came across a stone cross near Weminuche Creek somewhere above where it flows into the Piedra River. Nearby he found a cache of gold nuggets. The man obliterated the stone cross and hurried back to Mexico. Every few years after that he returned for more gold. He tied his horse to a tree and would be gone from that point for less than two hours, or so it was reported. The spot where the horse was reportedly tethered was very near to where Hossick Creek enters the Wemenuchi Creek, on the Hossick Creek Trail. Some time in the 1930's the Mexican stopped coming. Perhaps there was no more gold, perhaps he got sick or died, or simply got too old. Perhaps somewhere above that stream juncture there are still some rotted sacks of gold nuggets.

***

Some time in 1978 a bulldozer operator, hired by a mining company to do some road repair, bladed out a boulder. Through the center of the boulder ran a streak of buttery gold, obvious enough to get him down off the bulldozer and shove him into national attention. He reported it to the company, eventually they gave him about $50,000, then donated the specimen to the Denver Museum of Natural History. It is now on display there. It is worth noting the spot where the boulder was found is not far and downhill from where the Frenchmen were working. There has been some looking, for there probably was not just that single boulder. No other finds have been reported, but that should not keep others from looking.

Tabasco, or what's left of it, is one of the many coal camps to be found in Las Animas County, to the north of Trinidad.

BENT COUNTY

Go to the little towns across the High Plains of Colorado, talk with the folks who have lived there all their lives. You'll get treasure stories that have never appeared in the magazines and books, more than you ever thought. Most of them will be related to ranching, farming, freighting, and almost anything other than mining, but you bet there's treasures in those flatlands.

Notorious Clay Allison held up the Las Animas bank and fled with $52,811 in gold and silver coins. A posse pursued and after a time caught Clay. He did not have the money and he would not say a word as to where he'd hidden it. While later attempting to escape, the bandit broke his neck. The money, unless the posse recovered the money and broke the outlaw's neck, is cached not far from Las Animas.

***

In 1936 some treasure hunters recovered some Spanish armor in the sand hills south of Las Animas.

***

Not many miles from Las Animas, some twelve miles from Old Bent's Fort, a great cache of treasure is supposedly concealed in the sandstone cliffs along the Purgatoire River. Supposedly it is of Spanish origin, and its source was the mountains to the west and northwest of that area.

***

There seems to be some possibility the $200,000 stolen from Bent's Fort was buried in the Las Animas area. Perhaps, but the other theories are at least as credible.

BOULDER COUNTY

Some of the best things you'll run into while seeking treasure have no dollar value, they're beyond financial measurement. How could one economically evaluate walking into a meadow covered with wild iris in full bloom? Is there a dollar value to rolling out a sleeping bag on a bed of pine needles and trying to count crystal-point stars? Is it worth so many nickels and dimes to at last reach the top of a rise only to discover it wasn't even close to the top of the mountain? If so, how many dollars is it worth to go on to the top?

Nope, there's no possible price tag on the first little nugget in the bottom of a youngster's gold pan! That's as true even for an eighty-nine year old youngster, and probably for his older brother, too.

In 1966 a sixteen year old boy found three rolls of gold coins, all carefully rolled in paper from dynamite cartons. There were 175 $20 gold pieces in all, most of them in uncirculated condition, dated from 1880 to 1926. The stash was deep in a pile of rocks near Overland Pass, not far to the northwest of Jamestown. If other rolls were recovered from the same spot it was never reported. Plenty of looking went on for several years after that.

***

One miner's wife made each of her three children a necklace of small gold nuggets. The nuggets she took from chicken gizzards over the years. Their home was at the west end of Jamestown, and the chickens roosted in the barn behind the house. Several gullies come down the steep slopes nearby. The free-running chickens evidently picked up the nuggets with the gravel all barnyard chickens consume for their gizzards. The woman realized that, and carefully examined every gizzard for years, slowly accumulating those nuggets for her three necklaces. This was a long time before detectors capable of pinpointing nuggets came along. You'd probably do better with a good detector these days than you would with a flock of chickens!

(Story told to author by the late Al McGowan, life-long miner and milling man.)

***

In 1968 another cache of 175 $20 gold pieces wrapped in old dynamite paper was recovered near Jamestown, less than five miles from the earlier recovery near Overland Pass. One source claims the second cache was within one mile of the first.

To make 1968 even more interesting for Jamestown area residents a second gold coin cache was recovered that year. It was the third such find in the Jamestown area. The same number of coins were in this second find, but not any details of where it was found have been given.

***

Ben Leeper was a notorious outlaw, pulling off many robberies in Colorado. He is supposed to have buried his loot in various caches between Eldora and Denver. A few recoveries found in Ward and Nederland have been attributed to Ben Leeper. A very nice stash of old coins was found in the walls of a ward house while it was being fixed up.

***

Several caches of raw gold are known to have been hidden along a stream in the Jamestown area during the 1930's. A cache worth a few hundred dollars in those hard years is considerably more valuable now.

***

Happy Houlihan was the town drunk in Wall Street, to the west of Boulder. It surprised those who knew him when he came into one of his favorite drinking places with a nice bit of gold, about $700 worth. He boasted he'd found a deposit of extremely rich gold ore not far from Wall Street. For once Happy Houlihan could buy a round of drinks for his friends

The very next day Happy Houlihan was gone. Nobody knew where he went, and that irritated some of them, for they had big plans for his gold strike.

Later it was learned he'd gone to San Francisco, California, where he showed his nuggets in bars, caging drinks by telling of his rich gold mine in Colorado. Happy died shortly of acute alcoholism in a California mission, rambling on in his terminal deliriums about his glorious Colorado mine. People have looked, but his discovery has never again been located.

Some scoff at the tale, and believe that poor old Wallstreet drunk found and recovered a highgrader's cache.

***

A cattle dealer put down a substantial cache of gold coins not far to the north of the entrance to Left Hand Canyon just west of the highway between Boulder and Lyons. The man lived his later years in Boulder and often

-17-

took his horse and buggy to near the site in the morning, looked over the area for a time, then drove back to Boulder.

(From conversations of author with local residents.)

***

Near Jamestown the Golden Age, one of the best gold producers in the county, was found by Indian Jack and a fellow named Frank Smith. They were bamboozled out of the claim for $50 dollars and a barrel of whiskey, or so one story goes. Once sober, Indian Jack was understandably angry. He left Jamestown for a time, vowing never again to tell any white man anything. Some time later he returned, flaunting some extremely fine gold ore. It was entirely different from the Golden Age ore. He kept his word, never telling anyone where the ore came from. He did tell one friend the ledge was atop a ridge between The Golden Age and Red Dirt Hill.

***

The old wagon road up Boulder Can- yon was steep, crossed the stream more than twenty times, and was an ordeal for those who traveled it. There were in those hard, early years a half-way house midway between Boulder and Nederland. In the late 1960's or early 1970's a Boulder treasure hunter recovered almost a dozen various gold coins from what had been the foundations of that halfway house. I don't believe this has been reported elsewhere, and one cannot but wonder how many coins may have been missed by a weaker early metal detector. A picnic site has been developed atop the footings of the place that once took care of hungry wagon drivers' needs.

(From personal observations and conversations with the man who found the coins.)

***

Waxy horn silver was found by Sam Conger in the Kiowa Peak area more than two miles northwest of the Caribou town site. It was a very high-quality native silver. The Indians had long credited "Storm Mountain", which is Kiowa Peak, as concealing a very rich silver lode. A great amount of silver was mined in the Caribou area, but none of it was ever mined on Kiowa Peak.

***

Outside Louisville a treasure hunter recovered from an outhouse pit a collapsible silver drinking cup. Within the cup was a wedding band, and engagement ring, half a dozen Louisville saloon tokens, and several coins all dated back near the turn of the century.

(From author's conversation with man who found these things.)

***

There is scarcely anything left of the booming silver camp, Caribou, uphill to the west of Nederland. One of the old timers there is quoted as saying, "Summer's almost here. Geez, I hope both days is nice!"

Noland is a good example of Colorado resources other than gold and silver. The town, just uphill to the northeast from Lyons, boomed around the turn of the century. The extensive formation produced many tons of fine red Lyons sandstone. Noland became a ghost town soon after cheaper Portland cement was perfected, alowing poured concrete sidewalks and foundations to replace the attractive, durable, but more expensive sandstone.

Al Capone summered for several years in a secluded home just west of the town of Lyons, to the north of Boulder. There are rumors of his stashing some money in that area.

CHAFFEE COUNTY

You say lots of these treasure stories are legendary? That is the truth. It's especially true with tales dealing with the Spanish times. One hears that this tale or that is documented, but the documentation is in Santa Fe, or Mexico somewhere, or back in Spain. Legendary or not, the bits and pieces of Spanish manufacture have been found in some of these sites. If what is left of an old arrastre is there in the creek, right where it is said the Spaniards recovered gold, it is hard to say nothing happened and the story is just made up. Who knows where the truth ends and pure fabrication begins?

A donkey skin filled with gold dust is said to have been buried atop Round Hill. A miner buried it there, concerned about Indians and weather, who knows in what order. If the man did cache it there, and never came back for it as the story claims, the site is ten miles south of Poncha Springs, two miles from the summit of Poncha Pass. It has been looked for, but there has never been a report the gold was found.

Another story concerning Round Mountain involves a group of miners, not just one individual. They had accumulated a large amount of gold. The group was attacked by Indians. Two were killed early in the fight, the other two made it to the top of Round Hill. They threw up some hasty fortifications, and somehow buried the gold while holding off the Indians as best they could. Their best wasn't good enough. Another man was killed. The survivor made it to Denver but died shortly after arriving there. He told his friends what happened, and the story came out in an 1877 Rocky Mountain News. The fortifications have been found, but not the gold.

The fact is, the Indians could have buried it elsewhere and at some distance from Round Mountain, which would certainly have helped make it harder to find.

Juan de Onate, according to legend, brought people into the Poncha Springs area in the late 1500's. This group was supposed to have done a great amount of mining and placering. Various evidences of very old mining efforts have been found. A number of treasure stories in this area are connected with this.

One such widespread tale is that of a cache of golden ornaments stolen from Indians. The loot is said to have been hurriedly buried somewhere in a cave or crevice of the Chalk Cliffs downstream from the site of Saint Elmo. The Indians were pursuing the Spaniards and killed most if not all of them.

***

You may or may not find those golden trinkets, but there is semi- precious aquamarine to be found in and around Chalk Creek Canyon. Much of this excellent gemstone has been recovered high on Mt. Antero.

***

Newett was a quarry town and a railroad stop near the top of Trout Creek Pass in South Park. Reports of several caches being found there have been made. These seem to have been loot secreted away by highwaymen.

***

In July of 1968, while clearing away debris on the Monarch Pass Ski Resort property, a bulldozer operator and the fellows working with him discovered an old natural cave and gold mine. This is very near the old mining town of Garfield on the eastern side of Monarch Pass. Workers and the owner, Elmo Bevington, could hear what they took to be the roar of an underground river. The treacherous condition of the cave walls prevented much exploration. They did feel they were at the mouth of a vast series of caverns.

That goes along with 1880's legends of "a hollow mountain" in that area where the gold of centuries had accumulated. Conjecture has it that these caverns may be part of the fabulous Isherwood-Esther gold lode, located in 1885.

If there is an underground stream there, it could be tributary to either the north or middle fork of the Arkansas River.

***

A few prospectors coming back from Gunnison country in 1860 paused to prospect about three and a half miles down stream from where the town of Granite now sits. The oft-told tale of their lost source of gold is how Lost Canyon got its name. After minimal prospecting they began coming up with nuggets "the size of hens' eggs".

Before the winter weather forced them to leave, and in only a very few weeks, they had recovered enough $17 an ounce gold to have some $60,000.

When spring came to that canyon so did those prospectors, eager to go right back to what they had been doing until the snows drove them out. They found some gold, but most of it wasn't even pea size let alone as big as hens' eggs. They looked, to no avail, then at last went on to do other things elsewhere.

Twenty years passed before others came, found gold, and did some heavy placering. No more egg-sized nuggets, but a substantial total amount of gold recovery.

***

One modern day prospector, using no more than a gold pan, is said to have taken about twenty pounds in dust and nuggets from the stream between the ghost sites of Romley and Hancock. This is upstream from Saint Elmo.

***

Saint Elmo, by the way, was a rowdy town with over a thousand inhabitants during the 1880's. Dance halls and houses of ill repute ripped and roared. Often called Forrest City, some sixteen miles west of Nathrop, this was one wild place for a decade or so.

St. Elmo is upstream from the Chalk Cliffs, downstream from Hancock and Bromley. Tourists have replaced the miners years ago. The old buildings have remained fairly intact under private ownership.

CLEAR CREEK COUNTY

In the years between 1859 and 1939 the area surrounding Georgetown and Silver Plume produced more than $90,000, 000 in gold and silver. Not all that vast sum went into the legitimate banking system. Georgetown boasts of being the only major Southwestern mining town not to ever be gutted by fire, and both Georgetown and Silver Plume retain much of their original looks. Cache potentials are substantial in this area, and there were good ore veins discovered and lost. Some likely were never discovered in the first place, and await some persistent, lucky person's close attention.

There's a persistent story in Georgetown about a hidden bank vault beneath where the first bank in Clear Creek County once stood. This is at the corner of Fourth and Rose Streets. The bank was established by George T. Clark and Company, and conducted business in Georgetown's busy mining era.

Runs on banks were common enough in those days, and this bank suffered one in the 1870's. A wagon loaded with gold bullion was escorted from Central City to the bank in Georgetown. The gold was unloaded and taken in through the front door, and probably down into the secret vault most banks had for greater security in those violent times. The run was over, and the bank went on about its business.

When the bank's glory days were over it went out of business. One Edward Riley purchased the property.

In 1912 a large sink hole developed directly behind where the bank building once stood. It immediately became known around town the old secret vault was caving in. It had been built of timbers, but years in the moist soil had rotted them away, and the heavy overburden of rocks and soil broke through.

Riley at once fenced off the area. He investigated, but said never a word of what he found to the good people of Georgetown, their burning curiousity be hanged. What a marvelous way to fuel rumors and tall tales. Indeed, more than dust sometimes is to be found in long-sealed, forgotten places such as old vaults. Many valuable, sometimes sinister, and forgotten things have turned up in long-sealed Colorado banks.

$250,000 in gold bars, more at today's gold prices, was buried in the Georgetown area. Could those have been part of what was in the old vault, or was it hidden away elsewhere?

Riley kept whatever he discovered, and for that matter what he may have done with it, to himself.

The story has not diminished over the years.

***

One Gabe Espinoza buried some of his wealth on or very near Mount Evans. He was shot in a duel and his treasure has not been found.

***

In the Idaho Springs area, somewhere, is hidden what is known as the Quito Treasure. This was some $500,000 in gold coins.

***

Recently a rich silver vein was discovered near Silver Plume. Mining had fairly well ended around the small town some three miles to the southwest of Georgetown by 1900, but this ore was assayed as high as $6,000 to the ton. Even should a mine be opened there likely will not ever again be the population in Silver Plume of 2,200, as there was in the peak year of 1880.

***

Douglas McLean was diagnosed as having tuberculosis and was not expected to live long. McLean was an electrician, he also founded the Firemen's Fund Life Insurance Company. He had plenty of money, he just did not have long to live unless he moved to a higher, drier climate. He was advised in 1893 to immediately go to Colorado, perhaps that would improve his deteriorating condition and give him a longer lease on life.

Douglas spent two years in bed, but by the summer and fall of 1895, in the cool, high, dry air, he began to improve. He began to go for walks. Short, at first, then more and more active. He was recovering from his almost terminal condition and was at last able to do light work on his Doctor Bancroft's Evergreen ranch.

In 1895 Douglas McLean found and lost a vein of pink quartz laced with $1,000 worth of gold to the ton (those day's prices). It was unusually attractive ore, or he'd not have picked it up.

He was out rabbit hunting one fall day, leaving the ranch about ten in the morning, hiking on what then was called Mt. Strain, on the side facing Hicks Mountain. Mt. Strain is now Mt. Bergen. He became confused, actually got somewhat lost, wadering until nine o'clock that evening. He had to stop often to catch his breath, and while pausing in a gulch at the base of a high dirt bank he saw a ledge of pink quartz about a foot and a half wide. Darkness was falling and it had begun to snow. Douglas McLean was too worried to pay all that much attention to the ore or to the location of where he found it. Fighting snow and gathering darkness he at last stumbled downstream and found himself at the Witter Ranch. Only then did Douglas examine the specimens he'd taken and see they were loaded with gold.

The storm worsened, so there was no way to try to backtrack to where he found the exposed ledge. Douglas therefore took a stage into Denver where he showed the ore to his doctor. Doctor Bancroft had some of the ore assayed, gave Douglas some blank location notices, and even loaned him a pony. That did little good, because the snowstorms had worsened. McLean had no way of returning to the site of his discovery. He would have to wait for spring.

Spring did come, at last. In the summers of 1896 and 1897 Douglas McLean looked long and hard, walking over the entire flanks of the mountain. He could not find the exposed ledge. He reached the conclusion the earthen bank had caved in upon the ledge. He and others realized he could have been farther around the mountain than he thought, lost and confused as he was.

The ledge was in a high, overhanging earthen bank deep in a stand of thick timber on the Hicks Mountain side of Mount Bergen. McLean forever insisted he found the pink quartz on either Witter Creek or on the stream coming into Bear Creek below Witter Creek. Old timers have pointed out he could have also been on Mount Strain if he was paying more attention to rabbits than he was directions. Want to go rabbit hunting? That rose quartz would at least be $20,000 ore these days.

***

There was another rich discovery near timberline on Mt. Evans, around the turn of the century. A young prospector made the discovery as the first snows began to fall. A blizzard caught him before he made it to the foot of the mountain. He got lost, he nearly froze to death, and he became sick.

He at last stumbled into a woodcutter's cabin. The young man feverishly rambled on about his find to the woodcutter. He soon died. The samples he carried were visibly gold-rich. Numbers of people have searched hard for this deposit, more especially around timberline, but it has never been relocated.

Lamartine sits almost atop the hill between Georgetown and Idaho Springs. Three small high grade gold ore caches have been recovered from this area.

CONEJOS COUNTY

You go ahead and drink that cold pop. I'll just finish up the dab left in this pot of coffee, and get some more started. Can't tell treasure stories without coffee!

There was a La Jara gang of outlaws in and out of Conejos County for a time. They cached an accumulation of gold, jewelry, and gemstones in several places. Ten miles east of the upper end of Navajo Lake on the San Juan River. On the headwaters of La Jara Wash. Atop the La Jara Mesa.

***

Somewhere along La Jara Creek is said to be the Hidden Valley Lost Mine.

***

One Josh Thomas is said to have buried treasure on Conejos Creek.

***

A possible search site for one of the Aztec chief Montezuma's huge caches is in the area around Antonio.

***

In Cortez Valley, also known as Hidden Valley, the Spaniards are said to have worked a rich Indian gold mine. This was very near today's New Mexico Colorado line. Great numbers of Indians attacked and killed the Spaniards, and the site has never been located.

***

Two miners were successfully working a deposit somewhere on Mogate Peak. While celebrating in Taos, using some of their gold, the two men were murdered and robbed. Their rich location has never been found.

***

In 1881 a Negro robbed a stage near Conejos. There was too much treasure for him to get away from the posse, and the man buried part of the loot along the Conejos River. This helped briefly, but his horse was nearly exhausted. The posse was approaching. The robber cached the remainder of his loot and tried to flee. No such luck. He spent many years in prison, and it is believed he was too old to return to the cache sites after he got out. Some years later gold coins and several gold ingots were washed from their hiding place. The recovery was made very near the Conejos River. The rest of the loot has not been recovered as far as anyone knows.

COSTILLA COUNTY

You have to give the Spaniards a lot of credit for being a hardy, brave lot! Costilla County was settled before the United States was a country. Different small groups of Spaniards were exploring the mountains of Colorado, mostly looking for gold. It was a raw, dangerous place, and even when they found gold can we even imagine the problems they faced in getting it back to Mexico? There's many a story of some of it still being here in Colorado.

Near the town of Blanca, somewhere on or near Blanca Peak, there is reported to be a cache of gold coins.

***

In the Culebra Range of the Sangre de Cristos, west of Trinidad, is said to be the Scarlet Shadow Treasure. A cave somewhere in those steep mountains is said to be paved with gold dust and nuggets.

***

In 1860 Juan Carlos came to the San Luis Valley from Taos. He was a wealthy don, surrounding himself with the finest trappings. There was a miserly stinginess to the man beyond his own self- indulged image. He was always Don Carlos to those about him, never just Senor. There was a mystery surrounding the man, which was not eased by his secretive ways. For one thing, he paid all his bills with gold dust.

To the north of Alamosa, at the foot of Mt. Blanca he built a fine home and furnished it elegantly. All bills were paid with gold dust in full. His mysterious ways drove all who knew him wild. For three years he disappeared in May and was not seen again each year until the end of October. When some braver souls attempted to follow him the fourth year Don Carlos simply returned to his home. He did not go that year nor any year thereafter.

Juan Carlos was a hermit, but one with enough money to have his servant get out to transact his business. He kept absolutely to himself until in 1868. In that year he had a number of adobe houses constructed on the shore of the San Luis Lakes. Again, all bills were paid in full with gold dust. He not only paid his workers, he threatened them if they ever came around those houses again. Two men he retained, two of the least intelligent, it is pointed out. The two men worked for Juan Carlos for a short time, then they disappeared. They were there, then they were not.

The families of the men got no answers from Juan Carlos, nor did anyone else in the area. He suggested that Indians may have done something to the missing men. Nobody believed him, but that is the only answer they got.

Colonel Head, who became Colorado's first lieutenant governor, was as close to being a friend as Juan Carlos seemed to have. That friendship ended when Head married a lovely Mexican girl with whom Juan Carlos was infatuated.

As the eccentric old hermit lay dying he is said to have penned a confession and a will to a priest. His long time, faithful servant was murdered on the way to deliver that letter. It seems less than coincidence that two Mexican men showed signs of sudden wealth somewhat less than a year after that. They said they had earned their money in Santa Fe, and nobody was able to prove otherwise.

The death of Don Carlos was not long after the construction of those adobe houses. Most treasure hunters believe the last adobe structures are not where Don Carlos may have cached his gold. It turns up he had a rich placer operation in the Summitville area, and it is likely his caches were near his workings. Another location is twenty miles or so to the northeast of his San Luis houses. Another obvious question comes to this author's mind: What about Mt. Blanca, so near his fine home?

***

A young army deserter brought some excellent nuggets into the hunting camp of William Perkins in the 1870's. Perkins was on a hunting trip with a friend, high on Sierra Blanca Peak. The young man told Parker he'd found the nuggets on the other side of the peak. He had climbed up the mountain to better throw anyone off his trail should they be following him and had found the placer deposit entirely by accident.

Perkins and his friend didn't let the dust the young man left behind settle before they headed around the mountain to see what the young fugitive had found.

They didn't find the spot. Parker searched long and often, as have others, but the deposit has never been found.

***

The Spaniards were supposed to have had a very rich gold mine close to the New Mexico line in the 1870's. The miners were either called back to Mexico or were killed, but for whatever reason they sealed shut the mine and never returned. One speculation is that the mine is west of Tercio, southwest of Trinidad, somewhere on or near Culebra Peak.

***

A store of vast wealth is said to be covered by a landslide in the Sangre de Cristos. A waybill was discovered in a falling-down old shack. The direction in the waybill are to go to the northeast of San Pedra until one sees the stone profile of an old Indian chief close by an outhrust precipice. One then is to go fifty paces to the north of the stone face, turn east and go up- slope for another fifty paces (pacing uphill is a tough proposition in case you've never tried to do so). However, at this point is a steep cliff running along the canyon, east to west. Half way up the cliff the treasure is buried.

***

Josiah Greg reported a rich gold placer in 1844. His directions lead to the area of the southern Sangre de Cristos about nine miles north of Blanca. He could not work the placer at the time because its exposed location would have left him open to Indian attack. He could not find the spot when he came back to work it later.

***

An army paymaster's wagon was attacked one spring by outlaws at Gray Back Gulch. Some say this happened in 1866 or 1867. Others say, no, it happened sometime between 1881 and 1883. The wagon was going down the steep grade into Trinchera Creek. A payroll was brought north to Fort Garland from Fort Union twice each year, and as was the custom was being escorted by four well- armed mounted troopers. The wagon had been dispatched from Fort Union, New Mexico, to Fort Garland, carrying an iron-bound chest containing a $17,000 bi-annual payroll for the Fort Garland soldiers.

The story persists, unfortunately records for that time and place are simply missing. Fort Garland started out as Fort Massachusetts. It was built near Ute Creek, at the foot of Mount Blanco. The location was in a horrible location defensively, one of the poorest choices possible.

The fort was moved in 1858 from its original setting to where the Ft. Garland Museum sits today. The original location enabled Indians to fire at will directly down upon the fort from surrounding hillsides. It at that time was renamed Fort Garland, in honor of Bvt. Brig. General John Garland, then commander of the Military District of New Mexico.

Two hundred troops were stationed there at first. It reached a peak occupation about 1880-81 of almost 1,500. That was three years before the fort was abandoned due to near cessation of Indian hostilities.

The incidents that created this tale could have happened almost any time in between 1858 until 1883. It is most likely it took place in the last four year period of the fort's occupancy. Otherwise it would have been Indians raiding the payroll wagon, not bandits. The Utes had no more use for bandits than they had for the U. S. Army.

It must have been a bloody scene. The outlaws fired at both the wagon and the troopers, severely wounding the paymaster and killing three of the four troopers. The wounded paymaster fell into the back of the wagon as the driver whipped the team into a frantic run for Fort Garland. As they bounced across Trinchera Creek the wounded paymaster somehow managed to heave the iron chest from the wagon into a deep hole where he had often fished. The man died when the wagon arrived at Fort Garland, only managing to gasp out he'd hurled the heavy chest into his favorite fishing hole.

Soldiers promptly headed for Trinchera Creek. They saw that the wounded fourth trooper stood off the bandits long enough to allow the wagon to get away.

They searched for the chest. The problem was there was a good deal of confusion as to which spot was the paymaster's favorite fishing hole. It could have been any one of dozens. They could not find the iron-bound chest, nor have others ever found it since.

Yes, the outlaws may have had time to recover it, in spite of the one trooper's futile defense. The soldiers may have found it and not told the truth, or someone else could have recovered it since. Or it may be covered deep by rocks and gravel in the bottom of that paymaster's favorite now filled- in old fishing hole.

***

In 1870 a sheep rancher located between Walsenburg and Fort Garland sold a large band of sheep. He cached the proceeds of the sale. He later was kidnapped by thieves, who tortured him to force him to tell the location of the cache. The robbers were too hasty, too clumsy in their efforts, and they killed the man when he would not tell them where he'd hidden the money. His sheep sale proceeds are still well hidden in that immediate area.

CUSTER COUNTY

Here, dice up some of these onions into the potatoes. No good without onions. Yes, right into that big skillet, we have to have enough to feed all us hungry yahoos. Can't tell treasure tales on an empty stomach, and sure can't listen to them, either. Little more black pepper, if you will. I wish we had a green chile or two, but we don't.

We'll be done with this, soon, and then we can talk about treasure.

In 1882 twenty-five well hidden sacks of tellurium gold ore were found near Querida. Beautiful ore! The cache is thought to have put down either by high-graders or robbers who somehow were unable to return for their loot. It made the finders happy that lead poisoning, rope burns, or whatever prevented whosoever filled that hidey-hole from ever coming back for it.

***

During 1863 George Skinner found a rich gold deposit. It was very good ore. He built a cabin and began to develop a mine. His accidental death prevented him from working the mine more than a single summer.

Had it not been for the persistence of his brother, Bill, the fate of George Skinner would never have been learned. George had gone from Illinois to Colorado to seek a fortune in 1860. No word of him reached the family. Bill went to Colorado about eight years after George left, determined to find out what had happened to him. Living or dead, doing well or not, Bill wanted to know.

Bill discovered in Denver that George had bought supplies there. George had even left a couple of hundred dollars with a grocer for safe keeping, and had said he was heading into the Sangre de Cristos to look for gold.

Bill Skinner therefore traveled to the Wet Mountain Valley, to follow the cold trail. He could find no information on George, nobody remembered anyone of his description. Bill therefore spent the summer searching the mountains for any possible trace.

Fall was soon enough there, threatening to turn into winter when Bill and the guide he'd hired to help look found an old log cabin right at timberline on the eastern flank of Horn Peak. The cabin had begun to fall in. Bill took the time to look inside in spite of the urgings of his guide not to linger. There was a bitter threat of snow, and they needed to get off the mountain. In a chink near where a chimney went through the wall Bill found a wire-wrapped wallet.

He took it, and left for lower elevation with the worried guide. It was not until they reached warmth and safety that Bill examined the wallet.

Inside the wallet was a folded letter from George. It had been written shortly after he'd made a tremendous strike. He was preparing to head out to sell some gold and stock up with supplies for a return to the workings in the spring. George asked the finder of the letter, in case anything happened to him, to get word to his brother in Illinois. He wanted Bill to have his mine, in such an event. The letter gave directions to the location of the strike.

Bill kept the information to himself. He bided his time until Spring, then hired the same guide to return to the old cabin.

When they arrived they found that an avalanche had taken the cabin, the shelf it was perched upon, and the trees at timberline off the side of the mountain. Everything was a steep, jumbled mess of boulders and broken timber. All the markers George had described in his letter were gone. Trees, a spire-shaped outcropping and other boulders, the cabin, all of what George mentioned was gone.

Bill searched hard enough for his brother's workings, but he had nothing to go on. He could not be sure where the cabin had been. Fall came and it was time to go.

On the way out he and his guide lost a burro off the treacherous trail along a precipice. Loose rocks gave way beneath him. They carefully clambered down the steep rocks to retrieve the pack. The dead burro was close to the skeletal remains of another burro and that of a man. Near the remains was a dry, brittle pack saddle.

In the pack saddle was a pouch containing a substantial amount of gold dust. There also was the diary of George Skinner. Bill had found his brother's remains.

Bill buried his brother's bones right there. The diary spoke of the letter left in the chink beside the chimney. He mentioned again that he wanted Bill to have his mine in case something bad happened. He described in some detail the richness of the ore he had discovered, and his hopes for great reward when he got back the following spring.

Of course there had been no following spring for George Skinner. There was for Bill, but it did him no good insofar as finding his brother's workings. It's still there, but is somewhere high on the east side of Horn Peak and well concealed by many old rockslides.

If one wants to look for it, climb to timberline on the eastern flanks of Horn Peak in the San Isabel National Forest.

***

The best known treasure story in Custer County involves the fabled Caverna del Oro. This legendary tale is over three hundred years old. Indians say their people led Spaniards to a deep cavern in which a splendid ledge of rich gold ore was located. The Spaniards enslaved great numbers of Indians, working many of them to death. At last the Indians attacked their greedy tormentors and killed almost all of them. A very few Spaniards managed to escape through a tunnel leading to the opposite side of the mountain.

This fabled cave, rumored to be in several places throughout the west, may be Caverna del Oro, located in the Marble Mountain and Milwaukee Peak area, popularly called the Spanish Cave area near the Crestone Mountains. That area is a bit more than twelve miles west of Westcliffe, in very difficult terrain.

It is told that some seven hundred feet below the surface are two huge oaken doors. Behind these massive doors is a Spanish vault, filled with gold taken from the incredible vein. On the slope of the mountain, at about the same level as the oaken doors, there was supposed to be a log house. There was supposed to be a narrow tunnel from the vault to this house. If some of the Spaniards did escape being slaughtered, they may have used this tunnel to flee.

One confirmation of the truth of the legendary tale came with a Mexican's recovery in 1811 of gold nuggets scattered along a length of an old trail in that area.

The cave's entrance was rediscovered by Captain Elisha P. Horn in 1869. The cave is at 11,500 feet in the Sangre de Cristos. Horn noted a two foot square Maltese Cross, even a hundred plus years ago the red pigment faded, painted on the rock at the entrance. He located an old fort well below the cave, and came upon an arrow-pierced skeleton of a man within a suit of Spanish armor.

Subsequent searches of the Music Pass Trail near timberline located old rifle pits and bits and pieces of ancient Spanish gear.

In 1919 a hundred-five year old woman told Forest Ranger Paul Gilbert that when she was a child she had journeyed to a cave where miners were bringing out great amounts of gold. She said the name of this fabulous mine was the Three Steps Mine. She stated that five hundred feet within the cave there was an oaken door, put there to safeguard the rich mine. This was supposed to be near the Maltese Cross. On down, she said, seven hundred feet down, there were two even larger oaken doors. If those were to be opened one would find great amounts of gold.

Gilbert did some exploring the following year. He thought of the entrance more as a volcanic vent than an ordinary cave, having at ninety feet down a circular diameter of about twenty feet. Outside this shaft he found a badly rusted shovel and a tattered old piece of rope.

Gilbert at last, in 1929, got a party of men to explore the mine. One Ranger Truman of Westcliffe, and team members of the Colorado Mountain Club. They did not reach the lowest levels. There was a Maltese Cross, long before painted red on the rock near the entrance. They found old artifacts in the depths of the cavern, but did not see any doors. At seventy feet they found a ladder they estimated was at least two hundred years old. A hammer of 1700's craftsmanship was found at three hundred feet.

In 1932 Peter Moser, a Denver resident, found a skeleton chained to a rock wall in the caverns. A group then organized to conduct a thorough search in the same area reached the Maltese cross. They found many arrowhead points in that vicinity, seeming to indicate a fierce battle there. There also had been a major explosion at that level, blocking further access to lower levels. They went no farther than about five hundred feet, finding the shaft cold, muddy, with very loose rocks forming the walls.

In 1932, spelunkers, members of the Colorado Mountain Club and the Colorado Historical Society, descended about a hundred feet into the cave. Peter Moser went down an additional two hundred fifty feet into the mine. He then followed a passageway for some fifty feet to a somewhat lower level. There he discovered a skeleton still chained by its neck to the clammy rock wall. Rather upsetting for one down in such a place all by himself. He found roughly forged tools, hoists, and old, decaying ladders. They found no oaken doors, but then they were not even close to being down any seven hundred feet. One unsubstantiated report claimed that Moser had reached a thousand feet down, and found even more than he said. That does not jibe with what Moser reported.

Many explorations of this cavern have been made, from the late 1600's right up until very recently. A number of people dabbled at this in the 1960's and 70's, not as many since. The upper levels seem to be relatively safe, but it is not safe at all as anyone attempts to go deeper.

A serious attempt to reach those lower levels was made in 1957. It proved to be a most risky endeavor, and they failed to find doors, gold-bearing rock, let alone gold-filled vaults, but did find more artifacts.

Then in 1960 a side passageway leading off clear up near the entrance, back-filled with loose rocks and always before overlooked or ignored, was opened up. It offered a section of unexplored cave as large or even larger than what had been explored earlier.

There are, interestingly enough, a number of other caves of similar nature on Marble Mountain. Fifteen or more such caves. Each of these has a certain potential for hidden caches. One must realize any exploration of these caves presents great dangers even to experienced spelunkers.

And what few clues to all this still exist also are in danger. The Maltese Cross is now almost entirely gone. Poor souls with nothing better to do have taken numerous pot-shots at it, and have about demolished the marker. One now can find more cans, wrappers, and graffiti than they can bits and pieces of the past.

As stated, the tale is legendary. Nevertheless, somewhere deep in the Caverna del Oro, or perhaps in another nearby cavern, past crumbling and backfilled passageways, behind great oak doors, there indeed could be a vault filled with Spanish gold. Legends at times become realities.

***

Near Silver Cliff there is a long- sought cache of gold bars. The value of the stash was reported as $290,000 a number of years ago.

***

DOLORES COUNTY

Many an unknown treasure exists, no tales of it told around campfires such as this, but often every bit as real as anything we mention here. A lot has gone on down through the years that was never written about, never told, that died with those involved. A few such troves are found, and the sources of those pose mysteries that probably will never be solved.

The amazing thing, a searcher after treasures may well find such a cache long before recovering one better known.

There are some strange symbols carved into the walls of a cave near Dove Creek. Several people have stated their belief these relate to one of the incredible caches of Montezuma, and that the markings indicate the burial to be somewhere in the Four Corners area.

***

It is said that a cache of gold coins remains buried somewhere along Cherry Creek near Rico.

***

Also along Cherry Creek, up near the head waters, there are supposed to be $400,000 in gold bars.

***

Rich gold ore was found in a canyon high on the slopes of Mt. Wilson in the late 1800's. The strike was made by two former prospectors along the front ranges of the Colorado Rockies disappointed with what they found there. At least the story of this happening was printed in an 1892 as being the truth. This has come to be known as the Lost Trail Mine.

They trekked in to the middle of the western side of the San Juans, to a spot where they were looking directly at Mt. Wilson. They began to prospect from that spot, up the steep, narrow canyons cutting into Mt Wilson. Before long they found a vein of ore they considered to be rich enough to make working in such an isolated, difficult spot worthwhile.

Near their new workings the two men built a cabin in a small, open park. They worked long and hard through the summer, taking out their accumulated gold in late fall after the first snows promised a long, hard winter. They sold their gold, skillfully avoided all questions put to them about where they were working, bought supplies, and got ready to return to their spot as early as they could in the spring.

That is just what they did, making sure they were not followed. It was about ten years afterwards when their cabin may have been found. In 1890 what was thought to be their skeletons were found scattered here and there across the park. There was nothing to show what had killed them. It did not seem to be the results of an avalanche or Indians, two dangers to all isolated prospectors in those days. Very rich ore specimens were discovered in the cabin, so thieves had not killed them.

The workings could not be found. Maybe a rock slide had covered the entrance to the workings, but not even a trail was found. The two men had gone back after more good gold. What they sought is probably right where it always has been.

Railroad tracks went along the Dolores River, up Lizard Head Pass. To the west of those tracks, in a side canyon close to Rico, was found an extremely rich chunk of float (gold ore). The discovery set off a frenzy of looking, but the vein from whence that glorious chunk came has never been located.

DOUGLAS COUNTY

A number of treasure tales involve the Devil's Head Mountain area of Douglas County. That great hunk of rock glowers down over a huge area. The thick timber, deep gulches, and many caves of this area were a refuge for outlaws over the years. Before we start talking, though, I'm going to have to finish this plate of beans!

Stages operating between **Cripple Creek** and **Denver** had to come through a place called **Big Bend**. This is where the **Badwater Wheel Trail** crossed the **Gold Road**. Many a stage was robbed in this area, and the proceeds from several of these holdups are thought to be cached in and around this area.

***

The most widespread tale involving the Devil's Head area concerns a train robbery pulled off in Nebraska in 1874. An iron bound box containing $60,000 in $10 gold coins was taken. The robbers sought refuge in the Devil's Head Mountain area. They buried the box of gold eagles in a shallow hole when they discovered a posse was almost upon them. As a marker, one of the robbers plunged a knife into a spruce tree as they fled.

Years passed. In 1923 an old man was seen wandering the area by Forest Ranger, Roy Dupre. The ranger supposed the old man was either one of the robbers or a relative of one of them. A forest fire had burned off the forest in the intervening years and the old man could not find the tree with the knife stuck into it.

One version of the tale is that the loot was placed in three caches, all in the Windy Pass area near Devil's Head.

A badly rusted knife blade was found in this general location in 1970. Not in a tree, mind you, and any numbers of hunters and fishermen could have lost that old knife as well as did the train robbers.

$60,000 was supposedly recovered in this Devil's head area in 1975. Another report says the amount recovered was only $20,000. If there actually were recoveries amounting to more than $60,000, some other cache was involved.

There was a single $20 gold piece found in this same immediate area. Perhaps a robber or one of the recovery groups dropped it.

***

For those who've given up on the gold in the Devil's Head area, in 1883 W. B. Smith found a vein bearing excellent topaz on the west side of the mountain. The topaz crystals here are among the very best ever found within the boundaries of the United States. Top gemstone material. Smith was looking for other minerals and probably did not pay enough attention to precisely where he picked up the excellent specimens. The vein was exposed for about fifty feet, was two to fifteen feet wide, and about four feet in depth. Smith discovered it on the southwest side of a creek. His discovery has not been relocated by today's seekers of gemstones.

In 1885 Smith documented his find. It was written up in U. S. Geological Professional Paper No. 20. He did not state a precise location. The paper also noted his discovery had been described in the December, 1883 issue of The American Journal of Science, by Rev. R. T. Cross of Denver.

Dr. A. J. Argall, after reading an article by R. T. Cross on the finding, decided to hunt for the deposit. He and his wife spent the summer of 1935 looking for topaz on Devil's Head. They actually found three excellent gems, but felt they had washed downhill , perhaps for miles, from the matrix from which they came.

Others have also looked for topaz there, but the mother lode remains lost.

***

The same W. B. Smith is said to have cached $60,000 in gold near Sedalia. Some heavy research on W. B. Smith could prove to be extremely interesting!

***

Thomas R. Gavin, James Bullock, and Peter Larkin were partners in 1860. They contracted with Clark Gruber and company to purchase gold at a below- market price so the company could melt it down and mint coins.

The three men are said to have somehow obtained $400,000 in gold. They were carrying gold slugs in the shapes of four leaf clovers. The unusual shape was due to the shape of some Indian pottery they used as ingot molds. They were not completely prepared to conduct their crude smelting techniques after buying raw gold. Each slug weighed three and a half pounds.

Doing it that way seemed preferable to having about seven hundred pounds of raw gold, most of which was easily lost dust and small nuggets.

One version of the story has the three of them playing cards the day and evening prior to them heading back to Denver. Gavin came out a clear winner, and the other two were sore losers. There was a running gun battle between Gavin and the other two as Gavin tried to reach Denver.

A number of other stories say they were returning to Denver when they were ambushed, no wonder if anyone had an idea they were carrying that amount of gold.

Whichever version is the correct one, Bullock and Larkin were dead, and Gavin was badly wounded, there on the headwaters of Cherry Creek. Sceptics of treasure hunting surely put this tale at or near the bottom of their lists.

Gavin hid the gold in some groundhog holes, and attempted to make it into Denver. Though Denver was not too far to the north, the trip must have seemed to the wounded man to last an eternity. Gangrene had already set in, and he died shortly after reaching Denver.

The gold has never been recovered although it is supposed to be only three miles or so northwest of Parker.

EAGLE COUNTY

I hope you've got extra blankets. It's going to get cold tonight. I piled some spruce needles under my roll of foam rubber before I put down my sleeping bag and threw my tarp over it. It could snow tonight, but I don't think so. Just get cold. When I get into that bag I don't want to poke my head out until someone has the coffee ready in the morning.

Sometimes I don't know how anyone got much done in these mountains, but they did.

In 1892 Arthur Fullford worked a gold deposit to the southeast of Eagle. It was in the area of Brush Creek. The entrance was covered over by one of the severe snow slides for which that area is notorious. This deposit has never again been located.

***

There has recently been successful gold panning in Fullford Park, high above Eagle.

***

The fabulous Crazy Woman Mine may be located near Minturn. A few think so. It is thought to be within a fifty mile radius of Placita. Maybe so.

***

Perhaps the best known treasure tale of Eagle County is the so-called Lost Buck Rogers Mine. In October of 1879 Buck Rogers and a large group of hopeful argonauts, mostly Illinois tenderfeet, not miners, had been heading for the California gold fields. Evidently their plans were anything but solid. Having reached the vastness of the Colorado Mountains they stopped long enough to do some prospecting. Buck and five of his friends found a rich gold deposit in the Brush Creek area. This is not far from Red Cliff. Greed must have set in because these fellows decided to keep their discovery to themselves. The six of them remained in the area, the rest of the group went on to whatever fame and fortune awaited them in California.

Fall came early and bone-chilling cold, as it often does in the Colorado Rockies. These tenderfeet miners had no full concept of the severe wintertime problems they faced. The men had by then amassed gold amounting to sixty to a hundred thousand dollars, an amount varying according to which story one reads. Supplies were almost gone, the snows were falling more frequently and were heavier. The weather was much colder. The gold-crazed men, refusing to think about consequences, all wanted to continue working.

There seemed to be but one solution, other than shutting down the operation. None of them wanted to do that. They drew lots and Buck lost, which meant he was the one who had to stop mining and go for supplies. Buck took $500 worth of gold and headed out to get supplies. Upon reaching civilization and a warm saloon, Buck had his first drink of whiskey in a long time. He went on a binge with some new-found cronies.

Two weeks later he sobered up. He agonized over being so thoughtless and stupid, so he loaded up the supplies he'd come for, and headed back to where his undoubtedly angry partners were still working.

Buck was dumbfounded and horrified to find the camp obliterated. It had been completely covered over by a devastating avalanche of snow, rocks, trees, everything. He could not find his friends or the diggings, let alone their cached gold. The site was somewhere beneath a steep, jumbled incline of snow and rocks.

Things went on downhill for Buck Rogers after that. He became a wretched alcoholic, blubbering to anyone who would listen about his friends and fortune lost on "Slate Mountain". This was no doubt only the name he'd given it, due to the plentiful slate where they made their discovery. Only for a time could Buck get anyone to go with him in efforts to relocate the diggings. A few who did go with him were accidentally killed, and Buck got the name of being unlucky as well as being a slobbering drunk. Buck Rogers drifted into oblivion.

Then in 1891, give or take a year or two, an old prospector claimed he'd found "Slate Mountain". He had come across some notes in a room lived in by Buck Rogers. The notes were enough to get him into the right area, and he was lucky enough and observant enough to find the not entirely covered diggings.

This man was a friend of Red Cliff miner, Marshal Arthur H. Fulford. He had samples of the ore to prove what he said, too. The rock samples were extremely rich in gold. Fulford and this prospector made preparations to return to the site. The vein was the sort of thing that could make men rich. Unfortunately Fulford's friend got into a saloon fight and got himself killed before they could leave.

Fulford did little better. He searched his friend's cabin and found enough leads to head off alone for "Slate Mountain". Fulford was covered up and killed by a snow slide on New York Mountain trying to get there.

Not many years after Fulford's death a doctor obtained directions to "Slate Mountain" as payment from a bartender on a medical bill. The bartender said he'd gotten it from a miner who then disappeared, then became too ill himself to make any search for the site. The doctor tried a number of times to follow the directions, but was never successful.

For whatever directions are worth from a man who promptly got lost, given to a bartender who promptly was too ill to follow the directions, obtained by a doctor who was unable to follow the directions, the following advice is given:

"Take the trail that follows the Eagle River and go to the mouth of Brush Creek. (Easy, up to that point). Go along the creek for five miles to the forks, then follow the east branch for five miles until there is a shift of rocks almost to the water's edge. At this point go up a dry gulch on your right running north where you will run into four large trees that stand close together. At this point turn east up the hill to the third dug hole, then turn north for 200 feet. At this point three trees form a triangle and are 300 feet from timberline. The vein runs north and south."

If one stands on this high place the Taylor Range is off to the west, and The Mt. of Holy Cross is in view. What is not in view are any of the trees mentioned, no holes, nothing but one vast rock slide. This gold deposit has not again been found.

***

A treasure seeker came up with thirty-two silver dollars in a narrow crevice within Fullford Cave in 1977. The cave is about seventeen miles to the southeast of Edwards. The man claimed he saw, but could not reach a larger cache deeper in the narrow crack.

***

In Bowman Gulch there is supposed to be cached between $60,000 to $100,000 in gold dust and nuggets.

***

Andrew Recen discovered a high grade silver vein somewhere in Gore Canyon about 1890. Recen died in his cabin of natural causes in 1907. His brother, Daniel, found samples of the rich ore in the cabin, and spent two years looking for the deposit. This silver vein is thought to be located on the south slopes of Gore Canyon perhaps a mile to the southeast of Vail. Recen's cabin was situated some five miles along the foot trail along Gore Creek from I-70 through the Eagle's Nest-Gore Range Primitive area.

EL PASO COUNTY

You're right, the search is probably more important to most of us than actually finding one of these caches would be. The search goes on and on, brightly lit by the glitter of the gold one hopes to find. The glitter of gold once found somehow dies away and it suddenly is just another commodity.

An outlaw stash with a value of about $100,000 is said to be hidden somewhere near Manitou Springs.

A few caches have been recovered in the Manitou Springs area in recent years but it is believed there are others yet unrecovered.

One man was reported to have recovered a huge cache near Manitou Springs shortly after the end of WWII.

***

Some time in the 1890's William Burch left his wife behind at home and took off for Pike's Peak Country. He'd heard too many tales of sudden riches made around Victor and Cripple Creek, and perhaps dreamed too much of getting for himself part of that flow of golden wealth. Burch was not a big man, being only five feet seven inches, but his dreams were gigantic.

He did what most other newcomers did at first, he tramped the hills and gullies, looking for promising outcroppings. Then in the early 1900's William Burch supposedly found an unusually rich vein of gold some ten to fifteen miles northeast from Victor. For a long time that is where he was seen, coming and going. The find was supposedly made somewhere on the southern slope of Pike's Peak. There is no certainty about this, because Burch was a quiet, self-contained man, and simply did not talk about what he was doing.

Just when rumors were becoming legendary tales about Burch, the man disappeared from the area. As far as the people were concerned, his landlady was right. He had struck it rich, and went back to wherever he came from, to France, to where the sun shines and the girls are pretty. Wherever, they had plenty to do themselves. They soon for- got all about William Burch.

In 1948 Burch returned to the area, at the age of 90. He wanted to re-locate the discovery he'd kept secret for almost half a century. Nothing much is known about what he did over the intervening years. A niece, worried about the old man, called local authorities and begged them to search for him.

Sure enough, the old man was found wandering on the south side of Pike's peak. He was nearly done in. He was feebly wandering, confused, dazed, physically and mentally a wreck. He died shortly afterwards without telling anyone why he had been searching so hard. His vein of rich ore, if there truly had ever been one outside his dreams, has never been found.

***

A stage was robbed to the north of Colorado Springs in 1862. The band of outlaws then rode north, at first unaware they were being pursued by a cavalry unit that came upon the robbery scene shortly after the outlaws left. It did not take long for them to find out of the pursuit.

When their horses became exhausted the group stopped near a de-serted miner's shack in thick timber. They buried their loot in a false grave, their grave marker stating "Manny Preston--1862". This cache has report-edly never been found.

***

In 1859 another stage was robbed not far to the north of Colorado Springs. The site is very near today's U. S. Air Force Academy. Three outlaws got away with about $100,000 worth of gold dust and nuggets.

A posse was soon organized. They followed the thieves into the Ram-part Range to the north of Pike's Peak. The pursued group split up. Two men rode north into the Saddle Mountains where the posse overtook and killed them in a fierce shootout. The other man took a heavily loaded mule westward from where the group split up. Somehow he avoided the portion of the posse that followed him. Years after this robbery an Indian woman found the skele-tons of the lone bandit and his horse, and his supplies, in Dead Horse Canyon. The loot was not there. It was believed that the man hid the stash in a cave in that area. One discouraging possibility is that the posse caught up with the third man, killed him, and divided up the gold.

***

During the glorious Cripple Creek gold rush a railroad car filled with rich gold ore derailed, spilling its contents to one side of Highway 24. This spot is some 6.6 miles west of the intersection of I-25 and Highway 24.

About twenty miles northeast of Colorado Springs eight barrels of whiskey were recovered. These were full, sealed barrels of whiskey, as good or better than gold as far as some people are concerned.

FREMONT COUNTY

I went through Junior and Senior High Schools in Canon City. I should point out that although I didn't live too far from the state prison, I spent no time in that institution. Fremont County is like many places, more could have been said and written about it than ever was said and written.

One Tom Park buried a cache of gold coins somewhere near Cotopaxi. This treasure is probably still exactly where he put it.

***

Almost from the day its construction was completed, people have been throwing coins off the Royal Gorge Bridge into the Arkansas River Canyon west of Canon City. One brave soul recovered some coins, far beneath the span. Just in case you try to do the same thing, wear a steel helmet. The tourists still throw coins off the bridge, and a quarter falling that far becomes a lethal missile.

***

A Canon City man found $8,000 in the bottom of a pill cabinet.

***

A Mrs. Proctor told Bill DeBaca (yes, one of the men who found old coins near the Washington Street Bridge along the South Platte River) a story about a possible cache in Copper Gulch, near the mouth of the Royal Gorge.

Mrs. Proctor's family homesteaded near Copper Gulch. She grew up in the area, played and wandered there. She found a concealed cave near the Elsie Mine, and some odd blaze marks on trees that seemed to point to a circular group of rocks. She did not think much about it as a young girl, but as she grew older she began to realize those markings must have been significant.

She rembered tales of outlaws hiding out in the gulch, and a $75,000 gold shipment robbery chalked up to that gang by local people. Nobody ever knew what happened to all that gold, or the outlaws.

The big problem for Bill DeBaca, and anyone else hoping to hunt for the cache, he was drafted into the army. He served, and during his absence Mrs. Proctor died. So much for her showing him the cave, the circular rock patterns or anything else.

GARFIELD COUNTY

Of course most treasures are frustrating, difficult things to go after! I doubt there was ever any money put down in such a way as to make it easy for people like us to find it. Someone puts down a cache, they mean for it to stay there until they come back and get it. What's more, they usually don't draw maps, they don't leave waybills, they don't tell people, or if they do those things they do them as carefully and well as they hid their wealth.

A train was robbed in the 1800's near Grand Valley of a gold coin shipment. The coins were stashed very close to the holdup scene. This cache has never been reported found.

***

On or near Douglas Pass is the Lost Uintah Basin Gold Mine.

***

The Sterling Price Sloss Ranch is some eight miles up the valley from Basalt. While rounding up cattle in high country three or four miles east of Lime Creek, a stream running into the Frying Pan River, a rancher was caught by a drenching thunderstorm. When he sought refuge beneath overhanging rocks he came upon an extremely rich gold deposit. He came back a few days later to get more samples but could not then or ever again relocate the rich vein.

GILPIN COUNTY

You hope you won't run into a hundred other treasure hunters? My friends, you get two miles off the road you may not see anyone else in these mountains for days at a time. Half a mile is definitely enough to thin out the crowd. If one gets serious about most of these stories they don't need to worry too much about the competition.

Forty-two six ounce gold ingots were stolen from the Eagle Mine, near Central City, in 1864. Each ingot was stamped, Eagle Mining Company. The thieves were tracked to an old cabin in Red Rock Buttes. They were pursued and killed when they tried to escape. The ingots were not found, however, and it is believed those unique ingots are still hidden near the cabin site. If so, those are each worth the better part of ten thousand dollars today.

***

A Chinese man named Lin Sou Chin was a mine supervisor. He obtained enough wealth to purchase his own mine near Central City. After doing so he became very wealthy. He distrusted the banks, preferring to store his wealth in a vault at his mine office. In 1882 a group of whites plotted to rob him. One of the group, however, did not think what they were planning was right. He secretly told Chin about what was intended the night before it was to happen. Chin took his wealth, some $40,000 in $10 and $20 gold pieces, and fled town quietly in a buckboard. The would- be thieves followed his trail. Two days later they caught up with and surrounded him on Mule Ear Pass in the Arapahoes. There was no gold in the buckboard and Chin would not tell them where he hid it in spite of their graphic threats as to how they would torture him if he would not tell.

Before they could carry out their dire threats the Chinese man stabbed himself with a thin dagger, instantly killing himself. The group had no idea where to look for his money, and neither has anyone else since then.

***

It is not just the "old days" that produced treasure. David Mosch of Idaho Springs, fourteen years of age at the time, found a rich vein of gold ore within two hundred feet of an abandoned mine. It was exposed in a trail over which thousands of miners had trod daily years before. Thus a working mine has been developed in a "worked out" mining area.

***

Several high grade caches are thought to be hidden in the North Empire area, twelve miles to the northwest of Idaho Springs.

***

Apex, north of Central City, was a rather well preserved ghost town far longer than other such places. Treasure hunters came up with a full box of coins beneath the stairs in a building standing on one corner of the crossroads at the center of town. These men did not break up a single board in doing it.

It's shameful what happened afterwards. Almost every old building in that ghost town was torn apart after that recovery.

(From author's conversations with friends of the men who recovered the box.),

***

Somewhere on Berthoud Pass, near Empire, is the Lost Saxon Mine.

Perigo is nestled ing the hills to the north of Central City and is south of Nederland. Not long before this picture was taken, in the very early 1970's, a detector user located and recovered three ten dollar gold pieces from close beside the old house.

GRAND COUNTY

You wonder why some counties aren't mentioned, that probably there's no treasures in those counties? Just remember, we're only talking about the better known stories. For every treasure tale that's told, hundreds, maybe thousands of treasures exist that have never been talked about. There's not a town, not a hamlet, not a corner of the state that doesn't have some treasure potential. That's the best kinds of things to seek, too, the treasures that are not well known.

Isaac Alden discovered a vein of gold in the 1880's that assayed $1,600 to the ton. This was located on Soda Creek. He used an upturned tree by a large boulder as a landmark. Lightning must have struck the high, upturned tree, or something close by, for that and the surrounding vegetation was burned to ashes. Alden could never again find his vein of ore, nor has anyone else. The Lost Bonanza or the Lost Soda Creek Mine, whichever one prefers, remains lost.

***

Somewhere up Gore Pass, in 1905, a greenhorn prospector found and hacked off a hunk of good-looking reddish ore from a ledge exposed for about ten feet before disappearing into a rock face. This man was hunting elk at the time, not prospecting, and was not exactly sure where he was at the time. The ledge was almost a foot thick. The ore later proved to contain close to ninety percent silver and at that time assayed at a $17,900 to the ton. This deposit could never be located again, but up there along old Gore Pass, somewhere, is a ledge of nearly pure silver ore.

***

In 1859 a band of Ute Indians attacked a group of California gold miners close to today's town of Steamboat Springs. The miners were on their way back east with their collective accumulation of gold.

The attack was vicious. Only four men survived the skirmish, and they were wounded. They continued east, camping for a time on the east shores of Grand Lake. There they did some hunting, fishing, and recovering from the fight. When the Utes attacked again, the men understood their plight. Even if they could eventually elude the Indians they still faced distance, outlaws, bad weather, and hunger. If they continued to try to haul their heavy gold it could slow them down and get them killed.

They buried $40,000 in coins and nuggets in a heavy cast iron dutch oven. They chose a spot close beside a tombstone shaped boulder. A silver handled knife was stuck into a nearby spruce tree as a marker.

The four men eventually made it across the mountains and out onto the plains. There they were once again attacked by Indians. Only one of the men ever reached home in the East. He told the story to his family, knowing he would was unable to make any return trip to search for the gold.

The following spring family members led a group back to the Grand Lake area to recover the dutch oven. They could not find the right spot. They found all sorts of boulders more or less shaped like a tombstone, they never found the knife stuck into a tree. As far as is known, neither has anyone else.

Years after these things took place considerable work was done in that area, construction of the Colorado-Big Thompson water diversion project. Huge movements of earth took place immediately to the east of the cache site. The dutch oven could easily have been bladed out and spread elsewhere, or covered over deeply. It also could still be right where it was placed.

GUNNISON COUNTY

Sure, those old timey prospectors and adventurers had to put up with grizzlies, Indians, rattlesnakes, downpours and winter weather, but they didn't have any government officials. I suspect those rascals would be perfectly content, come to think about it, to keep their grizzlies and Indians and leave the government officials to us. I doubt they'd want to even trade off Colorow for one of our current governmental officials, not even if they could throw in a grizzly or two.

Twenty miles or so from Aspen, in the old Sylvanite Mine area, there are excellent wire silver specimens are sometimes found.

***

Joseph Johns was hunting deer in 1890. In a small cliff close to Muddy Creek he found a quartz vein and took some samples. When assayed the ore proved to carry a $5,000 to the ton value. Search as he would, he could not relocate the vein. Johns believed a rock slide must have come down over that small cliff and buried the vein. Probably so, for many others have looked for this one.

***

Otto Mears was a renowned railroad builder in Colorado. During the 1880's he amassed a fortune. Part of this, some $35,000 in gold bullion (1880's value) is thought to be buried somewhere in or around his corral in White Pine.

Another tale has Mears putting down that cache, or another one similar to it, at North Star.

***

There is thought to be bank robbery loot cached in or very near to the Marble townsite.

***

W. D. Murdie was an automotive engineer who lived and worked in Topeka, Kansas. His son was a prominent man in the Gunnison area. Each summer W. D. came into Gunnison County to visit with his son and enjoy his favorite use of summertime vacation, prospecting.

While in Taylor Park one year, on the very last day of his vacation, he crossed a small creek. While doing so he found a fifteen inch wide vein of gold ore in the bottom of the clear stream. It caught his attention, because he actually could see the gold in it. The material looked good so he picked some ore samples from the seam.

He some time later had the samples tested, and they proved to be extremely rich in gold. 2,400 ounces of silver and 95 ounces of gold to the ton. About $5,000 a ton ore at the time. He returned to the area as soon as possible, but could never find the right stream, let alone that fifteen inch seam of rich ore. Neither could his son.

***

Near Crested Butte is the Lost Cow Creek Gold mine. One can travel far while hunting "near" to Crested Butte.

***

A deposit of gold ore ten feet thick was found in 1890 about six miles north of Tincup. The deposit was located in the Cross Mountains and proved to average $440 to the ton.

***

A Spanish pack train is supposed to have met an untimely end near Crested Butte. They were carrying gold bars and coins.

***

Three prospectors stopped working on their worked-out claim near Ruby City in 1880. They intended to go to Pitkin and do some placering there. They had about $5,000 in gold between them. One of the men killed the other two and took it all. The bodies were quickly discovered and a posse gave chase to the cul- prit. He was caught near Pitkin, and taken to Gunnison. He did not have the gold with him nor was it ever found. That ill-gotten gold is probably still hidden somewhere between Ruby City and Pitkin.

***

Cement Creek pours into East River about six miles south of Crested Butte. In 1883 a mineralogical society committee explored the so-called Cement Caves. Matt Hayden and Pat Daly were two members of that expedition.

The survey crew found the skeleton of a man not too far into the Cement Creek Caves. Nearby the skeleton were old mining tools, cooking utensils, gold pans, a couple of ball and cap revolvers, and two rifles.

Was the man a miner, or as many have thought was he a thief using the caves as a refuge and hideout?

Daly and Hayden decided to investigate further. They found what at first seemed to be a hollow space under the cavern floor. It turned out to be a large gold pan, covered with dirt, atop a small hand-dug excavation. Within this small pit they found gold dust, some nuggets, some U. S. coins, and the picture of a lovely Mexican girl. Remnants of buckskin bags showed these items had not been placed loose in the cavity. The buckskin sacks had rotted away.

***

Lapis Lazuli of fine quality can be found on the slopes of North Italian Mountain in Gunnison County.

***

The Red Mountain Trail ran between California Gulch on the north side of the range and Washington Gulch on the south side. It was the earliest and most used means of prospectors going north or south in this area. There were many holdups, no few killings, and there are thought to be many outlaw caches along that old Red Mountain Trail.

***

On or in the vicinity of Sheep Mountain, in the southern part of Gunnison County, there remains lost a ledge of extremely rich gold ore. Work on the vein was not extensive, but it produced some extremely rich gold ore.

In early June, 1896, two old prospectors came upon a human skeleton about fifteen miles west of Sheep Mountain. These two men, going only by the names of Cantankerous Smith and Mo Ginsberg, found evidence to back up the wild ravings of a woman going insane thirty- six years before. These men's story brought back tales of a very rich strike in the 1860's, which nobody at that time had any idea of how to find.

Close by the skull and scattered bones lay a rusted muzzle-loader rifle. The back of the skull had a large hole, rather obviously caused by such a slug as would have come from that rifle. Among the bones were several pieces of quartz. The pieces were so rich in gold the old prospectors for a time thought they had made a major discovery. An assayer in Telluride found the material to be worth $2,700 to the short ton. Eureka stuff, for ore from the famous Smuggler Mine only ran $1,200 to the short ton.

A careful search of the area convinced them the pieces of quartz had been carried in by whosoever skeletal remains lay there. There was no significant mineralization in the area those pieces could have come from. This discovery, and the old prospectors' telling of it, gave credence to the babblings of Dora Cyre a third of a century before.

In 1859 one George Cyre, and his wife Dora, came to Colorado from

Independence, Missouri. He was maybe 30, his wife was only 22. They were drawn to Gregory Gulch, which soon became Central City. George for a time was printer for The Gold Reporter, a daily newspaper for the booming gold camp. By 1860 the hand press and Cyre moved down to Golden, and the paper became the Western Mountaineer. The newspaper business in Gregory Gulch seemed to be finished.

George Cyre was a good enough printer, but he was a drinking man. He got into the middle of a saloon brawl one night and was stabbed to death.

Dora's fate took longer. Knifing probably would have been a much kinder ending for her. Hardly a month after Cyre's death Dora married a would-be miner named Ira Tucker. He seemed like a good man, and she let him talk her into going far back into the mountains with him. He told her how rich he soon would be, that he was already cutting a drift to expose a vein of good ore he'd found on the surface.

Dora, now Mrs. Tucker, found out too soon what a hideous relationship she had gotten herself into. Tucker had a vicious, mean streak in him. He soon started hitting her for any little reason, or for no reason at all. He expected immediate slave-like compliance from her. If she didn't comply he would beat her.

Tucker's drift soon encountered the vein he sought. He continued to work through the summer. He was accumulating good ore, but his primary idea was to develop the property to such an extent a large company would buy his claim for a substantial sum. Good ore or not, it was too far, too risky to transport such rich loads out of the mountains.

The bad conditions deteriorated for Dora, and she wanted to leave. Tucker threatened her. He told her what his Ute friends would do to her. Most of all he continued to beat on her, anything to prevent her departure.

After he went to work in the drift one day, Dora saddled a horse and rode off. She was desperate. Before the day was gone the horse threw a shoe and soon went lame. She camped for the night not nearly as far from Tucker's mine as she had hoped. It wasn't far enough, and Tucker caught up with her. He beat her unmercifully for daring to leave him. He told her if she did not ride back to the mine with him in the morning he would kill her, and good riddance.

That night, after the man fell asleep, she picked up his muzzle loader and cocked it. She put the barrel of the weapon close to the back of his head and shot him.

Four days later three Utes found her, lost and starving. They said they would take her to Golden if she would give them her horse. She agreed, and they rode off with her horse after they got her within sight of Golden.

Dora kept all this to herself for a few months. When asked, she told vague stories of Indians murdering her husband. Then she could stand it no more. She felt her sanity slipping. She confided in Mrs. Thomas Gibson, the wife of the editor of The Western Mountaineer. Had not George Cyre had worked for a time for Mr. Gibson? Mrs. Gibson was someone she knew, and Dora had to have someone to talk to.

Mr. Gibson sent four men to look for Dora's husband. On the side he told them to search for the mine, and provided them enough provisions to last at least three weeks. They found neither the body nor the mine. Dora's directions were not clear.

The poor woman became less and less coherent, and as time passed less credence was given to her story. Dora at last slipped into her own personal insanity, and never recovered.

The two old prospectors found evidence that Dora's story had a strong basis of truth. But the rich gold ledge could be anywhere in an area of three to four hundred square miles. There is, somewhere northwest of Gunnison, to the west of Independence Pass, east of Cedaredge, and south of Glenwood Springs, an old drift exposing a vein of very high grade gold ore. Probably the drift is now caved in, and the area one must search is a rugged vastness, but it is surely there. Wherever there is.

In recent years it has been reported that two hikers, coming down from Sheep Mountain, broke some pieces from a thin exposed outcropping in a remote canyon. It was good gold ore. They saw no old workings. Their chance discovery may or may not have been near Tucker's drift, but it was good gold ore. They tried but could not find the spot again.

Look if you will, but don't end up in the same condition as poor Dora!

***

Two prospectors located gold near the west foot of Monarch Pass back in the 1860's. This was years before others did anything in the area. These two men built a long tom sluice, diverted some water. The tales relate they were recovering about a pound of gold a day. In spite of winter coming on they hesitated to shut down their operations. Ignoring approaching winter weather in that country has never been a wise thing to do, and it was worse back in those harder, more dangerous times. They finally headed back up and over the mountains to the east, but they had waited too long to go. They were caught in deep snow and blinding sunshine. They soon became snowblind, confused, and lost. Indians found them wandering in this condition and killed them.

The tale undoubtedly helped bring many gold seekers into the Tomichi and North Star area, hoping to find even part of a pound of gold a day.

HINSDALE COUNTY

Hinsdale County? The darned place is beautiful, but impossible to do much with besides visit. Mountains cut it up into three separate parts. In the north end of the county, where old Parker "et" his companions, is Lake City, the county seat. The Cochetopa Mountains cut off the middle part, the Carson, Lost Trail, upper Rio Grande section, from Lake City. The San Juans cut that middle section off from the southern third of the county. There's no easy way to go from one of these parts of the county to another. It's all mighty rugged, remote country, mostly up or down.

In Hinsdale County there's plenty of mountains, plenty of old mines, plenty of winter, and plenty of treasure stories.

Walter "Pat" Kelly found a rich gold ledge not far from Lake City one year just before the heavy snows set in. Pat was sheriff of Lake City for a time, and he also was a manager for the Golden Fleece Mine near Lake City. He also did as much prospecting as he could find time for, and it was on one such jaunt he felt confident he had finally made a big strike. He left a marker at the site. He was sure he would have no trouble going right back to the spot, so he made no notes, drew no maps, none of that sort of thing.

That winter Pat was killed in an accident. He fell and broke his neck. The story goes he was laid out in the morgue on a slab. The following morning his body was turned in the opposite direction.

Maybe Pat was trying to write some notes. The fact is, Pat's discovery has not been rediscovered.

***

There still is placer gold in much of the Lake City area.

Treasure hunters searched the ruins of a burned cabin in Lake City in 1967. They found in the ashes a number of jars of melted coins and sold the mess for about $600.

There are stories of other possible stashes in and around Lake City.

***

Emory Mitchell was a storekeeper in Lake City in the early 1930's. He grub staked a 25 year old named Todd Dawson with $20 worth of supplies to do some prospecting. Deep in the San Juans Dawson found rich gold ore. In 1932 it assayed at $6,000 to the ton. Dawson drowned in 1937 without telling Mitchell much more than the vein was located not too far from Lake City. Mitchell died in 1953, unsuccessfully looking over the years for the vein after Dawson drowned.

***

Henson Creek, just into the mountains to the west of Lake City had a gambling and prostitution center called "Hell's Acre". That immediate area is rife with tales of lost and hidden stashes.

***

There have been individual gold coins retrieved at Rose's Cabin, to the west of Lake City.

***

Lost somewhere in the rough area drained by Ute Creek is probably what is called la Mina de la Ventana. It was a rich Spanish mine, and many an effort to relocate it has been made.

***

These legendary stories of Mina de la Ventana and the Ute Mine are central to the many tales of caches of gold ore and crudely smelted bullion pertaining to this rough landscape. The Spaniards are said to have put down caches as they did their mining, to keep their gold and silver safe until there was enough wealth accumulated to warrant sending a well armed caravan south to Taos. If we think the area is hard to get into today, imagine what it was like in the Spaniards' day. The vast distances and hardships would have been bad enough, there were also hostile Indians. There were good reasons for putting down well- hidden stashes. In the area of the mine there were reputed to be numbers of such caches, many never retrieved by the Spaniards. One large cache was supposed to be located about two day's travel down from the divide, hurriedly buried there late one autumn. Some disaster stopped a treasure caravan headed to Taos cold in its tracks.

Old tree markings in various spots, of probable Spanish origin, dating back about two hundred years now, have added some credence to these tales.

This is an area at the head of Ute Creek, which is tributary to the upper Rio Grande. It is across the Continental Divide from the rugged head waters of the Pine, the Flint Fork, and the Vallecito drainages on the San Juan

-60-

side. There is no easy access from either side.

In the summer of 1937 three enterprising treasure hunters who'd heeded the old tales, studied the markings near Ute Lake and looked over the area carefully. Many men working in that area at the time saw them, but the three would not talk to anybody beyond saying they were fishermen. It was painfully obvious to the locals who observed them, these fellows were not interested in fishing. They had their minds on other things. Before the end of August these men at last recovered a cache of six rotted buckskin bags full of rich gold ore reported to have sold for about $40,000.

The spot where the gold was cached is known. Others interested in the same stories discovered the hole the three men left after the gold had been removed. In the remnants of rotted buckskin bags scattered in and around the hole there was one nice little piece of rich gold ore they'd overlooked.

The cache had been buried beneath a great, oblong flat rock at the base of a dead spruce tree crowning a high spot alongside the streamlet. The dead tree probably was a hundred feet tall with nearly a four foot diameter at ground level, a giant of its species. There was no other such rock as that in the immediate vicinity, and it obviously had been dragged there from elsewhere.

That cache may be gone, but its recovery should perhaps make other similar stories all the more fascinating.

***

In a rugged area about thirty miles to the northwest of Pagosa Springs is probably the fabulously rich Lost Ute Mine. This more than likely is somewhere along Ute Creek.

Spaniards out of Taos mined the lode beginning around 1760. Their work there continued throughout the later 1700's. This is documented in old records existing in Taos and Santa Fe. Both Spanish bandits and Indians were a constant threat to supply caravans coming to the mine or ore being transported out. A number of caches were put down along the trail back to Taos by the Spanish miners over those years because of the predatory gauntlets they had to run.

There were said to be seven men working at the Ute mine in 1780 when an exceptionally vicious, unexpected attack was made upon them by Indians. Five of the seven men were killed during the bloody fight. The first two were left dead in or near the entrance to the mine and their skeletons have remained there over the years since.

Two of the miners survived the flight out of those mountain and returned to Taos. As older individuals they tried to go back to the mine. Some of their descendants then attempted to relocate the mine, and failed. Others have tried, also with no success.

Two Mexican men, Candido Archuleta and Doneciano Aguilar, claimed they found an old mine, inside the tunnel of which they saw two skeletons. By that time too many people had looked too long and hard for such a place, and the men were derided. Everyone thought they were only telling stories to gain attention. With such treatment it is not surprising they clammed up and never talked again about what they saw.

Aguilar became involved in a murder and was imprisoned for life in New Mexico.

Archuleta met a mysterious, wealthy young Spaniard some time later. The man claimed that one of his relatives had worked in the Ute Mine and had survived the Indian attack. Archuleta some time afterwards found some markings. His conversation with the young Spaniard led him to believe the markings were key clues to the location of the old mine, but he never saw the man again.

Soon after Archuleta and Aguilar claimed to have found the mine, in the 1890's, a mysterious person began to furtively prowl the area. He showed up at times at the ranch of Jack Pearson, on the lower Pine River Valley. He said he was a Frenchman, but that is about all he said. Because of his sly prowling, and his secretive ways, he became known as La Sombra (The Shadow). What he was doing was never known over a good many years, not until he told the story as he lay on his death bed, eaten up with consumption.

His one driving purpose over the years, the cause of his endless searching through those rough mountains, he had hoped and tried very hard to relocate the Lost Ute Mine. He said that his grandfather had worked in that mine. He died in Taos and was buried there. At the time of his death he had upon him a badly worn map of the Ute Creek area.

In 1911 there was a carefully organized effort to find the mine. It failed.

Jose Garcia, prominent San Luis Valley man looked for the Ute Mine for years. Lots of looking, nothing found. Ed Speel of Pagosa Springs, same luck. Others, usually nothing but plenty of exercise.

The discovery of two skeletons on Starvation Creek in the 1930's caused a good deal of excitement. These turned out to be remains of members of Fremont's disastrous fourth expedition. No connection at all with the Lost Ute Mine.

In 1938 two men quietly recovered $400,000 in gold cached two miles south of Ute Creek. They were careful not to reveal their identities. Perhaps some of the Spaniard's burros got sick or injured on the way out.

The mine, however, is still guarded by two skeletons in some well-hidden, hard to get to spot. The ore they were mining is still there, rich as it was in 1780.

There have been many fruitless searches for the old mine. It is believed that the mine has a direct line of eyesight to the window notch of the Rio Grande Pyramid.

***

When Silverton became the hub of great mining activity in the San Juans, the way one got there was through Del Norte, and westward up the upper Rio Grande Valley and across Timber Hill. That's the way virtually all horse, stagecoach, and wagon traffic had to go in those days. Timber Hill was a very steep section of trail east of Beartown. That wooded, isolated steepness made wheeled traffic slow down, and that made the stretch of road a favored spot for outlaws. Ambush, robbery, and escape were easier there than elsewhere. Goods going in and gold going out was a magnet to the shiftless hardcases preferring robbery to work. There were many holdups along that rough, lonely stretch of road.

There was one three-wagon load shipment of rich gold ore in which three scouts well up the hill on the Silverton side were ambushed. Two of the scouts were killed, but the wounded third man somehow got back to warn the wagoners. There was barely enough time for two of the wagon loads of ore to be shoved off into a good hiding place. As the robbers came upon them sooner than expected, the haulers and the already wounded scout attempted to flee. The thieves attacked and killed them, and got away with the third wagon load of ore.

The empty wagons, horses pulling them, were found several days afterwards. The remaining two wagon loads of ore probably remain where they were dumped.

***

Also somewhere coming down Timber Hill four gold bars weighing forty pounds each were cached by the men who stole them from a smelter near Ophir. Don't put on your hiking boots just yet, it's quite a story.

In 1886 a somewhat dishonest employee of the Boston and Ophir smelting Company and his absolutely dishonest companion decided to try to steal some of the many gold bars being produced by the smelter.

The two of them were a rather unlikely pair that got together in 1883. Soapy Robinson was a sneaky, rowdy, never-do-well, a getting-gray sixtyish lout, totally incapable of wanting, getting, or keeping a job, always looking for a chance to beg, borrow, or steal anything not nailed down. He had gotten out on parole from a midwestern penitentiary where he spent time for being in on an armed robbery resulting in murder.

Buster Reede was about thirty years old when the two of them got together, good mechanically, and could have been about anything he wanted to be. They drifted into Colorado from further east, came over Timber Hill and Stony Pass into Silverton, didn't stay long, then came into Ophir.

Buster had some real skills, was willing to work but had seen enough of trying to prospect. Buster didn't mind working for wages, especially when some company would pay as much as $3.50 for only ten hours work, as they were offering in Ophir. There must have been a yard-wide streak of dishonesty in Buster for him to team up with the likes of Soapy Robinson.

Their plan was simple. Soapy would tend camp, cook, do all the running needed to be done, keep an eye out for dangers and opportunities. Buster had no trouble getting a job in the smelter. Most other fellows capable of doing anything were out doing the prospecting that Buster didn't want to do. So Buster went to work, hoping to get a chance to latch on to some of the gold bars transported eastward by trains of pack burros several times each summer and fall.

They finally were able to make off with five gold bars. The opportunity actually didn't happen until the last day Buster worked for the smelter. There never had been any actual plan. It simply so happened that late on that Friday afternoon, Buster's announced last day of working there, the man who worked in the plant with him got sick and had to go home early. That left Buster in that part of the plant by himself.

Buster was elated. Soapy was posted where he could watch a back window. The week's shift ended in a few hours, Buster figured if he and Soapy could do what they wanted to do that night, any missing gold bars wouldn't be noticed until the following Monday. By Monday morning they hoped to be long gone.

There was a little problem in getting into the locked laboratory, where the gold bars already poured were stored. Having a good mechanical mind, Buster soon took care of the lock, without damaging it. He soon found five gold bars and carried them to where he could throw them out the window that Soapy was watching. He was careful not to leave a mess in the laboratory.

The lock was undamaged. Even if someone were to check the room over the weekend the theft might go unnoticed.

Buster waited until nightfall, trying to look casual until the work crew all began to leave. He then threw the five forty-pound bars, a total of two hundred pounds, out the window to Soapy. About $60,000 worth of gold in those hard money days. After which Buster simply walked out of the plant with the last few workers.

The thieves used three burros to haul the gold bars and supplies. The animals were overloaded, what with the gold and all their needed supplies. Overloaded or not, they made their way over Ophir Pass that night with no real problems.

They edged around Silverton, doing their best to stay out of sight. The cautious duo went up Cunningham Gulch, then continued up and over Stony Pass. This was a steep and difficult route, and the men did not want to go as slow as they should have. Their confidence over the distance they'd already come had to be growing.

They hurried along the stage road going down into the upper Rio Grande Basin towards Del Norte, trying to stay as much as possible out of the sight of possible travelers. The men drove the animals mercilessly to try to get away.

This proceeded reasonably well, over the Continental Divide and on down Grassy Hill. All seemed to go well until they got to the downslope side of Timber Hill. One of the three burros gave out there. It would not or could not go further. They decided to camp there, as it was late. Perhaps camping overnight would rest the burro so they could continue early the following morning.

That night it started to snow. They awoke to find that the burro had not been pretending. The beast had died during the night. Another burro seemed about ready to do the same thing. The two frantic thieves were still at least fifty miles from Del Norte, the snow was beginning to stick, and they knew their good luck had run out.

It was not difficult to know what to do, not if they had any chance of getting away. The scoundrels had to bury four of the bars or risk having the second, maybe the third burro die. This way they would have one bar, could travel eastwards light and fast. The sale of the one bar would give them all sorts of money. They would have a wonderful winter, then in the spring could come back to get the other four bars.

They cached the bars close to the wagon road on a timbered, rocky knob. The mountainside across the stream from the knob was marred by a steep rockslide. A small glade along the stream below the knob had three great boulders standing alone in the open. Reede cut an odd blaze into a nearby spruce tree and noted all the nearby landmarks so they would have no possible troubles in relocating the spot. Before leaving, to make double sure, Reed used his axe to blaze some twenty aspen saplings on their east, or downslope sides, easily visible to anyone coming up the trail. The last thing they did was to take the pack saddle from the dead burro and hide it deep in the branches of a spruce tree well up the sides of that steep knob.

All this done, they got out of the area a hop and a jump ahead of a monstrous winter storm. There was at last no way anyone could follow them.

In Pueblo Soapy and Buster sold the one gold bar. It sold for $12,800, no questions asked in those freer days. It was more money than the two of them had ever imagined. That sudden wealth is what at last did them in.

Soapy was at heart one wild character. The money bought him all the alcohol he could drink, he discovered the ladies, and the rascal went on a whirlwind spree. In one wild-eyed brawl that winter he was shot and killed. Spring never came for Soapy.

Reede was different. He had always wanted but could never afford to have a small cattle ranch. Suddenly he could, so that is what he did. He bought a place in the midwest. Spring came, for Reede, but the fences needed fixing, the cows needed rounded up for branding, there was riding and roping to do, and a hundred other things prevented his returning to Timber hill that first spring. Fine with Reede, it was likely best to let the story of the theft cool down for another year or two.

Then, being a fine, new upstanding rancher, Reede got married. Several springs went by, and then several more.

Reede almost reached the age of seventy years before at last he decided to go back for the other four gold bars. It was 1926, forty years after he and Soapy stole them. He no longer needed the money, but he nevertheless wanted those gold bars.

What a difference forty years can make in a man and in country he had only passed through, and that during a snowstorm. The old wagon road had long fallen into disuse, was now overgrown and difficult to see in many places. The new Farmers Union Reservoir covered much of the route below Timber Hill, making the whole upper Rio Grande Basin look different to Buster. The now old man was running out of time, he was soon expected back home, and he had no good idea of where to start looking.

During the last few days he was there, Reede talked to Levi Brinkerhoff. Brinkerhoff was a professional packer and guide, and at the time he talked to Reede was coming out of Silverton with a string of pack mules carrying camp gear and provisions for a group of men come over from Silverton to the new lake to do some fishing.

Reede related much of the story to Brinkerhoff, and asked if the man could help him find the right locale. The man recognized what Buster was talking about as being on the east side of Timber Hill, some eight or nine miles from where they were talking. Reede was delighted. Since the day was growing late and he was expected by friends back at camp, Reede made plans with Brinkerhoff to go up Timber Hill the following day.

Not to be. A message awaited Reede back at his camp, urging him to come home immediately for this reason or that. He left the next morning instead of going up Timber Hill with Brinkerhoff. Buster Reede never got to come back.

Levi Brinkerhoff did not at the time think too much about this chance meeting, nor take Reede's story too seriously. There are many stories that sound just as good all through the high Rockies. He had a string of pack animals to get back to Silverton.

While herding his mules uphill on Timber hill, several of the more contrary critters sidetracked up a long unused track winding away from the now more used path. Urging his horse after them to chase them back to following the main string, Brinkerhoff suddenly found himself staring at a group of old, dead aspen, trees blazed only on the downslope side. One of the clues Reede had mentioned.

That set Brinkerhoff to looking, letting his pack animals stop and rest. Being a real man of the mountains, it was not long before he'd located each and every landmark Reede had mentioned. He now agonized over not paying more attention to the story the old man told him.

There was nothing to do but go on. He had a fifty dollar packing job to finish by the following day, and he'd best get with it. He rode away from the spot, standing at one point only fifty yards from where Reede's $60,000 worth of bars lay. Brinkerhoff got together at a much later date with Cornelius, one of the authors of Golden Treasure of The San Juan, and looked back regretfully to that moment.

It turned out that Reede, who normally was not a very talkative soul, had also talked with two other men a day or two before he met Brinkerhoff. After all, he'd come back to Colorado to try and find those gold bars, and he was getting somewhat desperate. He more or less told the same account he told Brinkerhoff.

Pat Duncan and Rusty Makibbon, young cowboys, had visited Reede around his campfire one evening. They knew the area below the big new reservoir, but did not know much of anything about the land above it. Reede hadn't mentioned Timber Hill to them, because he had never before heard the name. Not until he later talked to Brinkerhoff. When he asked them about the old trail going over the mountains, they told him it was no longer used much.

A man at the age of seventy years, now respected, does not like to expose too much of the skeletons in his closet. He told neither the two young men or Brinkerhoff much, but it was more than enough to get their interest up to a fever pitch. After the old man departed these men talked over looking for and possibly finding the gold bars. The group grew to include others, including that author, Cornelius.

There was a lot of looking done, and a few men got to know well the knob and glade along the old Timber Hill Trail. Plenty of probing, looking, and no little digging went on. The soil at the base of the rocks in the glade was dug until water filled the holes and turned the rocks into islands. The old pack saddle was found. Several fellows sat on the knob only feet from where the bars lay. Brinkerhoff and the book author felt they were getting closer all the time, but all they'd found after a lot of probing was one big piece of babbit that probably fell from some mule's backpack as the beast trudged up or down the trail. All these searchers had grand visions of what they could do with four forty pound bars of gold.

Then one day a Mexican sheepherder friend of the author, one Crecencio Martinez, came to him with an incredible story. The author had seen two men while he was out chasing a few stubborn, runaway mules. He hardly evem waved to them, and after what Crecencio told him, he wished that he had taken the time to talk with them.

Crecencio had seen the two men several times, their route seemed to be paralleling his. He came upon them by the bald knob, and saw them dig up the four gold bars. He knew enough of the story to see at once what was happening. They saw him, and pointed a rifle his way, shouting something. Afraid they would shoot him, Cresencio whipped his horse into a run and left.

The author and Brinkerhoff went up a few days later and found the hole they dug. There were four rectrangular impressions in the leaf mold.

Buster Reede may not have gotten his four gold bars, but some of his family or friends did. They went almost directly to the right place, knew where to dig, and took little time doing it. Probably at least one of the two men were Buster's grandsons. It came out they were driving a Chevy with Nebraska license plates. They had told a fisherman their grandfather had years before come across the mountains down Timber Hill.

The hiding place is somewhere on Timber hill, between Silverton and Del Norte. There was about 160 pounds of gold in those four ingots Crecencio saw being dug from the side of the knob. Enough for a terribly wild spree or a ranch or about anything else.

Could they perhaps have missed one bar?

***

An aged prospector in 1905 found a rich gold mine in the Bear Creek area. He was less secretive than many of his prospecting brethren, for he talked to many people in Durango about his find.

There were old workings, he described, and the old man believed the workings were Spanish. Rotted sacks of rich ore were stacked in the mine entrance, guarded only by three skeletons. There was no clue as to how whoever it was had died. Gasses, claim jumpers, Indians, cave-ins and other sudden endings killed many miners and prospectors in those rough days, but the old man had found no hints of what had finished off the three men.

He sold some of the rich ore in Durango. It was well concentrated material with a very high content of actual gold. It was as he had taken it from the old sacks he had found in the mine tunnel. The old man bought supplies, then headed back into the hills.

He may have talked, but he was most careful not to be followed. The old man was never seen again and his remarkable discovery was thought of and talked about for years.

Pedro Martinez came into Durango in 1918 with much the same story. He carried a sack filled with rich, well concentrated gold ore and described much the same situation as the old man had described in 1905. He wanted to return to his find as soon as possible.

It was not to be. Pedro Martinez fell victim to the raging flu epidemic that year before he could return to his discovery. People once more could only speculate as to where this remarkable, skeleton-guarded cave might be.

Twenty years slipped by. In 1938 a sheepherder came into Durango with a considerable amount of well concentrated gold. He told of how he'd found a cave guarded by three skeletons, and his description of the place entirely matched the earlier stories.

This time some of the townsfolk in Durango did not allow opportunity to escape them. They coerced the man into taking a group with him back to his discovery. They would give him top shares, but in that way the discovery could be developed into a remarkable, paying mine.

The man tried to take the group back to his find, but could never again relocate it. He may have been an excellent shepherd, he certainly was no miner.

Nor have many other searchers been able to do so. As far as is known, three skeletons still guard the mine tunnel and sacks of well concentrated ore that have had only a few pokes removed from them. The mine itself has not been touched since the original miners worked it.

***

Lieutenant Jim Stewart went west from New Mexico in 1852 because he had some mail to deliver in California. Stewart was a capable man, a good soldier, one of those who worked his way up through the ranks to later become a captain. He was assigned at the time to carry some mail and probably take care of other military matters in northern California. He set out from Abiquiu, New Mexico, with a small detachment of cavalrymen and a sufficient pack train to sustain the group's proposed long journey. To avoid the hot, dry desert areas of Arizona and southern California Stewart chose to travel along the Old Spanish Trail, which runs through southwestern Colorado, into Utah, and eventually to Sacramento. There is nothing strange about Stewart going that way, as some have thought. The Spanish used this route for a century and a half prior to 1852. Santa Fe traders were using it on a steady basis in the early 1800's.

Stewart had some concern over danger from the Ute Indians along this route. The traders had stopped using the trail because several of their caravans had been wiped out by the Indians in the late 1820's. Stewart knew the Utes had lately been less aggressive, so decided to risk going that way. In Abiquiu he asked about the current conditions along the trail, and was sure to ask how to avoid getting sidetracked on the Escalante Trail.

These things taken care of, Stewart and his group set out. With them went a Mexican youth, named Jesus Garcia. That was only after the boy at last persuaded Stewart he would be a real asset to the group. He was fleeing from a difficult, orphaned condition there in Abiquiu.

The group headed northwest along the Old Spanish Trail up the Chama River. They crossed the Continental Divide into the San Juan River drainage. It is hard for many people today to visualize the times, distances, and dangers inherent to such journeys in those days.

Their first major landmark was the great hot springs on the east bank of the San Juan River, located where the town of Pagosa Springs sits today. This site was beloved by the Utes, who resisted white men coming into the area and simply taking over such natural treasures.

Utes were camped there, so Stewart's party was forced to bypass the hot springs, detouring far to the north, until they reached a secure campsite in dense stands of pine.

Their second major landmark was La Ventana. La Ventana (The Window) is a sharply cut natural gateway piercing the Continental Divide about 75 miles to the northwest of Pagosa Springs, at the head waters of Pine River. This stark hole in the mountain was visible for many miles along the Old Spanish Trail.

It was not at La Ventana, but elsewhere they crossed the divide, because of having to skirt the hot springs. By following a dim Indian trail they found a notch in the divide, above timberline, and came down into a high, green valley where the placer was discovered. Stewart and others were to later realize there are a hundred such swales beneath the rimrock along the divide.

We can't be certain of Stewart's first name let alone know just where he was supposed to have discovered some excellent gold placer. The initials R. E. have shown up in some tales, he was called Dick by some tale-tellers, and very likely some other words we won't even mention here. He was a captain, before his career was over, but it was Lieutenant Jim Stewart who fell into the creek and in drying off discovered the gold.

That's what happened. Probably either in Antelope Park, near Creede, or to the northwest of Pagosa Springs, the young courier fell into a creek and got his clothing wet. Different versions of the story have said this happened anytime from 1846 until 1864, but the most accepted date seems to be in 1852. All this makes the story seem fuzzy, but it is one of the best known tales in Southwest Colorado.

What he did do, no matter his exact name, no matter exactly where, and no matter exactly when he did it, the incidents are the basis of a treasure tale that's excited many people across the years. The fact is, it well may have been the youth, Garcia, who spotted the gold, then called Stewart's attention to it. Some tales tell it that way.

Maybe it just sounds better if Jim Stewart got sopping wet. He may have been washing dishes, as some tales tell, or as others say, his mule may have rubbed a mail pouch off into the stream and he had to retrieve it. Who knows, it happened almost 150 years ago. Whatever the case, while his clothes were drying he saw some good gold and bare-assed naked he retrieved some of it. Not panned it, only scooped a small amount of it from the shining sands.

He wrote directions to the spot in his little black notebook. Then, as you would have done, he put the gold and his notebook into his saddle bag, put on his clothes, and took his mail on to California.

Jim Stewart sold his gold there for $18, $36, or $88. Take your pick, the best guess is $36 according to what seem to be the most reliable stories.

What counts is that it caught Jim Stewart's attention. He eventually returned to Colorado to find that stream again. He took up residence in a cabin he built not too far from the New Mexico border. He spent the rest of his years looking for his rich placer, but never finding it.

Garcia, the youth along on that trip, returned to Colorado as an adult. He also looked for the placer for many years. As he dressed in traditional Mexican cowboy garb he became known in the area as El Vaquero.

He tried hard to relocate the spot on that stream, convinced it would make him rich, but was never able to do so.

There are all sorts of reasons given for not ever being able to find it. Spring floods changed the course of the streams. Rock slides covered the placer bearing bench. And so forth and so on.

The best, most rational, more probable such story is when Ute Indians, seeing Stewart pick up some gold, and fearing his discovery would bring a horde of white men into their lands, concealed it. First they put dirt over the placer area, but the dirt washed away. They then rip-rapped logs across the width and length of the placer, and placed clumps of grass over the logs. That easily could be the true story of what happened, and it goes a long way in explaining how such a well known placer could remain lost for so long. We may never know for sure. The Utes certainly would never say anything about the matter.

Plenty of others after Stewart have searched just as long and hard, and with no better results.

It is believed the best place to search for his discovery is somewhere forty to fifty miles upstream along the Piedra River from Pagosa Springs. Perhaps, but it could be almost anywhere in the high southwestern Colorado mountains.

***

Then there's the tale of Kit Carson's discovery of a shining golden placer in Colorado. If it sounds like the Jim Stewart story it's because it sounds like the Jim Stewart story. About the same time, about the same circumstances, about the same fuzzy locale. A good case can be built here for having a marvelous tale attached to a romantic figure, and Kit Carson was that!

Kit Carson was commissioned to carry messages between Santa Fe and California. Kit Carson left Santa Fe on August, 27, 1847, headed to California with a consignment of messages. That much is certain. In the party was one Lieutenant Stewart and a Mexican named Archuleta.

For whatever reasons they came to the mouth of the Blanco River, where a sixteen year old Mexican, Jesus Garcia, joined their party. The boy warned them of heavy Indian activity in the area. The group made camp on what was then called Stolsteimer Creek. They had deliberately taken a circuitous route to try to avoid conflicts with the Indians.

The next day they passed just to the south of where Pagosa Springs now sits, traveling upstream along Four Mile Creek. They are said to have changed course, going up what they believed to be Turkey Creek. People who looked into the story later believe they may have actually remained on Four Mile Creek.

Whatever the case, it was Lieutenant Stewart's turn to wash dishes that evening. He saw gold in the sands and more panning than dishwashing got done that late afternoon. By campfire he noted locational directions and the incident in general.

When they finally reached California, Stewart sold the gold for $87.00. That was three months army pay so he eventually resigned from the army. He headed back to Colorado and that good placer. His little black book containing his notes on the placer had somehow gotten burned up in a fire, but he felt certain he could go right back to the little stream with the rich placer.

Not to be. Stewart did not find it again. Kit Carson looked for it several times afterwards, he never found it. Many others have sought it and not found it. But then it could be covered over by rock slides and spring floods, hidden by Indians, or perhaps actually be over in Antelope Park near Creede or maybe on the Weninucha. Or some other little creek within a fifty mile radius. If you'd care to search for it, too, it will be in some high, rough, beautiful country!

HUERFANO COUNTY

Huerfano, the orphan. There is hardly a county in Colorado with more tales of treasure. Sure makes for some fine talk around a camp fire!

Fort Taipa was built in 1820 some twenty-one miles northwest of today's Walsenburg. The site is across Highway 129 from the general store in Farista. This is a good starting point in a search for numerous small caches thought to be in the area.

***

There is a tale of the Spanish governor of New Mexico having ten burros loaded with gold diverted to Taipa instead of heading For Santa Fe. He feared losing it to American bandits. That gold was supposedly cached in or near Taipa, and has never been recovered.

***

Somewhere near Red Wing the Lost Green Mountain Mine is yet to be found.

***

Also near Red Wing is the Lost Jasper Mine.

***

Henry Sefton once maintained and operated a toll road he hacked out across La Veta Pass. Many miners wanting to go further west in Colorado had little choice but to go that way. He collected tolls, led a frugal, simple life style, and put most of his tolls into a hidden barrel for safekeeping.

He conducted a steady, profitable business, and being almost a miser, when the first barrel was full, he sealed and buried it. The fact is he buried at least two such barrels during his tenure as toll collector. It is thought that he started on a third. These barrels contained a face amount of some $100,000, all coinage before 1910.

When Sefton knew he was dying he came to the Gomez family and told them about his buried barrels of coins. These people had known Sefton for years and had no reason to doubt his story. After his death they purchased his ranch. The Gomez family for many years did far more probing and digging than they did ranching.

This cache has never been found, but its recovery would cause jubilation in the numismatic world. Might make the finder happy, too.

***

Some ten miles north of La Veta, and about seven miles south of Badito, is the site of old Spanish fort. This was in use from 1819 until 1850. All sorts of things went on in that country, and what better place than old Spanish Fort to start checking it out?

***

Some tales are tougher to chew on than others. The story that in 1892 an ancient Indian or Spanish mummy was found in some caverns near La Veta by two miners is one such tale. Jim Coleville and Taylor Markley were at the time working in the Coyote Mine on Silver Mountain. Having completed their project they decided to take what they thought was a shortcut off the mountain. Their haste was due to increasing snow. They cannot be blamed for wanting to avoid being trapped in a blizzard. In their haste to get down the mountain they fell through a snowbank into a cave.

They found themselves in what was obviously an old mine tunnel, but they were in no mood to explore. Falling into the place only prevented them from getting down off the mountain to warmth and safety. They wanted to find a way out.

In trying to get out they discovered a niche in the cavern wall, and in it was what the at first thought was the mummy of a child. It was too heavy, though, perhaps 140 pounds. Beads around its neck, bracelets, and other jewelry upon it, were of finely worked gold. The mummy was adorned with solid gold jewelry.

A fierce blizzard forced the miners to hurriedly leave the area. Who knows exactly why, they never returned.

***

There is a legendary tale about Bottomless Lake in Mustang Canyon. The tale goes that Indians, most likely Aztecs, hurled a vast store of treasure into the 170 foot deep lake. If so it is still there, for nobody has ever recovered it.

***

Jack Simpson prospected in the La Veta Pass area in 1869. While on Silver Mountain he discovered a fabulous vein of gold ore. Specimens of the ore as- sayed, at about $17 per ounce prices, some $40,000 to the ton. It was the richest gold ore to be assayed at that time in Colorado. At today's gold prices it would be give or take a few dollars one million dollar a ton ore.

He avoided a group of would-be followers and rushed back to his discovery. Before he got there, Indians killed and scalped him. After his mutilated body was found there were those who braved the risk of meeting the same Indians. Those folks never found it then, and his rich vein still has not been relocated.

Alex Cobsky was a quiet, lonesome goat herder as a young man. That changed to some small degree in 1890 when he found some ore that assayed about $40,000 to the ton. Sound familiar? Many believe the goat herder became a miner when he found Jack Simpson's lost ledge of gold ore. It was in the right area, eight to nine miles northwest of the town of La Veta, in the Silver Mountain area.

Early in 1901 the little known goat herder suddenly became a well-known figure nationally, not just in Colorado. It happened because he brought two burros loaded with bonanza ore, the richest ever to come from a Colorado source, to a Pueblo smelter. The ore assayed at $40,000 to the ton. Remember, that's in pre-FDR prices. Cobsky was paid $12,500 for the two burro loads. He demanded that be paid in gold coins.

Alex Cobsky did not stay to bask in attention and listen to any praise, he returned to the mountains as fast as he could go.

He didn't stay that long in the mountains that time. In a couple of months he was back at the Pueblo smelter to sell more ore. This time he was paid $17,500, probably because he loaded up a third burro. $30,000 for five burro loads of gold ore, a vast sum of money in the early 1900's!

Alex Cobsky was something of a dual personality. He enjoyed friendly conversations when he came down out of the mountains. People in La Veta enjoyed talking to the bewhiskered fellow. His buying two ice cream sodas and consuming them with childish relish each time he came into La Veta showed a very human side to the man. He spent some time with relatives in Denver, bringing them presents, flooding them with pent-up tales of the mountains. He gave some gold nuggets to the children of his realatives. The other side, once he headed back into the mountains, was a dark one. He became secretive, threatening, downright spooky. He refused to talk with anybody, went far out of his way to avoid meeting or talking with anybody.

Cobsky sold about $100, 000 worth of the ore over several years, converting the proceeds into freshly minted gold coins. He was a miserly type and never spent much of that money. He would have had to consume more ice cream sodas than he ever did to make any appreciable dent in his profits!

He buried his coins around his cabin, somewhere. The man let it be known he had built the cabin over his rich mine, and that the mine was full of cleverly set death traps. As he seldom told anyone anything, but did tell that, it now makes one believe he was deliberately trying to throw people away from the truth.

The primary source of such rumors was Theodore Gibbons. Theodore was one person with whom Cobsky ever let down his guard in at least thirty years.

As a fourteen year old boy, out doing some hopefull prospecting with his older brother and some friends, Theodore had given out and would go no farther with them. They left him with the strange old man they met there on the mountain. They recognized him from his trips into town. Alex Cobsky, strange at times even with Gibbons, was no inhuman monster.

Cobsky invited young Gibbons into his cabin. Once inside the cabin the entrance to the mine was in plain view. Within it was an almost vault-like door. Cobsky told the youngster nobody other than himself ever went past that door. He somewhat vaguely threatened what would happen to anyone who dared do so. If he didn't just shoot such a person, the multitude of death traps he'd set past the door would take care of the matter. Gibbons also noted the large number of guns hanging on the wall and the stalls on one side of the cabin. These observations more or less confirmed the rumors about Cobsky keeping his animils inside during the winter.

Alex Cobsky was struck by a vehicle along Highway 76 in 1936. The man was guiding his burro along the state highway at the time. One leg and several bones were broken, and there were internal injuries. The man did not die immediately. It probably would have been a blessing if he had. He died about a year later in the state hospital at Pueblo, no money to pay any bills, his mind gone, a weakened wreck of a human being.

Cobsky had been very secretive about his doings for forty-five years and nobody knew much of anything about his rich gold mine or the gold coins he'd bought with the ore he sold. His babblings, which probably were not much listened to in his final months, offered no revelations.

It was well after his death when local Undersheriff, Carl Swift, and a deputy climbed up to Cobsky's cabin and braved going into the mine beneath the structure. There was local concern about the tales of lethal booby traps in the cabin and mine. Swift had once had a run-in with Cobsky over the man carrying a gun and threatening people with it, and knew of the man's dark humors. He did not find a true mine. It was merely an empty hole, no good ore of any kind let alone bonanza material. There was some old dynamite found. To Swift's relief he discovered no death traps of any kind.

Cobsky willed his mine to his relatives, but it turned out that he had never patented his claim. He had nothing to will to the relatives, and the proprety actually belonged to a local rancher. Howard Roepnack, an Arvada attorney, was the lawyer of Mrs. Anna Reicht and Mrs. Elizabeth Weibelt, those mentioned in Cobsky's will. He hired a La Veta mining engineer to inspect the premisis, which was done. The engineer found almost no ore values. Soon thereafter the matter was dropped. Will or not, the relatives never got a thing. It is not believed that anybody else has, either.

It has been surmised the actual mine was somewhere off and away from the cabin, as probably was the cache of coins. The few stories he'd told in La Veta were simply to keep people away.

It is doubtful, however, that either the rich workings or those gold coins are a great distance from Cobsky's old cabin.

***

A man found gold near the source of North Veta Creek not long after the Civil War. He was one of the many nameless survivors of the brutal conflict, perhaps as much fleeing horrid memories as he was seeking anything in particular. The man in fact lived with friendly Indians for a good long time, almost becoming a "white Indian". Hunting with them, dressing as they dressed, doing as they did. Even so, he did hunt for gold as he roamed the mountains.

When he at last found free gold in quartz somewhere on the headwaters of North Veta Creek the man stopped being an Indian and became a miner. He put up a cabin near his workings and accumulated four sacks of good ore, which he stored within the entrance of his mine tunnel.

The man made several trips to Denver, to sell some of his ore and buy supplies. He never gave his name to those he met. He was unusually secretive, cautious with all he met not to say exactly what he was doing or where he was doing it.

Time marched on, of course, and he found himself aging. He knew that his rough way of living and the harsh, often dangerous area in which he lived could suddenly bring his days to an abrupt end. The man made out his will in a lawyer's office early in the 1880's. gave everything he had to his only sister, a Mrs. Clark, then living in Kansas. He stated that other than what was in his cabin, his assets were four sacks filled with prime gold ore sitting in the entrance to his gold mine, and the mine itself.

Directions included with the will stated the mine was near an old fort close to an old Indian trail. It is believed this puts the site into the area of the old Spanish Fort near Sangre de Cristo Pass. He said the mine was well concealed, but he had hidden a pick in the roots of a tree to let one know the mine was close by.

When the old man returned to the mountains from his visit with the lawyer, he was never heard from again. There is no knowledge of what happened to him.

Mrs. Clark's husband left Kansas for Colorado in 1884, coming to La Veta. He searched hard for the mine that year, with no success. The following year he returned, more frantic, more talkative. Too much so, actually, for he not only talked to several people about what he sought, he also showed them the directions. In short order a number of others were looking for the mine and did so throughout that summer.

Late that fall, however, Morgan Peterson and George Dotson were heading out of the mountains just ahead of an impending snowstorm. They did not know of the hunt going on for the free gold in quartz. They chanced to pass by a tree, the roots of which had been dug up, and in the loose dirt they found a rusted pick. They carried it for some distance, but the snow was falling and they decided to simply throw it aside.

Later, when they heard the story, they had no clear idea where they threw the pick away. More importantly they had no idea of where they found it.

That most important clue was gone. The old man took special efforts to make his tunnel hard to find, and the intervening years have undoubtedly covered it up some more. The mine and the ore stored in it have not been found.

***

The Spanish built a fort at the foot of the pass that later was known as the Sangre de Cristo Pass Trail. They wanted to keep Anglos and other trespassers out of Spanish lands, and by building a fort they briefly thought they could better do so.

The idea did not work out. In the fall of 1819 a band of about a hundred Indians attacked the fort. It is believed some of the Indians were actually Frenchmen and Yankees dressed as Indians. Maybe the whole group were not actually Indians. Whoever it was, the defenders of Spanish Fort were slaughtered to a man.

Later that same year Spain and the United States agreed the

Arkansas River would serve as the boundary between Spanish lands and the newly obtained Louisiana Purchase territories. The gutted Spanish Fort was no longer needed so it was never used again. Its ruins lay abandoned for more than a hundred years.

Then in the 1920's an elderly man bought supplies in the town of Gardner. He paid his bill with eight-sided Spanish gold pieces. Never many at any one time, but the old man continued doing this at times for several years.

He once let it be known he had found the coins within the walls of old Spanish Fort. LeRoy Hafen, well-known Colorado historian, heard the story and did some investigating. He found the adobe ruins of the old Spanish Fort. He did not find any more eight-sided Spanish gold coins.

The site of the old fort is about twenty-five miles northwest of Walsenburg if you ever want to seek some Spanish gold coins the old man may have missed.

***

Two boys found eleven post-1900 $20 gold pieces between two boulder in Walsenburg. This happened in 1977.

***

A lost Spanish gold mine is thought to be in the Walsenburg area.

***

Spanish miners worked a rich mine in or near Apache Gulch. Indians killed them and their mine has never been rediscovered.

In the Apache Gulch area there have been found a number of Spanish artifacts. One local farmer claimed he found a crude gold ingot while doing field work.

***

While attempting to reach Whiskey Pass in 1892, Ashton B. Teeples got caught in a blizzard. He found some refuge from the storm at the base of a cliff. When the storm abated he found himself to be in a small valley, in which a small lake was the main feature. He saw gold nuggets in the lake's sandy bottom. He removed about $200,000 worth of nuggets from the sand before he left. When Teeples tried to return he could not find the valley and the lake within it. It should be in the Culebra Range, near Whiskey Pass. The area is five miles or so west of Monument Lake, and is about seven or eight miles northwest of Stonewall.

***

The twin Spanish Peaks arise east of the major mountain ranges in Colorado, out in flatter lands. These two majestic cones are visible for many miles, as far away as Pikes Peak on bright, clear days. These mountains were revered by the old Indian tribes, and legends go back into the days of the Aztecs. Huajatolla it was named by early Indians, meaning the "breasts of the Earth", and they thought the good things of the earth came forth from there. Sustenence, good health, well- being, those kinds of things.

Now commonly called the Spanish Peaks, these mountains have been known by many other names, as well. Huajatolla is the oldest, but Dos Hermanos, Las Cubres Hispanolas, by the Spanish, Dream Peaks, Twin Peaks, Double Mountain by the later Anglo arrivals.

The legends persist that Aztecs probed the peaks for gold long before the coming of the Spaniards, let alone the Anglos. They were said to have hauled vast amounts of gold southwards, to decorate their temples and chieftens. Some disaster brought an end to their workings. It was attributed to various gods, but today's vision of the matter suggests violent volcanic activity. It's difficult to continue mining in or around an active volcano!

The Spanish Peaks hide many secrets, and have done so from the times of the Aztecs until today.

Ruins of ancient sluices have been found on both of the twin mountains. Andrew Merritt, mining engineer and geologist believed the Spanish sluiced most of their gold from streams on the flanks of the peaks. Merritt told of one such sluice being located below Lover's Leap by William Krier of La Veta, at the mouth of the canyon below the cliffs.

In the 1500's one Fray de la Cruz is said to have headed a group of Spanish miners working rich or in one of the peaks. They used enforced Indian labor, and that mistreatment eventually got them all killed. A large store of gold being secretly hauled from the area, after the bloody rebellion, was hidden by the Indians, who also carefully covered all the Spaniards' workings. There are said to be many old trails and tunnels high up in the peaks used at that time.

Rufus Sage, "Hobo Historian", wrote of his experiences around the Twin Peaks in the 1830's and '40's. Sage and some friends chased what they thought were Mexicans, found they were an American and an Englishman driving two mules east. The mules were loaded with rich gold and silver ore. Seeing the rich specimens confirmed tales he'd heard of gold coming from that region.

In 1811 a man named Baca, while traveling through the area on an old trail south of the Spanish Peaks, found some gold nuggets.

About 1860 a traveler found a golden cup wedged in a crevice beside a tiny stream on the lower flanks of the east peak. The word, "Hermoine" was graven upon it.

Several trappers came to Bent's Fort with gold ore, wanting to sell or process it. It was thought they had found it on one of the Spanish Peaks. The trappers made a number of trips to the fort and local stories about the men and the source of their loads of gold ore expanded. It was those stories that suggested the Spanish Peaks as the source. Efforts to follow the trappers were unsuccessful. George S. Simpson, of Bent's Fort talked with the two men, and got to know them as well as anyone did. He saw their gold but they would never tell him where they got it. After a few trips to the fort the duo failed to return, and it was assumed Indians or accidents had claimed their lives. What they found, possibly Fray de la Cruz' workings, has long remained lost.

Another cache site of Montezuma's golden horde is said to be in or around the Spanish Peaks.

Colonel Fransisco came into the area in 1850. In 1860 he built a fort on the Aspishipa River. The fort proved to be a good starting point for the growing numbers of prospectors looking at the Spanish Peaks or anywhere else they might find gold and silver. Mining was done on the peaks during the 1880's and 90's by John Hudson's Spanish Peaks Mining Company. He nor several other groups made much profit from their efforts.

The stories have kept searchers coming, however. Efforts to find old workings and trails in recent years have not been too productive. Most who look believe such evidences were long ago covered by volcanic activity, avalanches, and rock slides.

The notorious Reynolds gang is believed to have put down two caches in the Spanish Peaks area. There was $63, 000 taken in an 1864 wagon train robbery in New Mexico. There was $180,000 in gold and silver coins, loot from two different train robberies. One story suggests these caches were placed under or near an arrow made of stones pointing straight at the West Spanish Peak.

Do backfilled tunnels, covered by jumbled rock slides, conceal veins of gold, rich ore probably worked by Aztecs, Spaniards, outlaws, and trappers and who knows else? Those peaks, beautiful from a distance, revered by Colorado Indians, may hide some remarkable secrets.

***

There is a persistent tale of Spanish gold buried around Muneca Rocks, to the northwest of the Spanish Peaks. A group of ten or fewer Spaniards came into the La Veta area in the early 1800's. The found the Arapaho Indians there friendly. The Spanish leader even married a local Arapaho princess and had a daughter by her. Not long after their arrival the Spaniards began to prospect and eventually found a very rich gold prospect.

The gold was supposedly taken from this rich mine by forced Indian labor. The pay streak was in the form of a planchet, or sheet of nearly pure gold, in places half an inch thick. Such formations sometimes are formed along contact zones in heavily mineralized areas where intrusive material comes into contact with limestone formations. The story could well be true. If so, Even the crudest smelting techniques would have sufficed to produce the fifty pound ingots they are said to have poured, intending to transport their new wealth back to Spain.

This scenario seemed to have been terminated when Ute Indians came into that immediate area. Long-time enemies of the Arapahos, they surely liked the Spanish friends of the Arapaho no better. A fierce battle began, during which six of the Spaniards were killed. At some point of all this hectic action, knowing they could not take the gold with them, the surviving Spaniards buried their gold ingots before the Utes could return, and fled. The princess bride and her offspring were left behind. The tale goes that the cache was in a line from some houses and about three hundred feet from the Muneca Rocks. The houses were adobe, but it would be interesting to search for traces of them.

The Spaniard is said to have returned after a number of years. He discovered that his wife had died in his absence. His daughter was grown up. He is supposed to have lived there, and died in his daughter's house. She knew the story, but she and her father had decided to not retrieve the gold nor to mine any more. She remained silent as to where the ingots were buried until as an aged woman she knew she was dying.

Muneca Rocks are located not far to the south of La Veta. The rock formation is thirty feet or so in height, standing alone in a rather open area. The rocks were so-named because the Spaniards thought them to be shaped like a doll.

This author was shown by a local man in 1973 six of seven Spanish names carved into the top of the larger rock. The seventh, he said, had already been eroded away by water collecting in natural basins atop the rocks. Two of the remaining names had grown faint by the time I saw them.

The cache near those rocks was supposed to have been eight burro loads of smelted gold bars, each bar with a weight of about fifty pounds. Obvious signs of digging show multiple efforts to locate the cache.

The dying daughter of the Spaniard had at last told her sons to look for an old iron shovel. She told them it had been placed upon a rock as a marker. A local man, some stories say one of her sons, is said to have found it, used it for some task, then cast it aside. He had no idea of which rock it was on when much later he was asked where he found it. Indeed, it would be almost impossible to dig under all the many rocks in an undetermined area around the Muneca Rocks.

JACKS0N COUNTY

Out of the way, even today, Jackson County. Beautiful country, but mostly bypassed. Quite a few things started in the past, but much of it never got finished up. Maybe that's good, it's a great place to go trout fishing or deer hunting!

A rich outcropping of gold was discovered near Rabbit Ears Pass. It is in the area of the headwaters of Muddy River high in the Gore Range.

***

Also in the Rabbit Ears Pass area a rich silver deposit remains hidden. In or near the workings is a cache of silver bullion crudely smelted from the deposit.

***

Teller, a ghost site twenty miles east of Rand, once boasted a 2,000 pop- ulation. There was extremely rich silver ore in the area, but terrible transportation problems shut down mining there. Several small caches have been recovered in Teller, and the probability of others still being there is high. No running down to the bank back in the boom days!

***

To the east and a little north of old Teller is what's left of the rich Entre Mile silver mine. The ore is still there for someone to extract. It's not a lost mine, it's a case of lost owners. The ore body is at the head of Michigan Creek on the western flanks of Mt. Richtofen. The ore had a high silver content, a shaft was sunk to about two hundred feet.

Isolation did it in, no doubt. There was mismanagement. There was never a profit, and the debts ran up. Creditors stopped being nice. In 1885 the property was sold at auction in Vandalia for $60,000 to meet its debts.

To many peoples' surprise the mine did not reopen. The new owner was not to be found, in the records, in real life, not anywhere. A lost mine owner. Many wanted to buy or lease the property but the property owner could not be found. This is 600 ounce silver ore.

Now water has filled the workings, the price of silver is down, and there it sits.

JEFFERSON COUNTY

You ask who treasure really belongs to? Well, if you don't think it's wrong to pick up a penny from the ground, and stick it in your pocket, the only difference in that penny and a million dollars is seven zeroes and a period between where the one is in each case. Treasure does no good tucked away, unused, forgotten. The person who finds a treasure deserves it as much or more than anyone else does.

I guess if the government, lawyers, your relatives, or anyone else would like to have whatever treasure you may find, they ought to do a little research, some thinking and looking. Then maybe they will find their own treasure. If you do find it, keep your mouth shut just like most of the old time prospectors did, and enjoy the products of your efforts.

The Ralston Creek Road was a major short cut between Denver and Central City in the mining boom of Central City, a far easier route than others for many years. Ore wagons and stages had a rough, steep route to travel with natural and human dangers to face. Outlaws took advantage of the rugged area. For years there were numerous robberies along the Ralston Creek Road.

The ruins of a stone house right at water's edge along the Ralston Dam Reservoir shore was a frequent rendezvous point for outlaws. There are a number of thieves' caches supposed to be buried around or near there.

The most impressive such story involves a chest of gold heisted from a stage. Hasty digging for stashes went on where the Ralston Creek Dam was to be constructed when plans to build the dam were announced.

***

A different chest of gold was stolen from a stagecoach traveling the Ralston Creek Road. It was buried near the holdup site and has never been recovered.

***

$50,000 in gold bullion, outlaw loot, was buried in this vicinity. The probable spot is now beneath the waters behind Ralston Creek Dam.

***

On the southwest corner of Standley Lake is the site of the Ralston Road Stage Station. There was a great amount of outlaw activity in both directions along the road in the area.

***

The waters of Standley Lake, not far from the outskirts of Denver, cover some most interesting mineral deposits. In 1902 drillers hit eight feet of gold-bearing material at an 800 feet depth. The ore at that time had a $30 per ton value. This property was in the area involved in plans to build a big dam and reservoir to impound waters just outside Denver.

The residents on what was to be the eastern end of the reservoir did not mind selling their properties in 1902 for the dam and reservoir construction. Those on the western end of it minded a great deal!

There were coal seams underlying that area, and more importantly from a financial viewpoint, the drilling had discovered a deposit of gold ore some eight feet thick at a depth of 800 feet. The property owners vowed to fight to the bitter end when condemnation papers were drawn up. An engineer testified there were only some gold traces, and that evident only in one of seven drilling records, and a few coal deposits. That, in his opinion, should not be a factor in blocking the progress of the dam construction.

A bitter fight was at last avoided when those constructing the dam agreed to take only surface rights, for the reservoir purposes.

Not many years after the dam was built and the reservoir was filled an engineer went over the drilling records. This had not been done before. All seven of the drilling records showed the seam of gold ore containing gold with values of $12 to $45 to the ton.

Futile efforts were made to postpone construction of the dam until the deposit was mined. The deposit is still 800 feet deep, and it is also beneath the waters of Standley Lake.

***

In 1888 in Harrisburg a glass jar half filled with gold dust was found only inches below the surface outside the front door of a deserted cabin. The two ranchers who found it sold it for about $6,000.

***

Ben Leeper was an outlaw in the 1880's. He lived in a cabin on or very near the road to Denver at Warder's Hill. Not only was the man an outlaw, he was very much a hermit. He is known to have buried some of his loot not far from his cabin. He died in jail, and none of his caches have been found.

Ben Leeper buried some $200.000 in gold coins near Golden in the late 1800's. The stash has never been recovered.

***

Fourteen gold ingots were taken from a Ulysses stagecoach on the Gold Road while going over Eagle's Nest Pass. This was on a route between Denver and Cripple Creek. The outlaws were caught in a cabin west of the South Platte River and killed but a search of the cabin and the area around it did not produce the stolen ingots. Hundreds of Denver residents for a time afterwards searched for the gold, but it is not believed the ingots were found.

***

Indians worked a rich gold ledge somewhere in Stevens Gulch not far from Strontia Springs. They filled eagle and goose quills, knowing they could trade it to white men for more useful things, such as cloth, beads, iron utensils, and whiskey. Many early prospectors attempted to locate their rich workings but failed to do so.

Strontia Springs was a station on the Colorado and Southern Railroad in the Platte Canyon.

Shortly after the Civil War two young men from St. Joseph, Missouri, came into the area. They listened to stories of gold being found near Strontia Springs told them by Henry Jackson, an old half Indian, half negro man who'd been born and grown old there.

The young fellows soon found the source of gold, but had to work very hard indeed to get supplies into the narrow canyon and begin to get good gold concentrates. It took months, but they eventually accumulated a wagon load of carefully hand picked gold ore.

This load they took back to St. Joseph and sold. While there they drew a crude map of where they had been working.

In 1867 they headed back to their mine. The never made it. Their bodies were found near Devil's Head Mountain and it was thought they had been headed along or near the Jarre Canyon Road. Their murder was attributed to Indians.

Relatives of the young men contacted Henry Jackson, asking him if he could not find their workings. They sent him a copy of the crude map. He searched, but never found the gold.

He did in 1910 find some rusted mining tools well concealed in a dense cluster of brush.

Then in 1911 a young fellow named Carl R. Johnson, out rabbit hunting, picked up some pieces of rusty quartz near the headwaters of Stevens Gulch. He noticed several veins of the rusty looking material.

Eventually he crushed the quartz and panned the results. A string of fine gold showed up from that handful of crushed material.

In 1912 Johnson returned to the headwaters of Stevens Gulch. He found plenty of rusty looking quartz, again, but he could not relocate that which contained the gold. He remembered he had been forcing his way through some very dense brush while after a rabbit, and coming upon a hole in the ground. That must have been where he got the quartz with gold in it. The hole likely was where the Missouri fellows had worked.

***

Amos Alright found a big, rich silver vein in the 1860's about twenty miles southwest of Denver. A huge rock loomed over the three foot wide vein somewhere in or near what is now Kenny Park. He dug out an amount he could carry, then carefully concealed his work. Amos returned about a month later and this time extracted enough ore to fully load several mules. He returned to his home in Illinois. The man became ill and died without ever returning to his strike or telling anyone its location. Many people have searched in vain for this bonanza.

***

In 1960 a Denver cigar store, actually a front for a bookie operation, was held up by three bandits. Two of the three were Denver policemen. They took about $34,000. Because of the nature of its operations the holdup was not reported.

It is said the robbers held out $4,000 for spending money. The rest they put down in two $15,000 caches. One they hid near a churchyard in Littleton. The other they cached somewhere along the road winding up to Lookout Mountain, near Golden.

One of the policemen was indicted shortly after this happened during the incredible police scandals to hit Denver at that time. The other policeman dared not go near the caches for fear of being caught doing so. The third man died.

The $15,000 in stolen money cached somewhere along the road that leads from Golden to Lookout Mountain should remain well hidden. The man who actually hid this money died of a heart attack soon after being exposed as one of the three thieves. The cache has not been found.

KIT CARSON

The nice thing about gold coins is that almost nothing bothers them. Our new zinc-clad cents begin to deteriorate the day they are minted, and in bad soil conditions can be completely eaten away in less than a year. Copper and brass gets green and rots away if there's moisture, soil acids, or heavy mineralization in the ground. Silver is better, but it can also deteriorate under bad conditions. Gold? Gold can be in the ground a hundred or a thousand years and come out looking as though it was minted yesterday.

Some $10,000 in Spanish gold is thought to be buried near Burlington.

LAKE COUNTY

There's a lot to be said for just sitting here breathing pine air, sipping coffee, and eating campfire ashes flavored beans. I talked for years about someday doing that with my dad, and I now regret that we never did it. So, dadburn it, drink up!

A fabulous vein of silver and gold ore was found in the Taylor Park area by a man named Murdie. The vein was over a foot in diameter, close by a stream. Liking its looks, Murdie took samples. It assayed at 2,400 ounces of silver and 95 ounces of gold to the ton. Murdie returned to Taylor Park the following year but could not find the vein. Differing water levels made him unsure he was even on the right stream. His relatives took up where he left off, but they could do no better. The vein remains lost.

***

In 1859 a man found a rich exposed structure of gold ore in a gulch somewhere between Twin Lakes and the headwaters of the Arkansas River. The man was pretty well lost at the time, surviving on berries and things he would formerly never have considered eating. He at last came wandering into the gulch that was to soon become Central City, on his way out of the mountains to head back east. He had enough of that horrible wilderness, and even the gold he found was not enough to make him change his mind. He had property back home, and a way of making a living. He decided looking for gold in those hard, cruel mountains was only for idiots.

To the group who welcomed him to their campfire that evening, and fed him, he explained where he got his marvelous gold specimens. No, he would not lead them back to that spot. He told them it was in a gulch somewhere between Twin Lakes and the upper Arkansas River Valley if they wanted to look for it. He even drew them a map, of sorts, from an admittedly confused memory of his tortuous wanderings.

Some of those who listened to his tale, or heard it from others, are those who found gold in California Gulch and set off the Leadville area boom. S. S. Slater, John Currier, George Stevens, Abram Lee, Rufus Alvord, James Miller, and Ike Rafferty. These were men who became well known in and around Leadville. They are said to have been encouraged by this tale to go seek those nuggets and wound up finding different good spots. They nor many others were never able to relocate the lost man's lost gulch.

***

Gold can still be found in the gulches around Leadville. The town began because of the original gold strike in 1860. Thousands of miners have lived and worked here off and on over all the years since. Caches, artifacts, and individual coins have been found in the area, and more is still to be found.

***

High grading ran rampant in and around Leadville. There are many stories of high grade ore caches. A few have been recovered, there are still many right where they were hidden.

***

There is supposed to be a cave in Capital Hill, near Leadville. A vague story persists concerning an unknown amount of treasure hidden within that cave.

***

It is believed the old silver king, Tabor, cached an immense fortune in or near the Tabor Hotel in Leadville. His estate was short huge sums after he died. There may also be one or more caches of those missing funds in or near

-91-

his Baby Doe Mine.

***

Baby Doe Tabor lived at Tabor's rich mine for years after his death, almost a total recluse. She continued to mine silver, and secreted the ore away. All that silver did her little good. She froze to death in the winter of 1935. Like her husband's missing funds her cache of silver ore remains unfound.

***

A group of Frenchmen are said to have cached $3,000,000 in gold ore near Leadville.

***

There were two Mexican robbers using a cabin near Leadville as a hideout in 1880. They were suspected of killing unwary miners and stealing their gold and money, at least $10,000 worth. Bat Masterson was called upon to take care of the situation. He eased up close to the cabin before dawn and shot them as they came out of the cabin. That took care of the robbers, but he could find no loot when he ransacked the place. Very likely the loot was cached somewhere outside the cabin, possibly near a spring close by.

***

Half Moon Gulch is not far to the southwest of Leadville. Jesse James was supposed to have had a hideout at Half Moon Gulch, during 1879. Perhaps he did. It's a narrow valley, with forested, overhanging cliffs, a rushing stream offering good water, plenty of look out points, and natural caves. It is not known for sure that he and his gang was involved in a number of local holdups, especially in California Gulch, but it was always suspected. He and various gang members were often seen in different towns in the upper Arkansas River Valley. The signatures of Frank James and several other gang members, dated 1883, are to be seen on the register sheets of Hotel Jackson in Poncha Springs.

The group was forced to flee the area, because whether or not he and his gang were involved in the many robberies going on at the time, his reputation made him one of the first suspects in anything and everything bad.

It is believed Jesse may have left several caches in Half Moon Gulch even though he had a reputation of never stashing much money. One stash he may have put down there is said to have contained almost $50,000 in gold and silver coins.

***

The Lost Gulch Gold Mine remains hidden in the Leadville area.

***

LA PLATA COUNTY

Good treasure stories are cyclical. About every twenty to thirty years they wear down a bit, get old, and people lose interest in hearing them. Then along comes a new generation. Those old tales come alive again, just as fresh, just as interesting, just as remarkable as they ever were. I guess that's why you're here snuggling up to the fire, listening, instead of crawling into a nice, warm sleeping bag like sensible folks would do.

Somewhere on the western flanks of Parrott Mountain is a rich gold lode. It's been called the Lost Lone Wolf Gold mine, so that's what we'll call it. This is one of the best of the best lost lode stories as far as this author is concerned. Somebody with the observational skills and stick-to-it grit of the old-timey prospectors perhaps can and probably will relocate this 1870's bonanza some day.

There is no doubt the ledge exists. One man found and worked it for a time. It was seen by an engineer employed by H. A. W. Tabor. Tabor liked what the engineer told him about it enough to write out a check for $25,000 for the claim. All that is well documented, as is much of the rest of the story.

When Parrott City was developed in 1874 to support placering activity on the great alluvial deposits at the mouth of the rugged La Plata Canyon it brought in all sorts of men seeking to make their fortunes. John Moss, working for the California Mining Company, headed the efforts to create Parrott City. In 1874 Parrott City was built at the base of the mountain to the west of the mouth of La Plata Canyon. The mountain de- rived its name from the new camp, thus, Parrott Mountain. Moss is said to have spent $100,000 in developing Parrott City. The belief was that the placers would pay that expenditure back many times over. $100,000 was enough money in the 1870's to guarantee an immediate, frantic, enthused inrush of men into the area. The camp boomed, and all sorts of hopeful, rowdy, some honest, most not-too-honest sorts were drawn there like moths to a golden flame.

One of these men was a twenty-five year old hard-rock miner arrived from Leadville, where he'd been working. He was quiet, kept to himself, said little to anybody about anything. He looked and listened. This may have been why he became known as Lone Wolf.

He was not interested in the fevered placer talk, so he bought supplies and headed away from Parrott City, around to the west flanks of nearby Parrott Mountain. He was seeking good ore veins, not placer gold. At that time nothing was known about the vein structures of the area, nobody had yet prospected for lodes. Lone Wolf's work in the Leadville area had given him a good working knowledge of vein structures, how to look for and work them if found. As almost everyone in Parrott City other than Lone Wolf was interested only in placer potentials, and were grubbing along the stream beds, the young hard rock miner had the mountains pretty much to himself.

Much of this part of the story was passed on by E. F. McCartney, early day freighter into the area, once county commissioner of La Plata County. McCartney came into La Plata county in the 1880's, after the Parrott City boom busted because there really wasn't as much gold placer in that vast alluvium as had been thought. But McCartney did know knew all the old timers who were there when Lone Wolf made his strike. He became interested in and well acquainted with the Lone Wolf story.

Lone Wolf liked the west side of Parrot Mountain. Plenty of springs, plenty of game, no streams so there were no placer miners. There was ample grazing for his burros. The area was covered by stands of spruce interspersed with dense thickets of scrub oaks. Ravines dissected the western flank of Parrott Mountain in places. Lone Wolf found various indications in one of these that made him look even harder.

Somewhere in that narrow ravine, one of numerous washes down the western flanks of Parrott Mountain, somewhere close to its base, Lone Wolf found a small protrusion. It caught his fullest attention. When he broke of several pieces he knew he'd struck it rich. There was visible gold laced through the rock.

Lone Wolf did enough work on the ledge to put heavy loads on two burros. There had to have been at least the beginnings of a tunnel along the ore seam. He sold the two burro loads of ore in nearby Parrott City to an ore buyer for some substantial but now unknown amount of cash. Then he hurried out of town, answering no questions.

Lone Wolf did not at that time return to his discovery. He instead went to Alamosa, two hundred miles east in the San Luis Valley. Alamosa was a railhead, and from there he sent samples he'd kept back from the ore buyer to H. A. W. Tabor. Why not, that was a name in mining circles everyone knew, with money flowing from his many silver properties. Perhaps the Silver King would be interested in buying a truly good gold property. If Tabor was interested, stated a note accompanying the samples to Tabor, Lone Wolf would take $25,000 cash for his discovery.

The presentation and the samples did interest Tabor. Enough so that he sent a mining engineer to Alamosa so he could go inspect the property. The man brought with him a check for $25,000, payable to Lone Wolf, should the engineer find the ore body to be as good as it was said to be.

The engineer rode horseback with Lone Wolf from Alamosa, visited the claim on the west side of Parrott Mountain, and was favorably impressed. He offered Lone Wolf the $25,000 check.

Lone Wolf may have known lode veins, how to look for them, how to work them, but he knew nothing of checks. Checks were not common in that time and place. Hard money was best, currency was fine if hard coinage was scarce. He told the engineer he had told Tabor cash, he wanted cash, not some piece of paper.

The engineer tried to explain to Lone Wolf that the check could be immediately turned into cash at any bank, all Lone Wolf had to do was endorse it. The engineer could not sign it for Lone Wolf. What did endorse mean? He had to sign his name to the back of the check.

No. Hell no. Lone Wolf was certain these rich men were trying to fleece him out of his rich discovery. He told the engineer to take the check back to Tabor, he didn't want to sell his property, anyway. He probably used so some colorful language in telling him, too.

The engineer left Alamosa and Tabor never thought any more about the San Juans. To his ultimate ruin Tabor did not ever acquire gold properties.

Lone Wolf, knowing his meager workings were well concealed, drifted off to see if he could get rich in Nevada. It is hard in retrospect to understand why he just didn't work the site.

Years passed by, as they have a way of doing. The tale of the lost Lone Wolf Ledge became just one of many such stories.

Then in the first half of 1927 there was a rich gold strike around Mojave, Nevada. Robert McCartney, grand son of already mentioned E. F. McCartney, and Milton DeLuche, the son-in-law of E. F. McCartney, went out to the Nevada area to check out what was going on. Strictly by happenstance they met a scraggly, taciturn old man who turned out to be none other than Lone Wolf. He wouldn't talk to them until almost incidentally they offered to buy him breakfast and a drink, whichever order he wished. That made him somewhat more sociable.

When he discovered over breakfast the young men were from southwestern Colorado he began to open up. He told them of his rich strike and the story of Tabor's man trying to bamboozle him out of it. For years he'd thought of that check as being some kind of deed form.

Then, as he realized he was saying too much, he mumbled something about planning to go back and doing something with the lode. He left the young man and wandered grumbling away into whatever was left of his life.

Upon hearing about this incident E. F. McCartney recalled that in 1908 the engineer who'd checked out the site with Lone Wolf visited the La Plata area again, checking to see what had become of Lone Wolf's rich strike. He was amazed to hear that nobody knew what he was talking about. There was no rich mine on the west side of Parrott Mountain. There was no more Parrott City.

For a time the engineer hoped to relocate the site and develop it. The fact was, he could not find his way back to what he'd been shown. There seemed to be more scrub oak, denser stands of spruce, the ravines more grown up. Several people became interested enough in the engineer's story and questions to begin to do some looking for the ledge.

One of these people was a man named George Brawner. Brawner was a long-time, experienced prospector. He felt confident, if he went about it systematically, that he stood a good chance of finding the spot. He knew there were few pronounced outcroppings on the west side of Parrott Mountain. He well knew how overgrown the ravines were. Even so, he felt the story was too good not to look into. So that is what he began to do.

For many weeks he avoided the ravines, feeling they were too overgrown to allow erosion to expose veins. Late in the summer, however, he came to one narrow ravine that for some reason demanded his attention. In a thick clutter of oak brush, protruding from an seemingly endless mass of leaf mold, Brawner saw a loose, sharp-edged fragment of rock.

The rock seemed out of place. Brawner picked it up, it had a good hefty, heavy feel. He wiped off the leaf mold and dirt, and at once could see the gold shot through the stone. He had picked up a very rich piece of ore.

Brawner looked about him carefully. He could see no exposed outcropping. He was crouched in the narrow, brush-choked ravine, almost at the very base of the west side of Parrott Mountain.

He soon noticed a slight depres- sion up the gully from him. It was several feet in length, at the very foot of the slope of the mountain. In the depression he found mixed in with the layers of leaf mold several short, rotted poles with axe marks at each end.

Scratching around in the leaf mold exposed several more ore specimens. Each was more or less the same as the first piece he discovered.

Brawner was convinced he'd found the remains of Lone Wolf's meager workings, but as it was getting dark he picked up all the samples he could find and headed back to his camp.

He needed to get financial backing to develop his find. He offered McCartney a chance to buy in, but McCartney had too little money to meet other obligations as the time. He talked to several others, then got R. E. "Ross" McGirr interested in going in with him.

Brawner and McGirr traveled from Durango on the Rio Grande Southern passenger train to where they got off at the Cima switch. At that point it comes close to the foot of Parrott Mountain. From there Brawner was to lead his new partner up to the claim, around on the west side.

They may have gone a half mile before Brawner stopped, complaining of suddenly being very tired. They rested, then started to go on, and Brawner fell over dead. He had suffered an acute, fatal heart attack.

McGirr had no idea where the ledge was. He did not pursue the matter, and neither did anyone else. There were those who did some looking, but they usually gave up rather quickly when they got to the west side of Parrott Mountain.

Are you equal thirds mining engineer, billy goat, and mule? If so, that rich ledge is right where Lone Wolf and Brawner left it. If you search hard enough in the leaf mold, somewhere in a narrow, tangled ravine at the base of the west flank of Parrott Mountain, you may be the one to find it.

***

To the north of Parrott Mountain, in the Root Gulch area, is the Lost Clubfoot Gold mine.

From the mid-1990's back to the mid-1870's is at least 120 years. The main character in this tale we only know as "Clubfoot". That's all anyone called him then, so that is what we'll call him now. His right foot was congenitally deformed and he could never walk as well as everyone else did. Otherwise Clubfoot was bright, active, observant He arrived, as other fortune seekers in the Parrott City area were doing, to seek his fortune.

The crippled man arrived in Parrott City well equipped, but he had no intentions of doing any placering as almost everyone else who arrived at Parrott City hoped to do. He was a "hard-rock" man, intending to look for a good vein structure that could be developed into a highly productive mine. His string of three pack burros and good supplies and equipment backed up his intentions. Two burros were to carry the supplies and equipment, the big, beige beast was to carry Clubfoot. Clubfoot told anyone who'd listen that his tawny jack had four good feet, every one of which was better than his bad foot even if it had been good. He was the eyes, the jack was the feet, together they would go find a good gold vein in solid rock.

For a time Clubfoot camped at the edge of Parrott City, where his animals had good water and grazing. He prospected out from that base camp over a period of time.

Unlike Lone Wolf, who was in the Parrott City area at the same time, Clubfoot looked over Parrott Mountain and did not like it. Not enough outcroppings, too overgrown. From the top of Parrott Mountain, however, Clubfoot saw an area he liked better.

A rough, tumbled basin, which eventually became known as Root Gulch, lay to the north of Parrott Mountain. It drained into the La Plata River in the rugged area north of Parrott City. It looked like the kind of place Clubfoot wanted to explore. There was less scrub oak, fewer stands of spruce, steeper exposed ridges where there was little chance for layers of leaf mold to accumulate atop good veins. Such conditions made his looking for exposed veins easier.

Clubfoot came down off Parrott Mountain and never had any reason to return. He concentrated on the rugged Root Gulch area.

Clubfoot's prospecting technique was simple. His burro could carry him into rugged spots where most men would hesitate to go. He only had to watch the surroundings, looking for exposed vein structures as they plodded along. When he saw something he wanted to examine, Clubfoot would get off the burro, and hobble or crawl to the spot. He never seemed to get in a hurry. The burro would patiently wait for him, glad to have time to nibble the greenery.

Little or none of this would be known had not Clubfoot become good friends with the big Dutchman blacksmith in Parrott City who sharpened his drill steel. This was a big, honest, friendly man, expert in his work, who knew how to keep confidences. This impressed Clubfoot, who needed more than just having his driving steel sharpened. It is human nature for even very private individuals, as Clubfoot was, to want to have at least one good friend. The Dutchman was concerned about Clubfoot and his announced intentions to explore the mountains alone. It did not seem safe to the Dutchman that Clubfoot intended to do his prospecting alone. He could fall, he could smash his good foot, he could run into a bear. any number of bad things can and often do happen to a man alone. Clubfoot told him not to worry, being with his big, beige burro was not being alone.

The fact was, Clubfoot located his rich vein not long after he ventured up into Root Gulch. He went around the east side of Parrott Mountain to get there. On up the La Plata Canyon to the mouth of Root Gulch, two or more miles up the then trackless gulch through heavy timber into the upper reaches of Root Gulch. As almost everyone else in the area was looking up and down the bottoms of the gulches Clubfoot had the country almost to himself.

He set up camp beneath a great spruce tree in almost the exact center of the rugged basin. He was there to prospect. Evidently Clubfoot found a good vein structure not long after setting up camp. There is the possibility he found it even before he set up his camp. Because of his clubbed foot it is doubtful the vein is too far from where his camp.

The man left Parrott City early in June. Nobody saw a thing of him until he returned to Parrott City in the middle of July. He was not seen coming into town, he simply showed up, going immediately to the Dutchman's blacksmith shop.

He had the big blacksmith take from one burro all his drill steel, tied up together in canvas. Every piece was dull and needed to be sharpened. Clubfoot took a small but heavy canvas bag from the back of the other pack burro. In reply to the Dutchman's unasked question he told him he'd driven about ten feet of tunnel. He mentioned that he covered it well before he left. By this time Clubfoot knew the Dutchman would keep what he told him confidential.

Then Clubfoot proceeded to show his big friend the sack's contents. It was extremely rich gold ore. Clubfoot repeatedly warned the Dutchman not to say anything to anybody about what he was being told or shown. The Dutchman reassured him that whatever Clubfoot told him was safe and would go no farther.

Clubfoot did not say precisely where his workings were. His secretiveness bordered on paranoia, which is understandable. Too many scoundrels in the area would try to take it away from him if they knew of it. He was therefore careful not to mention any landmarks or say anything that could allow anyone to know where to look for his barely started tunnel.

Clubfoot said he had located the vein soon after he came into Root Gulch. The rock along one side of the vein structure was not too hard, so he had no problems in working along the face of the lead. He carried no more material away from his developing tunnel than he had to, not wanting to create a dump to give away his workings. He threw what waste he had to dispose of into the nearby stream, and that at some distance from the workings and never in the same spot.

He stopped working not only because his drill steel was dull, he also was out of supplies. He brought out only enough ore to take care of those two problems. He explained he'd come back by the way of the west side of Parrot Mountain, probably coming out of Root Gulch through the gap in the divide between the East Mancos and the La Plata Rivers, a route that later was called Sunset Pass. Not only was going down through Root Gulch a hard trip, he did not want to create a trail for people to notice or follow. Crippled, maybe, but crafty, that Clubfoot.

Clubfoot did not want to sell the ore himself. He understood what happened when some naive prospector let slip the discovery of a rich vein. It was almost impossible for an ordinary prospector to sell rich ore without setting off a frenzy in a camp. He knew that suddenly he would not be all alone up there in Root Gulch, he would be surrounded by hundreds if not thousands of men trying to find something just as good or trying to wedge him out of his strike. He would be unable to make a move without being watched and followed. For these reasons he wanted the big Dutchmen to sell the ore, and for doing so he was willing to give him fifty per cent of whatever it brought. The Dutchman could do this without anyone raising an eyebrow whereas Clubfoot, should he show only one good piece of that ore, would create a firestorm of greed.

So the Dutchman agreed, and soon quietly sold Clubfoot's ore. The blacksmith was later to say it was the quickest, easiest $160 he'd ever made.

Nobody saw Clubfoot quietly leave Parrott City, and only the Dutchman had some idea of where he was. He kept his word, saying nothing about the matter to anybody.

The last time anyone saw Clubfoot alive was approximately two weeks later. He again quietly came into Parrott City, this time only riding his tawny jack. He wanted to see the blacksmith. The Dutchman was gone out of town on busi ness, to Clubfoot's disappointment. He posted a letter, bought a few more supplies, and quietly departed.

The very next day the tawny jack showed up again at the edge of Parrott City, where Clubfoot's camp had been for a time. Clubfoot was not on him. The saddle and bridle were intact, but the ends of the reins had been broken and the saddle blanket was missing. Old tawny did not have a scratch, no blood, no sign of a bruise. The immediate, natural question was, where was Clubfoot? His blacksmith friend wanted to know what had happened to the man, for he knew the burro would not be back in town without him. Had the burro not come, probably nobody would ever have known of Clubfoot's death.

A group of men rounded up horses. Most of them had no idea where to go, but one grizzled prospector was a pretty fair tracker and he knew as much or more about burros than most other people knew. He told the group to follow him, he would turn Clubfoot's burro loose and just follow the burro. Very likely the animal would go right back to wherever he'd left Clubfoot.

That's what they did. The burro went back uphill along the tracks he'd made coming downhill a couple of days earlier.

Near the upper end of the scrub oak zone on the mountain the group found the missing saddle blanket and the missing broken pieces of reins entangled in some dense oak roots. Old Tawny obviously had gotten the loose reins caught and held for a time. By the looks of the disturbed ground around those roots he'd tried hard to get loose, and eventually did so.

The men knew they must be close to whatever had happened, because the burro must have been running wild to get caught up the way he had. They found what they were looking for not far up into the gap that is now Sunset Pass. The mauled remains of Clubfoot. They figured out what happened as best they could from the tracks around Clubfoot's body.

For some reason the man must have been dismounted when a mother bear and her two cubs came into the scene. Mother bears are notoriously vicious when they feel their cubs might be in danger, and Clubfoot's slow, awkward movements must have annoyed and angered her.

The group split up. Two or three men and the grizzled old prospector took Clubfoot's body back to Parrott City. The others did a little exploring, enough to find Clubfoot's camp. They gathered up his few belongings, which didn't amount to too much. None of his mining tools were there, and they could not find where he'd been working although that actually was what they were looking for. They found no notes, no letters, nothing to give any hint as to where he had been digging. One man took the time to blaze the big spruce tree, to mark the campsite.

Clubfoot was buried in the little cemetery at Parrott City. They found a single $20 gold piece and some small change on his body. There were a few pieces of gold ore at the camp. They sold his belongings, getting enough together to have a somewhat drunken wake.

Only the blacksmith knew why no tools were found at the camp, and he said nothing at the time. He had no intentions of looking for the diggings himself. He had nobody to entrust with the information on such a prize. Still, he could not just forget it, the ore was too good, and he did have some interest in what Clubfoot discovered. Was he not a partner, of sorts?

There was some interest in what Clubfoot had been doing, for the few nuggets he had were enough to cause all sorts of speculation. The grizzled old prospector who led the search party actually did some looking. Rains after Clubfoot's death, however, had erased any signs of Clubfoot's activities. The workings obviously had been well concealed by the crippled man.

Everybody went on to other things soon enough, even the grizzled old prospector. The story was almost forgotten.

Then in the early 1880's a young man got off the train in Durango. New track had just come into the new town. He asked about Parrott City, and was told there was no more Parrot City by that time. The great placers in that vast alluvia at the mouth of had not been as rich as people hoped. Big amounts of work and money went into those gravels, only small amounts of gold came out. Parrott City faded away almost overnight.

The young man persisted, asking many people. A grand uncle of his had found a very rich gold mine near Parrott City a few years earlier. A club-footed man, his grand uncle. The man's sister had received a letter from him, describing what he'd found. He intended to bring out a large shipment of extremely rich gold ore in the fall and planned to visit the family.

Then never another word. The family did not know what to think, and the young fellow was in the area to find out the facts.

He did not find out the facts. Nobody seemed to know anything, for old Clubfoot had been tight-lipped about his efforts. The young man found nobody who knew much about him, most knew nothing at all. The young man left the area as he came, via the railroad, all his questions unanswered.

The Dutch blacksmith heard about the young man some time later. For the first time he told what he knew about the matter. He had given up any idea of any personal gain from Clubfoot's discovery.

The Lost Clubfoot Mine story was suddenly alive and well. It revived interest in more prospecting just as the mining fever in the area was fanned into flame by the discovery of the Lucky Moon gold vein on a ravine running into Root Gulch to the south of Clubfoot's old campsite. Then the Mountain Lily, a big gold producer, began operations maybe a mile to the north of the campsite.

When in the 1930's The Red Arrow Mine was opened, that really had everybody telling and retelling Clubfoot's story. The Red Arrow, the biggest producer of all the good producers in that area. It was directly west of the campsite. It was on the other side of the divide down into the Mancos drainage, but still very close. Nuggets the size of hen's eggs were plucked out of the Red Arrow veins. It has been thought the Red Arrow is merely the westward end of Clubfoot's discovery.

Still the workings of old Clubfoot have never been found. Perhaps that and other rich lodes remain to be found in that highly mineralized zone.

Maybe if you want to be the one to find barely worked outcropping you ought to buy a tawny burro and do some riding. Just avoid the bears!

***

In 1901 a man named Hollingsworth came across a rich outcropping of gold ore in the La Plata Mountains. Hollingsworth, even while hunting deer, always kept his eyes open for good-looking outcroppings. The ledge was on a sharp ridge somewhere between Snow slide Gulch and Root Creek. The rock was recognizable sylvanite, a telluride ore, and Holligsworth at once thought this material contained good gold values.

He took careful note of landmarks for he had at the time been tracking a deer. He intended to shoot the deer, lug it back to his cabin in La Plata Canyon, then come back and stake out a claim. He could see the Southern Boy Mine on the other side of the La Plata Canyon from the ridge where he stood. That was in an open area just below his own cabin. The Gold King tailings dump was also visible, on the side of Lewis Mountain. There was a wide-open stretch of rim rock close below him, on the opposite side of Snowslide Draw. These observations firmly in mind, Hollingsworth continued to track the deer he'd been following. He finally shot it, perhaps a half mile farther along the ridge, at the head of Snowslide Draw.

He wired the deer's hind legs to a spruce limb to dress it out. He'd brought a couple of lengths of wire for such a purpose. That done, he cut off the lower hind legs and left them hanging there in the spruce tree, thinking they would lead him right back to the outcropping. He was glad to be finished with the job, because it was starting to snow and he had to carry the dressed carcass quite aways back to his cabin.

Of course the snow continued to fall after he reached the cabin, but he was in no hurry. After examining the ore sample carefully he would have liked for the snow to stop, but it did not. The ore was the richest he'd ever found, by far. He put the sample carefully aside, where he could not get it mixed up with other samples.

The winter set in, and there was no going back to the ridge until spring. Hollingsworth, able to do simple assays from a long mining career, checked his piece of ore. He was astonished, and wondered if he had made some stupid mistake. He sent of a bit of his sample to get a more studied opinion.

Eventually the assay result came back. It was better, not worse than his own test. A ton of that ore would be worth almost $40,000. This was in 1901, and gold had not yet reached $20 per troy ounce.

You can guess what happened. Experienced miner, prospector and deer hunter that he was, knowing that mountainous area as well or better than most, Hollingsworth could never again find the rich outcropping along that ridge. He could see the various landmarks from almost anywhere along the ridge, so he soon discovered they were not much help. He knew he was close.

The increasingly frustrated man hunted by himself every chance he got for two summer seasons, telling nobody about it.

The third year he confided his problem to a mining friend, and together they hunted many years for it. They tried hard, they did find a few pieces of float, of the same ore, but they never found the outcropping.

When the Lucky Moon Mine opened in 1905 Hollingsworth visited the operation. The mine was not where he found the ore sample. The Lucky Moon was about a quarter mile north and somewhat west of Hollingsworth's ridge. It must be noted the ore from the mine was very similar, just not as rich. Many mining men believed they were erratic, offshoot veins of the same formation.

If you'd like to search for some of Hollingsworth's telluride ore, it's somewhere up there on the ridge between Snowslide Draw and Root Gulch. Maybe it would be best if you wait for deer season and be sure to take along a piece or two of wire.

***

A deposit of gold nuggets remains lost in an area some two miles north of Vallecito Lake. This is on the upper Shuahgauche, upstream from the mouth of the Weasleskin.

***

A fellow working a rich mine in La Plata Canyon above Hesperus did well enough in 1929 to buy his wife and himself each a brand-new Cadillac. When the snows began to fall, they parked one car well back inside the entrance to their mine, high on the cliff which overlooked Basin Creek. They drove the other car out of the high country for the winter.

They returned the following spring to find a huge landslide had covered the entrance to their mine. A huge jumbled slope made it almost impossible to know exactly where the mine entrance had been. All efforts to reopen the tunnel failed.

The location is about a mile and a half on past a ruined boarding house at the edge of the ghost site of La Plata. Treasure? That car is said to have had only about 500 miles on it.

***

In that La Plata vicinity some treasure hunters found a few gold coins near the old Gold King Mill.

***

The Lost Loma Gold Mine remains hidden somewhere in Animas Valley.

***

The Animas Treasure, a cache of gold ore, is said to be in the area of Bondad.

***

Pierre Giron had a ranch in Northern New Mexico but often rode north into Colorado to do some prospecting. On one such jaunt he found a small ledge of rich gold ore close by the Animas River. Taking samples home, he soon had thirty friends ready, willing and able to go gold mining with him. They went back to the place in Colorado where he'd found the ledge, constructed an arastre, and proceeded to work the ore.

When winter snows started, the group packed up their gold and headed back for New Mexico. Only a short distance from their camp one man sent out as a scout rushed back with news of an impending attack by Ute Indians. The miners hastily buried their gold and decided to individually flee for home. Only one Juan Sanchez and Pierre Giron survived the resulting flight. Because of the menace from the Utes, neither man wanted to leave the safety of New Mexico.

Juan Sanchez died a few years later. Giron changed from only reluctant about returning to Colorado to fearfully, superstitiously refusing to go. Had not his friends died because of that gold? He refused requests to go back and show others where to mine gold. After he became much older Pierre did try to give directions to family and friends as to the whereabouts of his workings, but his directions proved to be useless. He spoke of a wide valley, hot springs, and red cliffs overlooking the spot somewhere along the Animas

River. There are any number of places that could fit that description. The outcropping nor the buried gold has ever been relocated.

***

Hank Sommers took a shortcut in 1903, taking a trail that runs between the Neglected Mine on Monument Hill down the mountain to Durango. It was a heavily traveled trail at the turn of the century. This is near the headwaters of Falls Creek, northwest of Durango. Sommers was a cook, and had, until he quit the day before, been cooking for the boarding house at the Neglected Mine.

In a small knoll beside the trail he noticed some recent disturbance in the leaf mold. Hank was curious, because highgraders often used this route to carry their stolen ore into Durango. He did some digging. There were twelve sixty pound sacks of high grade gold ore recently buried there. He knew at once it must be a highgrader's cache. He also immediately recognized that the ore came from the Neglected Mine. It was some of the best sylvanite ore ever mined, shot through with raw gold. There were a few chunks of raw gold, speckled with bits of quartz, as large as hens eggs.

Hank Sommers first checked around the area to be certain nobody was nearby. He was far too wise in the way of things to be seen fooling with twelve buried sacks of high grade ore, especially if whoever saw him was one of the highgraders who put them there. It was not considered too bad, at least among the working men throughout the mining regions, for a man to appropriate some of a mining company's gold, but it was considered a terrible thing if someone took a highgrader's gold.

Sommers seemed to be all alone. The man put aside all notions of simply ignoring the cache. It was too much of a temptation not to take it. He carried the sacks to a point about three hundred yards away, one heavy sack at a time. There he carefully buried them, intending to return after enough time passed to make it safe for him to haul the sacks off the mountain. He made sure to leave no signs of disturbance. He noted several landmarks near his stash. A clump of trees on a bench beside a creek. The clump of trees was located upstream from a waterfall. There was a large dead tree of unusual shape on the other side of the canyon. He felt sure he could find the exact spot again without any problems at all.

Heavy snows kept him out of that area over the winter. He returned as early as possible in the spring but could not find the spot he had moved the sacks of ore. Snowslides had carried away entire hillsides, evidently flattening his odd clump of trees and the large dead tree across the canyon. Boulders did not seem to be in the right places. Panic set in, then despair. Frank Sommers never found where he buried the ill-gotten ore, nor has anyone else.

If one wants to search for this cache, the trail wound from the site of the Neglected Mine between mountain peaks for about five miles up to the Falls Creek Divide. It there climbed over a mountain called Cape Horn, which is a steep, rugged promontory. From there the trail wound back and forth down Barnes Mountain and on into Durango. Good scenery and plenty of exercise can be guaranteed, not so the cached ore.

***

In 1860-1861 Charles Baker and his group of prospectors buried a substantial cache of gold dust and nuggets along the Animas River. They returned after the Civil War was over to recover the big cache but could not locate it. Their marked trees had been cut down, things had changed. That buried gold has never been found.

***

Herbert McCaw worked for a screening and crushing plant located about a mile upriver on the Los Pinos River from Ignacio. Here was where the country produced crushed rock for road repairs.

On one of his shifts in 1932 a basketball-sized quartz boulder became jammed in the screens. He had to try several times before it was crushed. The hardness of the rock made him wonder, so he picked up a piece of the now broken boulder. It was shot through with gold. Herbert stopped the crusher, but a day's searching produced only two more pieces of the gold-rich rock.

A portion of the boulder was assayed, and the results came out at $36,000 to the ton. Although the rich float had to come from farther up the Los Pinos River, towards its headwaters, the source of the float has never been found.

***

A boulder shot through with gold was found by Martin Hotter in the summer of 1897 on the banks of Junction Creek not far downstream from the mouth of Wall's Gulch. The area is high in the La Plata Mountains, about fifteen miles to the northwest of Durango.

The chunk was worth $1,600 at the time, and was sold for that amount. Hotter did not get a dime of the money. Two "friends", Shears and Biggs, got him to show them where he found the rock. They waited until he left. They then broke the rock up, sorted out the gold ore, and sold it. There wasn't much Hotter could do about it even though lesser things have caused murder.

It did set of a flurry of searching for the boulder's source. Although the big rock could not have traveled too far from where it was found, its source has never been discovered. Many people have looked for the ledge from which it came.

***

High graders in 1910 cached about 840 pounds of extremely rich gold ore somewhere in the area called Burnt Timber Flats on Indian Ridge. There were twelve sacks, each containing forty pounds of high grade gold ore. Plenty of highgrading was going on at that time but to have that large a quantity in one place at one time certainly was no everyday occurrence.

In September of 1910, two large and extremely nervous men hired a young packer to transport some ore. They did not say they had taken the ore from one of the area mines, but he was sure that is how they got it. He was to haul it from the Bar, a flat tableland on the west side of the La Plata River, up along and then out of the La Plata canyon northwards across the mountains over the old Ute Trail and down to Rico.

This area was wild and empty in 1910, it's just about as wild and almost as empty today. If one is not careful gravity will pull the careless traveler along that old Ute Trail downslope, westward into Montezuma, then Dolores Counties. That's the way the railroad had to go, following the Dolores River in a great loop westward.

The men said they would pay him $50 for his service, because they could certainly not transport highgraded ore by train. The young packer could ignore what was going on, for all sorts of highgrading was going on at the time, and fifty dollars was a lot of money for a young packer to make on one short haul. One of the men would go with the load, the other intended to take the train from the May Day Switch and come up from the Monteloros switch on the other end to be sure the route was safe.

They were nervous because they were afraid of getting caught with the ore. Although highgrading was almost universally practiced among gold miners, and looked upon by those men as not being dishonorable, it was a crime for which long prison sentences were given to those who got caught.

The location is up out of the La Plata Canyon and across the highest and more rugged portion of Indian Ridge just into the Burnt Timber Flats. The trail coming up from Monteloros switch on the Rio Grande Southern line, on the Dolores River, joins the old Ute Trail there.

The other man was waiting for them when they arrived at this trail junction. He was terribly nervous, and drew the other man aside to talk. They soon told the boy to wait, they were under suspicion for ore theft, and had to hide the ore quickly. There was no way they wanted to be found transporting it.

It was cached back in thick timber by miners who knew very little about that rough terrain. From the cache site they could see a bluff on a hillside across the Dolores River. They marked the place where they buried the sacks with some logs and branches, not wanting to cut any blaze marks or have anything else too obvious near the cache. They never once considered what the winter weather soon to come would do to markings fashioned of logs and branches. They took the burros back through the timber for maybe two hundred yards from where the two trails met. This has to be near where the trail comes up along Ryman Creek from the Dolores River.

The young packer was paid his $50, and was also given a good sized ore specimen probably worth almost another $50. The two men told him they would lay low over the winter, and wanted his help when the situation cooled off.

Fate stepped in, for it has a way of doing that to the good, the bad, and the highgrader. That winter the second fellow, the one who'd come up the trail from the Rico end, was killed in a mining accident in Arizona. The other man hunted for the cache the following summer, but could never find it. He tried to find the young packer, who was working elsewhere at the time. The disappointed highgrader drifted off elsewhere, working in mines, often dreaming of that incredible stash, but never again trying to find it.

Years later the packer, grown up, located the once-upon-a-time highgrader in a Boulder sanitarium. He was near death from miners' consumption at the time. Knowing how close he was to dying, he urged his visitor to seek out the cache.

The once-upon-a-time packer looked for the stash, for years, but he never found it either.

If you want to do your own looking, take the Dolores River Highway 145 to Ridgeway. The highway bridge, which is at the dividing line between Dolores and Montezuma Counties, sits almost upon the old Monteloros Switch of the discontinued Rio Grande Southern Railroad. That's where the old trail led up towards Indian Ridge.

It's some eleven hard miles up the trail to the north side of Orphan Butte, where you want to go. Be careful, the trail up from Monteloros is not the only trail to join or cross the trail along Indian Ridge. There's the Ryman Gulch Trail, the Pasture Gulch Trail, and the Salt Creek Trail.

Those sacks of highgraders' gold seem to be a terribly small target in the downed timber and seemingly endless vistas of Indian Ridge. Good luck, if you must go see for yourself.

***

A man named Thurman and his brother located the now Lost Florida Mine back in the 1800's. The man's son was with him at the time they developed the mine. This was in a heavily mineralized area that extends along the southern flanks of the Needle mountain upthrust between the Vallecito Canyon on the east to the Las Animas River Canyon on the west. The mine was somewhere in the Florida drainage area of this vast district, probably along the east side of Lime Mesa.

The men proceeded to sink a shaft into solid rock along a vein structure situated very near a stream bed. The stream came down through a narrow valley. They worked hard for quite some time, accumulating good ore as they dug. A cabin was built nearby in the timber, facing east towards the edge of a nearby bluff. The cabin had two windows, and along the south wall were a couple of two tier bunks. and put together a substantial amount of good ore.

They had come into this area by going up the Animas River Canyon. When they at length had enough ore to take out and sell they took safeguards to keep what they had worked so hard to develop safe and secure. New supplies were needed. The men sealed their mine and concealed the entrance. At this time they blazed trees from the mine back into the Animas canyon, thus marking a trail east from the Animas Canyon back into the mine's location. They had a great deal of ore, and were uncertain as to when they might return. The blazes would assure them of having no trouble relocating the well hidden mine. After all, they well knew how difficult it was to find anything in such rugged country. Their discovery of the rich seam had been more or less accidental, located as it was in one of hundreds of small, narrow valleys.

For three summers the men worked the mine. They made five trips with strings of pack burros to Pueblo during that time. Pueblo was then the nearest place to sell their ore.

By the end of the fifth trip they had banked a grand total of $125,000. That was a fortune in those days. The brothers were tired of mining, and decided they could use the money to start a cattle ranch in South America. They did so, buying tracts of land and good cattle. Over the following years they vastly multiplied their wealth. The old Florida workings were all but forgotten.

When Thurman's boy returned, about fifty years after the last string of burros left for Pueblo, he could not find the mine by himself. This was in the spring of 1928. He tried to, for a time, thinking he remembered well enough. But things were not as he remembered, and his father and uncle had been dead for several years. The younger Thurman, now at least in his sixties, was a wealthy South American rancher, but he hoped to find the old Florida mine.

Thurman hired two local men to help him find his way around. From his descriptions they took him to the east side of Lime Mesa. Thurman and the two men spent several days searching, but found neither the mine shaft or the cabin. He decided he would search for the blazed trees, instead, so the three of them moved their camp over to the Animas River canyon. Sure enough, they found the blazes within a day or two. These led the trio up into the Florida watershed, just as Thurman said they would.

Thurman then began to search with renewed zeal. He could still not find the cabin nor the mine shaft. The summer was almost gone, and the time for Thurman to return home was getting closer. He was cheerful enough about it. He paid off the men, just as he said he would, and informed them he would be back the following spring. He would like for them to again assist him in his search.

As good as his word, Thurman showed up in the spring of 1929. He hired the two men again. He also talked to a good many local stock growers, told them what he sought, and offered a substantial reward to anyone finding either or both the cabin or shaft. One of these men was Chester Petty, a sheepman in the area.

Thurman received a message from home just after doing these things. He was required to leave. He again offered a substantial reward for anyone to find the cabin or shaft, and requested that word be sent to him.

Most of the local men soon lost interest in the search once Thurman left. Charley Waldner was one local cowboy who thought he could find these things. He was challenged enough to look for them every chance he got. It was two summers later when he came upon a cabin that fit Thurman's description. It was well hidden in a stand of spruce trees covering a rimrock close to but not actually on the main part of Lime Mesa.

He hunted hard for the shaft but never found it. Thurman had never told anyone Waldner knew of how far or in what direction the shaft was supposed to be from the cabin.

Waldner asked around, but everyone he asked no longer had Thurman's address or remembered how he was to be contacted. An old cabin without a mine is not worth much if a fellow is herding sheep or cattle. Waldner had plenty of that sort of things to do without worrying any more about lost mines.

If one could find that shaft it might be a profitable way of spending several summers.

***

It was during the 1930's, the depression was well underway, when an amateur prospector came into Newton's Cafe in Durango. He knew something of rocks and minerals, he told Newton, and he was willing to split profits from mining any gold or silver he might find with someone willing to grubstake him.

Newton liked the young man. He gave him his grubstake, seeing to it he had tools and food enough to do some prospecting.

Sure enough, the lad returned in about two weeks. He had with him some attractive, glittering samples to show Newton. Others in the cafe admired the specimens. While this was going on an old prospector entered the cafe. He briefly looked at a specimen or two and broke into laughter. His verdict was it was only some iron pyrite, damn fool's gold. Worthless.

The young man left, crushed. It was the last time he was seen in Durango and nobody had any idea where he may have gone.

Some time later a respected mining engineer was in the cafe and chanced to pick up the specimens, still on one of Newton's shelves, probably to remind himself not to be so quick to grubstake this fellow or that. The mining engineer did not think it to be pyrite, but some of the best gold ore he'd ever seen.

Newton was still not convinced, so he had some of it assayed. The assay gave the ore a $5,000 to the ton value. There was no way Newton could find out from where the samples had been taken. He had half interest in an undeveloped gold mine somewhere to the northeast of Durango.

***

The Butinski Gold Mine remains lost, somewhere to the northwest of Durango

***

Miner Al Stevens hid a stash of high grade gold ore on Bald Knob. This is near the headwaters of the Middle Fork River not too far from Durango.

***

In the 1700's there was a Spanish mining town named San Geronimo, thought to have been near the site of Hesperus. It was important to Spanish mining efforts in the region.

***

Gold panners still get some yellow stuff from the La Plata River and its tributaries.

LARIMER COUNTY

Pull up closer to the fire, why don't you. Have another cup of coffee.
These evenings are starting to cool down sooner.

There is said to be a cache put down along Boxelder Creek, which runs just to the west of the town of Boxelder.

Also, near Boxelder in 1862, a hunting party discovers soil heavy with lead particles. Enough for them to melt and cast all the musket balls they needed. Those were the days of gold placering, and who had time for deposits of lead? The discovery was ignored, and almost forgotten. When years passed, and lead mining became both practical and profitable, nobody could relocate the deposit.

***

Virginia Dale, to the northwest of Fort Collins, on the route up to Fort Laramie, was once a busy stage stop. Perhaps a mile to the north of Virginia Dale is a table top mountain. Indians used it as a lookout, from its top able to see far in most directions. When the Indians were crowded out, outlaws and renegades discovered the flat topped mountain and moved in. They were after loot, not elk and buffalo. They reinforced natural lookout points, built shelters, and went into business. They could see, without being seen, every single rider, every stagecoach, every caravan approaching for many miles. They could estimate how strong or how weak any individual might be before they jumped him. After all, even if they happened to meet fierce opposition, they could take refuge in this natural fortress and with a handful of men hold off an army. It should be no surprise to know the place was widely known as Robbers' Roost.

To make matters worse for travelers along this route, the notorious thug, Jack Slade, somehow weasled and cajoled his way into being for a time the superintendant of the stage station at Virginia Dale. Very convenient for the bad guys. Terrible judgement on the part of the stage line. When the position got too hot for him, wiley old Jack loaded up all the money and goods from the stage stop and skedaddled.

The army was forced to train artilery on the place to finally dislodge the outlaws.

There is evidence that two caches were buried on or near Robber's Roost, in the Fort Collins area. One of the caches contained $125,000, all stolen loot.

A different gang of outlaws put down a separate cache near Robber's Roost. This one is said to contain $60,000 in gold. If the stories are accurate, the two caches are not far apart.

***

Colorado has its own Lost Dutchman Mine. This is usually called the Lost Cache la Poudre Mine The site is supposed to lie hidden in very heavy timber near the top of a mountain near the site of Manhattan. The north slope of Black Mountain seems to be a logical starting point if one gets the urge to look for it. Rich ore is said to have been mined there. A cabin was built near the mine and there still could be some scattered, rotted logs at the site.

It began in 1860. The area was still a part of the Kansas Territory. Two men, we know them only as Hans and Mike, located a rich source of gold somewhere to the west of Fort Collins. They showed up at the military post of Fort Collins, loaded down with gold. They stayed long enough to purchase supplies and do some serious drinking.

Nothing remarkable, that. If it had happened just once it would soon have been forgotten. Again the two came, Hans the Dutchman, Mike the Irishman, again with gold. Then another time and another. Always with gold, and no matter how drunken they became, remained very secretive. Never a word about where their gold was coming from. That is a certain method for raising soldiers' curiosity just as it would have anyone.

The curious soldiers hired an Indian scout to follow Hans and Mike, to find out just where they were doing so well. The scout easily followed them for three days, making sure to remain unseen by the men he followed. He became careless enough to take time to hunt a deer, and by the time he finished doing that a snowstorm came up. All he could sheepishly tell the soldiers was that the burly men headed up the Cache la Poudre River.

The men bought a donkey the next time they brought out gold. They wanted to pack in more supplies and be able to bring out even more gold.

The trip in following that they traded in the donkey, and bought an ox. The donkey couldn't carry enough. The next time they came in, the poor ox was overloaded. As there wasn't any bigger equipment available in those days, after the pair did their drinking and had time to sober up, they and the ox once more headed west.

After a time the two returned, staggering under huge loads of gold. No ox. They reported the beast had been killed by a bear right beside their cabin. They killed the bear, but it was too late to help the ox.

The men seemed not to be in a good mood. They drank even more than usual. They increased the level of their arguing. About the donkey, about the ox, about the bear, about the gold, about all the hard work, about everything.

Suddenly Mike swung a terrible blow to Hans' head, which killed the Dutchman.

There wasn't much law in the area. The soldiers were as close to being the local law as there was. They seized Mike, believing they at last had a way of finding out where all that gold had been coming from. They informed him they would hang him then and there if he wouldn't tell them everything about the location of the gold source.

Mike said nothing. He never said a word even though they threw a noose over his head, not even when hoisted him up to a cottonwood limb. Thinking to force him to speak, they let him hang there a short time.

Mike had been a big, tough man, but he was dead when they lowered him, short time hanging there or not. Probably he was still raging drunk, angry from the argument and fight, and his heart simply stopped.

That seemed to be the end of that. People talked about it for years, and a good many of them did some looking, to no avail.

Then Billy Meline came to Fort Collins from Nebraska in 1899. He heard the story, all about Hans and Mike and their fabulous gold strike. Right down to the donkey, the ox, the bear and the hanging. Billy was often in Manhattan, and made up his mind he would find that lost mine.

Meline's interest was at a fevered pitch when a boy got himself lost near Manhattan. He followed his mule, not sure of where he was. The mule led him to an old cabin. There were bones scattered near the cabin, and rich gold ore samples were stacked inside on a shelf. Pretty rocks, as the boy described. Yellow spots all through them. He built a fire in the old fireplace and heated up an old can of beans off one shelf that seemed to be edible. He picked up some of the rocks and also some bones from outside the cabin, almost certain they were bear bones. He and the mule eventually found their way back to Manhattan.

Someone recognized the richness of his ore samples as equaling that of Arizona's Lost Dutchman Mine. Many recalled the story about a bear killing Mike and Han's ox near the cabin. Most were too busy making a living, and soon enough forgot the incident.

Not Billy Meline. He got an old prospector to go with him, even though he was warned the old man often became violent, downright crazy if he encountered any wild animals.

They followed the directions the boy had given, mixed up as they were. Sure enough, they found the cabin. Close by was the tunnel mouth of the mine.

The old man rushed in. Almost at once he came rushing out, waving his arms and bellowing, a mother bear and her two cubs close behind him.

The bears rushed off into the woods, but the old man went crazy. Only by tackling the old fellow did Billy keep from being shot. He badly sprained his ankle getting the babbling old fool with him back to town. He couldn't return to the mine site for several weeks.

No problem, he thought. It was a problem, for although Billy Meline looked for years he never found the cabin and the mine again.

It's still there. Gold isn't like an ox or a bear, it never rots.

***

Several lost gold mines are thought to be on the northern and eastern slopes of Black Mountain, including the Lost Cache la Poudre Mine.

***

The Musgrove Corral treasure, consisting of gold and silver coins is supposed to be hidden along the Cache la Poudre River.

***

An army payroll of $62,000, consisting of Clark Gruber and Company gold coins, was being transported by stagecoach. The incident took place some nineteen miles of Fort Collins in 1872. The Borrell outlaw gang held up the stage, taking the payroll box. The holdup site was in Coyote Pass and today's highway 287 takes one right past the spot where it happened.

The horses pulling the stage were spooked, and didn't stop for about two miles. The robbers took off up the mountain to the west, a troop of soldiers from Fort Laramie hot behind them. The thieves headed to a hideout on the mountain, but when after a time they tried to dash away for safety the four of them were shot dead by the soldiers.

Soldiers searched the area continuously for six weeks afterwards, but could not find the gold. Most of it is still somewhere on that mountain above Coyote Pass, in some place were desperate outlaws had only a brief time to hide it.

A few of the coins are gone from the cache. In 1883, eleven years after the stagecoach robbery in Coyote Pass, rancher Stacy Wehrer found the army payroll cache on the mountain. Other searchers demanded he tell them where he found the cache. Because he refused to tell them the location they killed him. On his body were found eleven Clark and Gruber Company $20 gold pieces.

Clark and Gruber Company coins are very rare. They command extremely high prices upon the numismatic market. There is little doubt that only eleven of those precious have been removed from their hiding place.

***

Colorado artist, Albert Bierstadt, found a single large gold nugget while out to do some painting near Estes Park. His best painting was perhaps the one of Loch Vale, he went there often, and in that area is where he picked up the nugget. This is somewhere between the Wind River and Loch Vale. Bierstadt nor others ever found more nuggets. He was doing more painting, his friends did some looking. He got more paintings, his friends got exercise.

***

Also near Estes Park, in 1875, another gold ledge was discovered. A fellow named Barber, more of a prospector than he was a hunter, was with a Boulder group near Estes Park hunting deer. Watching for good outcroppings more than he was for deer sign, Barber picked up some rich samples in the Wind River and Glacier Basin area. He placed them in the pockets of his hunting jacket and mostly forgot them for several months.

Finding them there months later, Barber showed the samples to an assayer. The assays proved the samples to be worth thousands of dollars to the ton.

Barber returned the following spring to Estes Park, and he thought he searched the same trail, the same area as where he'd found the samples. He could never find the right spot. Many other peoples' fruitless searches have never relocated the spot.

***

Not far from Estes Park is the Lost Issac Alden Gold Mine.

***

As a prospector lay dying he told his friends about finding a rich outcropping of gold on Specimen Mountain, near Estes Park. He even managed to draw them a crude map. His friends searched for the ledge after his death, but were unable to find the outcropping. The map and what little he'd told them had too few landmarks, too little information.

***

Natural Fort is about five miles to the southeast of Fort Collins. Artifacts have been found in the area. Outlaws are said to have cached $30,000 in loot deep in a crevice somewhere within Natural Fort. If so, it has never been found.

***

Near Fort Collins is the Lost Clay Peterson silver mine.

***

In 1863 six outlaws held up a stagecoach on Long View Hill. The site is but a few miles from Virginia Dale. The stage was carrying a $60,000 army payroll, all in ten and twenty dollar gold coins, being sent to Fort Sanders in Wyoming Territory.

The thieves carried the strongbox west into some wooded foothill country. They blew the padlock off the strongbox, removed the coins, then buried them. Shortly thereafter troopers on their trail caught up with them. Five of the six were shot dead in the following battle. The sixth outlaw got away, but was soon captured. The man was hanged even though he offered to show where the loot was buried if his life would be spared.

Soldiers made four different searches for the buried payroll, but were unable to find it. Many others have been no more successful.

***

LAS ANIMAS COUNTY

You bet, it was dangerous in the Colorado mining frontier. Never were many lions or tigers in Colorado, but there were enough bears, bandits, Indians, and bad weather to make up for it and then some. Bad food, and usually not enough of it. Accidents, illnesses, isolation, those kinds of things killed many a good man.

It is said that a rich silver lode is somewhere along the Apishapa River near Trinidad.

***

About 1930 a train was held up at a railroad station north of Trinidad. An amount of $250,000 was stolen. Since that time the station has burned and there now are only ruins. A posse caught up with the thieves and gunned them down. The money was not on them. The train robbers had enough time to have buried the money, and evidently did so. It has not been recovered.

***

What is known as the Lost Cockrell Silver Mine is located not too far from Trinidad.

***

In the 1800's a group of outlaws held up travelers, killing some, robbing everyone they could. They are thought to have cached the loot from one such robbery in a cave on Fisher Peak, to the south of Trinidad. The thieves were killed by lawmen. As far as is known that and other caches they put down have never been recovered.

***

The Reynolds gang pulled off a wagon train robbery in New Mexico, stealing about $60,000 in gold. Three members of the gang then hid out in the Sangre de Cristos for a time. Two of them made off with most of the gold, fleeing eastwards from the mountains. Perhaps five miles west of Trinidad one of the men somehow secreted away the gold without the other seeing him do it. The other man shot him when he would not tell where he buried the gold. The gold was not found then, nor later.

-119-

There are several caves to the east of Trinidad. There are said to be several caches in some of these caves, put there by outlaws preying on travelers along the Santa Fe Trail.

***

Sometime during the 1800's a man named Baca found some gold nuggets upon a trail a short distance south of the Spanish Peaks. There were fissures in the ground there, and evidence of a recent earthquake. Perhaps Baca found a portion of the site of the Fray de la Cruz treasure.

***

Several miles northeast of Branson is thought to be located the lost gold mine of Mesa de Maya. The general area is to the north of Folsom, New Mexico.

Branson was not established until 1916. Lawrence Athey chose to settle in that area, bought a tract of land for $1,350, and Branson got its meager start. A Texas handyman, hired to collect firewood atop Mesa de Maya, claimed he discovered a rich ledge of ore while doing so.

He said he was cutting firewood at the time he saw the outcropping. He used his axe to hack off a chunk of the ore. When he showed the spectacular chunk to his boss, his boss became excited. He offered to finance the development of a mine if the handyman wished. After all, Colorado was experiencing a gold boom, they could have their own gold mine.

The handyman said he had to think about it. He may actually have stolen the good ore from an actual mine, not found it there on the mesa. The man weasled a team and wagon from the rancher, so he could go back to Texas to visit his family. He then wintered over at the ranch until spring, then he and the wagon disappeared.

Look as the rancher would, he could never find the ledge. Neither has anybody else.

***

A Spanish pack train carrying gold ingots was attacked by Indians near the south end of Mesa de Maya. Two, perhaps three of the Spaniards survived the first attack, and fled. The Indians took all the supplies, mules, and horses, but had no use for the gold ingots. They the carried the ingots for a distance up the south cliffs of the mesa, wrapped them in buffalo hides, and hid them in a cave. The cave, said to have two chambers, and a small stream running through it, has never been found.

***

William Metcalf had a tollgate in Tollgate Canyon when traffic was heavy on the Santa Fe Trail. The site is at the south end of Mesa de Maya. It is thought many of his coins may still be buried around the old tollgate site.

***

In July of 1858 a weary old prospector named White came limping just ahead of a mule in as bad shape as himself into a prospectors' camp in Horsehead Gulch, in Northeastern New Mexico. The leader of this group of prospectors was Henry Sharron. Henry's brother was a New Mexico Senator.

The prospectors fed the old man, they fed his mule, and they let him rest up. Within a few days the old fellow was back to as fine a condition as is possible for a tough old man. He sat in during long evening campfire sessions with these seekers of Mother Nature's metallic fortunes, listening to their tales, each teller trying to overshadow the last tale teller. The old man became increasingly animated. He obviously had plenty to tell, himself, and his desire to fit in with these men who helped him probably clouded his better judgement.

He began to tell about his own prospecting experiences. He'd come west in 1849, as had so many others. He never found much gold in California. Mostly he worked for wages for those who'd found good spots. He eventually got fed up with that sort of thing and was returning east in a dejected sort of way. No nuggets or gold dust to show friends and family. Supplies scant, no money to buy any.

Then in the high Colorado Rocky Mountains, northwest of Horsehead Gulch, he chanced upon a white, cement-like deposit. White was no geologist, but he could see the deposit was loaded with gold. He had taken good samples. This deposit, he told his now breathless listeners, was a few hard days trip to the northwest of them, in Colorado.

The camp geologist took a few small pieces of the white material, crushed them, and ran a simple assay. 1,000 ounces of gold to the ton, the geologist announced.

Interest turned into greed in a hurry. There wasn't a man in the group who slept that night. They each one were figuring how best to get part of or all of White's amazing lode discovery. Henry Sharron saw what was developing. He knew the situation could at any moment turn more dangerous and ugly. He pulled White aside and told him since he'd hadn't kept his mouth closed, he had nothing else to do but lead this gold-hungry group, now a greedy mob, to the site of his rich white ore. White would be given his choice of claims, but there was no chance this mob would allow him not to take them to the site of his discovery.

Everybody left early the next morning, and traveled hard. It soon became obvious that Mr. White was stalling, not taking a definite trail. That night they camped, dead tired, and not at all happy with Mr. White. The second day was even rougher, going through increasingly mountainous country, and the men were getting meaner.

They camped, worn out, in a box canyon near what is now the Colorado line. White saw that many of the men were angrier with him. He explained they were now only about thirty-five miles from the deposit, that he was seeing some landmarks he recognized. He reminded them how worn out he had been when he came to their camp, and it was because he'd traveled through this same rough country. He assured them they could reach the site late the following day. He even volunteered to stay up and watch the horses.

The following morning, White was gone. Mr. White may have been foolish enough to talk about his find, he was not foolish enough to stay with a gold-hungry bunch wanting to take away what he considered to be his own.

The now furious group of prospectors attempted to catch up with the old man. He had too good a head start, and he knew the country better than they did. They lost his trail.

Almost a hundred men were in the group. They spread out, looking for several weeks either for White's rich deposit or White himself. Some of them got lost. They gave up the search after a time, and went on to other things.

That would have been all there was to it, White's chalky gold deposit entirely forgotten about, but an old man named White showed up in Salt Lake City a few years later. The old man was wealthy, and spent his money freely. He loaned $60,000 to a Provo rancher, then again disappeared. He never even returned to collect his loan.

The gold-rich white ore Mr. White discovered became ever more legendary in the Colorado mining frontier. Many have looked for it. None have found it.

***

Black Jack Ketchum and his gang is said to have once terrorized and robbed travelers going through Tollgate Canyon, which runs beside Mesa de Maya. Black Jack Ketchum was a mean, ruthless outlaw, coming out of Texas in the middle 1990's. There was nothing nice about him. He and various hard cases with him did most of their specialty, robbing trains, in New Mexico and Arizona, but they did not let state lines bother them any. They spent some time and effort in Colorado.

The robbers camped for a time in secluded, brushy spots near the old Metcalf cabin, taking refuge in overhangs and caves at the base of the cliffs. The toll road ran through the narrow canyon nearby. In these narrow stretches the gang did a little business while they were laying low from robbing trains elsewhere. To make their numbers seem greater, seeming to be an overwhelming mob of outlaws, the gang set up grass-stuffed dummies with real guns partly hidden in rock crevices but plainly visible from certain points along the narrow toll road. Then, whenever some unfortunate soul passed that way he would be told, maybe by only one or two actual thieves, this pilgrim would be blasted away by the gang if all his money was not handed over that very instant. It worked well, several different times, and Black Jack probably thought it a clever ploy.

Black Jack Ketchum was not known for actually putting down a great many caches, but there are those who believe some of his caches of gold and silver coins may well still be buried in those camp sites.

Black Jack certainly did not come back to retrieve any wealth he cached in or around Toll Gate Canyon. Several train robberies after his time in Colorado, in 1901, he tried to hold up a train all by himself. He was badly wounded in the attempt. He somehow escaped, but a posse soon caught him staggering across a desert area, almost done in. Not a bit sympathetic, the posse took him to Clayton, New Mexico. Black Jack was quickly tried, convicted, and hung.

Black Jack Ketchum and his gang is also thought to have buried about $60,000 not far from the mouth of Chacuaco Creek.

***

Pierre's Lost Mine is said to be located somewhere in Las Animas County.

***

There circulated for a time a story of some outlaws caching stolen money in Shell Canyon, less than twenty miles northeast of Kim. In about 1900 the sheriff of Baca County captured a gang of thieves in Shell Canyon, even though it was over in Las Animas County. That act not only stopped a lot of thieving going on, it started a bunch of theories about hidden treasures in and around Shell Canyon.

The same stories are still told, at times, even though two old men recovered two treasures in Shell Canyon in 1924.

Clifford Benson, resident of Fredericktown, Missouri, had an uncle living in Shell Canyon. He and his wife came to visit, and Benson wanted to check on several treasure stories he'd heard over the years while he was there.

His uncle soon told him that the treasure stories must have been at least partly true. There had been a child's grave marker on his land he'd kept fenced off, for years. Someone had tipped the gravestone over and dug a two foot deep hole where the grave should have been. In the bottom of the hole was a neat, square impression, likely from a box being buried there. It was too small to have been even a crude casket. He felt sure it was a cache, not a grave at all he'd been caring for.

His uncle thought the diggers had to be two ratty looking old men, who'd been poking around through Shell Canyon for a considerable time that year. Nobody knew who they were. What's more, he still saw them once in a while, and they had been doing some digging where an old cave had been dynamited in by the sheriff when he captured the thieves in 1900 or so.

Benson and his uncle went to the cave, and the signs of recent diggings were obvious. The two old strangers had not yet been able to open the caved-in entrance, however. Benson noted that a big rock, the caved-in entrance to the old cave, and an old tree formed a big triangle. It was too rocky between the tree and the cave, or between the big rock and the cave, but the dirt was loose and deep between the tree and the big rock. His uncle laid a stick atop where they intended to dig the following day. They wouldn't leave another cache for those ratty looking old men to dig up!

When they returned the following day they found an open hole where the stick had been. The remnants of a broken, rusted box lay scattered in the fresh dirt. Benson's uncle dejectedly assembled the pieces of the old box. The two of them could see ring markings where coins had been stacked within the box, leaving impressions as the box disintegrated. They counted enough ring marks to add up to 2,600 circles about the size of silver dollars. That or twenty dollar gold pieces, his uncle wistfully observed.

The two old men were never again seen in those parts. Are there other caches? The sherrif did not arrest all the thieves around in 1900. Nor do we know there were only two caches in Shell Canyon to be recovered.

***

Indians are said to have had a rich ledge of gold close to the New Mexico border. About the time of the Revolutionary War Spaniards are said to have discovered and seized the workings. They used Indians in forced labor to work the mine. They set up smelters, timbered the tunnels and shafts, and dug ever deeper along the ore chutes. Many believe that enforced labor eventually cost the Spaniards their lives in a resulting bloody rebellion. Others believe they were for some untold emergency forced to leave, and first had their Indians backfill the tunnels leading into the mine. Whichever way it was, or for some other reason, the Spaniards never returned to this rich mine.

Many sought to find the mine. The story came down across the years and the generations. One man among the many who listened believed, and did the long tedious searching required in such an undertaking.

Manuel Torres spent much of his life looking for the old Spanish Mine, in whatever time he could get away from his post office job in Trinidad. Torres was a member of a large, respected family in Trinidad. Through his younger years he heard and believed the stories about the Spanish gold mine.

Eventually Torres came to believe the mine had to be high on Culebra Peak. All the stories, all his research into the matter drove him to that conclusion.

In 1939 he found a rotting timber sticking out of a rock slide high on Culebra Peak. Torres began to move rocks, found a few more old timbers, and soon got into some running water. The water was coming from an ancient shaft driven into the bowels of the mountain.

Further exploration of the area revealed a large rock dump somewhat around the mountain away from the shaft. The rocks plainly came from the shaft. This material obviously had been carried that distance in an attempt to better hide the tunnel and shaft. Three miles from the shaft he found what was left of an old ore-cleaning slough and some masonry work.

Torres discovered the property was controlled by the Colorado Fuel & Iron Company. He obtained written permission from the company to continue his explorations. With the help of his son, Elias, and his grandson, Simplicio Vallejos, Manuel Torres begam a steady, well-planned effort to open the old mine.

In that summer of 1939 he and his younger helpers uncovered the tunnel leading to the shaft. This had been well timbered, but that had been long ago and the timbers were rotted away. In the cleaning process they found an ancient tool sharpener and some other evidence of former work.

Winter comes early in the high country. The small group had to cease their efforts all too soon.

The following spring Torres found some ore. It was of low quality, but it did show both gold and silver. He began to carefully retimber the shaft.

He got perhaps 180 feet of the work done, but bad gasses and increased water seepage slowed, then stopped him. Some say he got in as far as three hundred feet, where he saw a crosscut tunnel.

It may not have been as far as three hundred feet, but Torres did see the crosscut tunnel. The man was certain he was close to where the Spaniards found their rich ore. Perhaps, but it was out of his reach. The gasses were terrible, and the seepage was getting worse. He could not afford to buy equipment capable of solving these problems.

Torres never did get any deeper than that. As his years advanced the problem became agony too him. So close but so terribly far. Riches in sight but just out of reach. He died at more than the age of eighty in 1956, never having reached the gold he was so sure was there. But he had found the Spanish mine!

Go some forty-five miles west and a bit south from Trinidad. On a clear day one can see the tiny opening high on Culebra Peak if they look up from the village of Tercio. Local residents believe it will take someone about like Manuel Torres, but with more money than Manuel had, to ever finish the job he started years ago.

***

There's another story of Indian gold located near the New Mexico border being taken over by Spaniards. This supposedly began not long after the time of Coronado's trek. One successful group of Spanish explorers tracked the source of various gold trinkets to a hidden valley in what is now southern Colorado. They killed the Indians working the mine and took over. They found different Indians to work the mines, and for a time things went along very much to the new owners' liking.

A different group of Spaniards later discovered this setup. They accused these Spanish brethern of mistreating the Indians. With that good excuse, they killed everyone in the hidden valley, and then proceeded to do just what the others had been doing. They rounded up some more Indians and put them to work. It did not last long before there was a bloody uprising. The Indian victors blocked off the valley, hid its entrance, and forbade any word of anything about what had happened there. Even so there were some fascinating rumors.

Two young Leadville prospectors, William Ramsey and Charles Ackerman, wrote letters in 1880 to a Leadville newspaper claiming to have found the gold-rich hidden valley. What's more, they sent along rich specimens of ore to back up their letters. They found Spanish tools, adobe walls, and many skeletons. They found gold-rich quartz. Feeling certain they had discovered the legendary hidden valley, they headed back to civilization to file claim to the entire area.

They then fell from sight for a time. Nothing was heard about what they were doing with their remarkable discovery. One friend of the two men claimed he heard from them not long after their letters appeared in the newspaper. They told him they had been totally unable to again find the blocked entrance to their hidden valley. It remains hidden.

***

There is a cave east of the Willow and Vogel Creek Junction. In 1924 a rusted flintlock pistol was found by human skeletal remains. It is not known if a metal detector has been used at the site since, but there certainly wasn't one used there at the time.

***

There are many persistent, legendary stories of Spanish treasure in Purgatory Canyon. The Spanish gave the canyon its name, El Rio de Las Animas Perdidas en Purgatoir. The River of Lost Souls in Purgatory.

This comes from a time not long after Coronado's frustrating search for Gran Quivera, the seven cities of gold. A band of conquistadores, led by a Portugese don, with a Spaniard second in command, set forth on a quest that led them into Colorado. Priests, soldiers, and miners rounded out the group. It was deemed proper and necessary to have the priests, no Spanish expedition was sent anywhere without them. It was hoped they would need the miners. Every soldier was necessary, and in this case they could have used a few dozen more.

The trip did not start out well. The Spaniard could not stand to have the Portugese, no matter how capable, leading the party. He became increasingly jealous and angry. Shortly after they were underway the Spaniard killed the Portugese and took over leadership.

The priests would not sanction the murder. They refused to go further in the company of what they considered to be evil leadership. With others of the group they returned to Mexico.

The remainder of the group continued on, northwards into what is now Colorado. It is believed Apaches attacked and killed them. As there were no priests left with the group the slain men were considered to be lost souls, thus the name.

The French later changed the name to Purgatoire when they claimed the territory. Americans came and called it the Picketwire, but that really didn't stick.

One tale keeps popping up about twelve chests of Spanish gold coins being transported in about 1700 from Santa Fe to St. Augustine, Florida. The money was for the garrison there, soldiers' payments, garrison expenses, and so forth. The regiment transporting this money was commanded by one Carrasco Rodriguez.

He should never have even been in Colorado. What we know of the man tells us he should not have been in command of anything. He ignored good advice and went that way, anyway, prefering it for some reason over a more southerly route. Winter caught them and they had to winter over near where Trinidad is today.

When spring finally arrived Rodriguez again led his caravan in the wrong direction. Nothing was heard of them again. They simply seemed to vanish from the face of the earth.

There are stories of the Spaniards burrying those twelve chests of gold somewhere along the banks of the Purgatory River. Other suppositions claim the Indians who probably did in the Spaniards took their weapons, tools, clothing, and animals, but had no use for the gold. They probably threw it into some cave or gully. This makes some sense, for items of Spanish armor and craftsmanship later showed up in Indian possession. A skeleton and an ancient rusty firearm was found in 1924 in a cave east of the Willow-Vogel Canyon junction.

An even more nebulous tale is told, of a dark wagon pulled by dark horses on dark nights, always driven by a mysterious dark driver. Always at night, always near the sheer rim of the canyon. I don't know if they smoked marijuana back in those days or not, but this author feels the primary thing being pulled here is his leg. There are more concrete bits of evidence, such as pieces of arms and armor being found, showing the other tales are closer to whatever truth is there about possible treasures in Purgatory Canyon.

There have been rumors of recoveries of gold ingots hidden along the trail through Purgatoire Canyon. One man did find some Spanish gold coins. Don't entirely scoff this off! Would YOU tell anyone if you found a crude gold ingot in Purgatory Canyon?

In a cave in Purgatoire Canyon, one tale goes, a small iron-bound chest containing "a few thick gold coins" was found, after 1924. There were some tiles of Spanish creation. An old piece of harnass with well-carved, ornate silver trimmings were recovered.

The man who found these things is said to have driven a knife into a tree outside the cave. In some tales he drove two, knives into a tree. For some reason he felt confident he was close to recovering the twelve chests of gold coins. While leaving the cave he fell and badly broke his leg. He lay there for two days and nights, dying of exposure. Some people found him before he died. He had enough time to tell his tale.

One suit of Spanish armor was found along the banks of the Purgatoire River in early days.

***

A persistent story crops up concerning a wagon train carrying 1,500 pounds of gold ingots being attacked by outlaws and Indian renegades in 1858. At first the would-be thieves were driven off. In an effort to elude their tormentors the wagon train party detoured through Chacuaco Canyon. Once within the canyon they were again attacked by the outlaws. Three of the party loaded the ingots onto six mules, took the loaded animals to some caves at some distance along the creek. They hid the gold as well as possible.

While doing this the rest of the wagon train group was slaughtered by the outlaw gang. The three men escaped, recuperated in a Mexican village, but were killed by Utes when they tried to return to get the ingots. Their cache is thought to be right where they hid it.

LINCOLN COUNTY

You say you don't care for the High Plains as much as you do the high mountains? Well, I suppose some people think along those lines. Don't rule out those open miles if you're hunting treasure. The mining era produced more spectacular tales, but money is money, and plenty of it got stashed away in the eastern third of Colorado. Don't let anyone tell you different.

In 1849 a group eight outlaws began a career of thievery. Some versions of the tale say as early as 1847. In 1862 they made off with a huge sum of wealth they had stolen over a twelve year period in and around Sacramento, California. The sum is said to be about one hundred thousand dollars, most of it in gold coins. These thieves were pursued, but fled safely from California. They actually made it as far as the Clifford, Colorado area.

The group intended to go straight, the story goes. Good intentions, it seems, gave way to a seemingly surefire stagecoach robbery. Why not one more? It was a big army payroll. Do one more, they must have reasoned, then they could go straight.

The soldiers escorting the stagecoach were well prepared for people with such intentions. Six of the group were killed during the aborted robbery attempt. Two of the thieves survived, and for some reason decided to cache their wealth a few miles east of today's Clifford.

They made three grave-like mounds. Each chiseled his own name on one stone, and the false date, 1857. They chiseled "unknown, 1857" on the third stone. In the center of the three mounds they buried their loot.

A small, secretive man came to the Clifford area in the 1880's. He did considerable looking, but very little explaining what he was looking for. The only person he ever talked to was a sheep herder. He told him that he was looking for a treasure he helped bury in 1862. He also told the herdsman the cache was buried within a triangle of three gravestones.

After several weeks the man was seen no more. There is a definite possibility this furtive man located and dug up the treasure. There is no way of knowing if he did or not.

The site is on the old James Will sheep ranch. Many unsuccessful searches have been made there. One of the marker stones was found in 1931. In 1934 T. C. Hatton of Clifford found a second stone.

The stones were enscribed: "D. Grover--August 8, 1857, and Joseph Foxe Lawe--August 8, 1857". The third marker and the cache have never been found. It is most probable that either some unknown person picked up and moved the two stones from their original location or flooding washed them for a distance.

***

The old town of Wild Horse burned to the ground in 1917. This was near Limon. A charred keg containing gold coins was found in or close to the charred ruins of the Albany Hotel there. It is believed other caches, greater or lesser, are still to be found within the townsite.

MESA COUNTY

I guess treasure hunting is Easter Eggs, Christmas morning, the tooth fairy, and a game of hide and go seek all rolled into one. Get too serious about it, too grown up, and all the fun goes out of it.

The Lost Pin Gold Mine is located in the general area of Grand Junction.

***

A lost silver mine is located not far from Fruita. The story is known because when Virgil Hutton and a friend, named Jack, returned from Alaska they rented rooms in Fruita. They found an unusual stone in the attic when they were doing some rewiring work for their landlady. She told them she had broken it off a ledge in a canyon to the northeast of Fruita a few years earlier while out cutting a Christmas tree. It eventually had ended up in the attic and was forgotten.

Virgil and Jack had an assay run on the rock, just out of curiosity. It showed $200 worth of silver to the ton. The landlady liked the sound of that, she knew right where that ledge was.

The following weekend saw the three of them headed northeast out of Fruita. They went as far as the car they had would go, but because the landlady had an appointment later that day, decided not to go any further on foot. They would simply return the following week end so she could show them the ledge.

It began to snow before the next weekend. The snow lasted, then got worse. It became clear they could not go until the following spring.

Not long after that the landlady suffered a stroke. There was no way she could go with the two men, but she gave them detailed directions. She said the ledge was high on the side of the canyon and much of that canyon wall sparkled.

Hutton thought she had seen a chimney of calcopyrite. They looked for it, long and hard, but never found it.

MOFFAT COUNTY

You're right, there's not as much almost inaccessible country as there used to be. The problem is, there's beer cans and candy wrappers where you'd think nobody's been for a hundred years. A four wheel drive vehicle can get a person into places where a burro scarcely dared to go a hundred years or more ago. Even so, once you park that vehicle, there's still a few areas mighty hard to get to. Some of Western Colorado's canyon country is that way. If you want to get to that kind of places the burro still has its place. That or you have to use your own feet.

Near Powder Springs, north of Brown's Hole, Butch Cassidy and his Wild Bunch gang is thought to have buried $50,000 in loot from robberies. As far as is known this cache has never been recovered.

***

Trappers often used Brown's Hole to winter over. There is abundant game in the region, so there was ample food along with great relief from harsher winter conditions elsewhere. There are many tales of cached goods and relics still unrecovered in the area. A trading post was established there in 1837. Philip Thompson and William Craig, seeing the numbers of trappers wintering over there, decided to establish a trading post in Brown's hole that year. There are many caves, some of which at times housed various some of these tough men.

The site of Old Fort Davey Crockett is situated on the Green River bottoms about two miles north, upriver, from the mouth of Ladore Canyon. There was a stand of cottonwood trees there. It truly was a wild and wooly place, a real heller. It took tough, wild men to brave that sort of country, and the rowdy, boozing, rough and tumble violence of it is far easier to write about than to have experienced. Too much went on in this area to not have a few caches. Who knows how many relics remain lost or hidden in the vicinity.

As the number of mountain men began to diminish, the glory days of trapping going or gone, the outlaw element began to move in. They liked the protected isolation of the place.

Outlaw Elza Lay helped pull off the Wilcox, Wyoming train robbery. Elza, one of the Butch Cassidy gang, buried his share of the resulting $30,000 loot somewhere in the Brown's Hole area. Many think he came back and got it, because he was able to somehow finance a rather respectable, honest lifestyle in his later years.

In the late 1890's Butch Cassidy and his gang hid out at times in Brown's Hole. This author has found V nickels and trade tokens near a dugout saloon, just to the north of the Ladore Canyon mouth. Not far to the north of old Fort Davey Crockett. Cassidy gang members frequented the place according to an old Vernal, Utah man who worked on an irrigation ditch project as a teen-ager. The locals, little better or worse than Butch or his buddies, accepted them. The nickels or trade tokens undoubtedly were not part of the $50,000 in gold coins and nuggets they are thought to have cached somewhere there in Brown's Hole.

It must be emphasized, Butch Cassidy and his gang were only a few of a great many outlaws to often use the caves, canyons, and remoteness of Brown's Hole as a hideaway. There are a good many substantial cache leads in this region.

***

$30,000 in silver coins remains securely buried in Irish Canyon, close to the Utah line in northwest Colorado. Some say within a cave there in the canyon, but nobody knows for sure.

***

There is a considerable platinum deposit located in the northwest part of Moffat County, close to both the Wyoming and Utah lines. The location is in very difficult terrain.

***

A cache of gold ore said to be worth $10,000 at the time was buried in Pat's Hole, which is now deep within the Dinosaur National Monument. The cache is not thought to have been recovered.

***

One of the Butch Cassidy gang bank robbery caches is thought to be near Wild Mountain in Dinosaur National Park.

***

Seventeen miles north of Craig, to one side of the road leading to Baggs, Wyoming, is a rich deposit of placer gold in a hard, cemented formation. It is said to be at the base of a low sandstone bluff.

***

Two miners worked a rich gold deposit somewhere in the Pat's Hole area. Outlaws killed them and their workings have never been found.

A prospector named Pete Madison heard the story from a Uintah Indian and is the one guilty of passing it on. He was told enough to forever catch his interest by the old Indian. He then talked with Harry Chew, a local long-time rancher, who told him a great deal more.

Harry had once come across the two brothers, Red and Eli Hanson. They were not too friendly, did not say much, but Chew knew they were prospecting. Some time after that, because word had somehow leaked out the brothers had accumulated twenty-five pounds of gold and were working a rich spot, outlaws ambushed the two men. They took a small amount of their gold and were on their way over to a small settlement just across the line into Utah for supplies and some relaxation. They were attacked and gunned down, their backs to the base of a granite cliff. The robbers found far less gold on the brothers than they had hoped. There was only enough to buy a few supplies and have a binge, which is what the brothers were heading into Utah to do. Their killers pried off some rock to cover the bodies.

Chew admitted to Pete Madison he had later found two skulls at the base of a granite cliff. One of the skulls had red hair and there was no doubt in Chew's mind these bones were those of the Hanson brothers.

The incident that cemented together a picture of ambush and murder was Harry's hearing of a drunken ruffian bragging about how he and his friends shot a couple of prospectors for their gold. They were angry about finding hardly enough to get drunk on and replace the bullets it took to kill them.

Harry Chew didn't want Pete to repeat what he told him, afraid of having the area invaded by treasure hunters. Pete did tell a few too many people the story, however, and the story became known.

The fact is, none of those who searched have ever found the Hanson's workings. Nor has the majority of their twenty-five pound cache of gold been found. The brothers removed only enough from the stash to go over into Utah.

***

Near Elk Springs is the Lost Yampa River Mine. This contains rich gold ore.

***

During the Civil War a party of government engineers, well guarded and backed up with supply personnel, were surveying along the 41st parallel. The line eventually between Colorado and Wyoming. Somewhere in that seemingly endless job one of the party picked up an unusual piece of good-looking float. It was worth keeping so it went into his pack.

A year and a half later, back in Washington, another man in the party saw it and thought it was worth assaying. Sure enough, it contained 1,600 ounces of silver to the ton with some gold and copper content. The problem was, the man who'd found it had been killed in battle on the Potomoc after the party had returned from the survey trip.

Three of the survey party wanted to return, but the area at the time was crawling with hostile Indians. They hired Jim Baker, the noted old scout, and they looked off and on for a time. It's a long ways to look for an outcropping somebody else found back and forth along that Colorado/Wyoming border.

***

Jesse Ewing was an Englishman. He is thought to have been " one of the meanest, toughest characters the West has ever produced". He endured many hardships, and cut his way through problems he had with other people with a big knife.

Jesse rafted down the Green River in 1868 with a group of prospectors led by a man named H. M. Hook. They had been attracted by stories of rich ores in the almost inaccessible area. The raft broke up and Hook and several others drowned. Most of the others headed out of the area, back to Green River City.

Not Jesse Ewing. He liked the country and made up his mind to stay and do some prospecting. He soon located a large copper ore deposit on the upper reaches of Red Creek Canyon.

Ewing built a cabin and started to dig a shaft. The man was not afraid of hard work. All by himself he tunneled almost five hundred feet into the mountain.

He also "took in partners". When their money was gone and their work slowed, Ewing drove them off with threats, at knife point. If that didn't work, he killed them, and several men are known to have died at his hands.

That worked, for a time, and Ewing had a tunnel of about 1,500 feet before his way of doing things backfired on him. First of all, the vein he'd been following pinched out. He felt sure he had passed by the main body of ore, somewhere, but he was not sure where.

His second big problem came from the fact he also raised horses. Ewing was never too careful as to where they grazed. Most people abused by this indifference on Ewing's part were afraid to do anything about it. Not so

Clephus J. Dowd, a tough young gunfighter. Clephus claimed lands on which Ewing's horses often grazed. Dowd drove several of the beasts off the cliff into Green River.

Ewing accosted Dowd over the matter, pulling his knife. Dowd drew his revolver. He shot Ewing in the groin before the man could get close enough to use the knife. He walked off, leaving Ewing for dead.

One of Ewing's few friends, a man named Jarvie, found Ewing not long after Dowd shot him. Jarvie nursed Jesse back to health, and soon Ewing was back to trying to find the main copper ore body he'd bypassed.

It was in 1885 when Ewing told "Pick" Murdock that he had at last found the copper ore. Murdock was an Indian prospector living away from the Uintah Ouray Reservation, and Ewing liked and trusted the man. He still only told the Indian his tunnel was at the west wall of the upper end of what was to become the Jesse Ewing Canyon. Murdock sent off some of the samples Ewing showed him to a Denver assay office. Jesse would never know the results.

A third and fourth thing then occurred to bring about the demise of Jesse Ewing. He married a mail-order bride, one Madame Forrestal. About the same time brought in a tough no-good named Duncan to help work. One day Duncan said he was sick and did not go with Ewing to the diggings. Ewing soon got to thinking, and decided there was some hanky panky going on between Duncan and his new bride.

Ewing stormed back up the trail towards his cabin. Duncan was hidden beside the trail, waiting for him in ambush. Duncan almost took Ewing's head off with one shot.

Many looked for Ewing's mine after that, because the samples sent in by Pick Murdock showed sensational results. The Kennicott Copper Corporation estimated the body of ore to be worth three to fifteen million dollars, depending on how large the ore body was. Possibly more. Nobody found it although a few found other worthwhile deposits in their search.

Pick Murdock searched, even though he had little real knowledge, and for a long time had no better luck than others had experienced. Then in the fall of 1906 Murdock came into Vernal, Utah, very excited. He had found Ewing's tunnel. "In the damndest place anyone ever dreamed of," is what he said. Pick sent off some new rich samples to be assayed.

Pick never saw the results, which showed $1,500 to $5,000 to the ton values. He died at his reservation home in Whiterocks before the results reached him.

This is the richest copper ore on the continent if somebody can ever find it.

MONTEZUMA COUNTY

It is said that one of Montezuma's great caches, large amounts of gold and silver, is hidden within Montezuma County near McElmo Creek. Maybe so, maybe not. Know this, if parts of his treasure are buried wherever people say they are, you have half a dozen spots to search just here in Colorado.

George H. Osteen was prospecting in the vicinity of Ute Mountain late in October, 1890, knowing he ran the risk of encountering hostile Ute Indians. Sure enough, they found his camp, not too far from the base of Ute Mountain.

He lost one mule in his flight from them, and he heard sounds of the Indians stealing his foodstuffs and supplies back in his camp. He managed to keep control of his horse and the other mule.

In trying to escape the Indians he headed up the northwest flanks of Ute Mountain through thick clumps of timber and brush. It also began to snow, fortunately for Osteen. He couldn't see where he was going, but the Indians couldn't see where he was going, either.

After a long, slow, wary climb, from one bench up to another, Osteen broke out of the dense clouds, above the snowstorm, and saw he was still well below the mountain top. Bright sunshine where he stood, dense gray clouds below. He saw no sign of the Indians, nor heard anything, but felt sure they were all too close. They could come from the fog any second, and be all over him.

When he saw the mouth of a cave, maybe ten feet high, he realized it would make a good place to defend himself.

George Osteen led his riding mule into the cave, the other mule followed. He saw at once the cave widened into a artificially squared chamber, worked by unknown earlier tenants. It would not only be a defensible place, he would give him some protection from the cold winds and probable snow.

There was enough wood to build a fire. After a fire was going he made enough trips outside to bring in enough fuel to at least last the night. The campfire lit up the chamber, which he saw was the entrance into an old mine shaft. It was not a natural cave as he had thought when he saw the entrance. Modest exploration showed the workings were old, very old.

Along one wall of the chamber he found what at first he thought was a great pack rat's nest. In scooping off pine cones to feed the fire he discovered a great, neat stack of dusty gold ingots. He estimated their weight at fifty pounds each. There had to be hundreds of them. Nearby he found a cast iron ingot mold. There were two extended iron bars on each end of the mold, and any of the ingots would fit the mold's depression.

Thinking ahead to the next day, he hobbled his mules outside so they could graze on the thick grass growing across the wide bench in front of the cave. He brought them in about midnight, lay down to rest comfortably between the fire and the warmth reflecting off the rock face beside the cave entrance. He dared not fall sound asleep.

The next morning, while exploring the immediate area as the mules grazed some more, he also found the ruins of a two room rock cabin and an ancient arrastre.

Osteen put some of the ingots onto his mules and headed south. He knew the Utes would expect him to head for Cortez, trying to reach safety. He got that right, but he soon realized he had badly overloaded his mules. It wasn't smart, but Osteen had put fourteen ingots onto those poor mules. Not a good way of doing things if you know some Indians are trying to scalp you.

Close beside a small stream he buried eight of the ingots, taking careful note of where he buried them. He then continued his flight with loads the mules more possibly could carry.

The tale goes on. He at last got safely out of Ute lands. George ate his first food for several days at a sheepherder's camp not far into New Mexico. He reached the Shiprock Indian Agency not long after that, where he got some food and cooking utensils. From there he traveled through Farmington, Cuba, and on to Santa Fe.

Osteen made up his mind to return to the area after he had a friend sell his six ingots in Denver. The ingots contained eighty percent gold, and Osteen got a very tidy amount of money. George wanted to claim the old mine as well as haul out all the gold ingots. He spent the rest of that winter trying to find someone hardy, dependable and trustworthy enough so he could share his fantastic secret. That sort of person was as hard to find in those days as it would be today.

George bought four big mules and half a dozen good burros. He purchased pack saddles and panniers, and plenty of supplies and ammunition. He decided he would be better off to make the trip by himself.

He took a long route, around into Utah and then back to Ute Mountain from the north. Not the way any Utes would be expecting white men to come from.

He reached the foothills below Ute Mountain without seeing an Indian. He made camp, and the following morning was attacked by a band of warriors while he was out rounding up the animals. George was wounded in his left side by the first volley of shots. He rolled into some rocks, pulling out his revolver.

He killed two of the Indians almost upon him and wounded at least two others. It was more than the Utes had bargained for.

The survivors of that band turned tail, giving George time to rush back to camp and retrieve his rifle and ammunition. Bleeding, but armed, George barely had time to hurry into the shelter of some rocks and brush before some twenty mounted Utes burst from several directions into his camp area.

Screaming, shooting here and there, they evidently did not know exactly where he was. George remained silent, and did not shoot until they began killing his stock. Then he blasted three of them from their mounts before any of them spotted him. They tried to attack, but he was able to force their retreat. He possibly wounded one or two more of them, but was unsure.

Through the afternoon, although various braves tried to crawl towards him, Osteen held them off. After dusk he was able to move up the hillside to an even more defensible position.

In the early morning the Utes attacked, running up the hillside in a widely dispersed line. George held them off, but was wounded again, in the left shoulder. His foe moved around and above him, and finally a shot ricocheted from a nearby rock and struck George in the back of the head.

Much later he awoke to pain and silence. He felt it was not even the same day, and was not sure of how much time had elapsed. He was alive, there was no sight or sound of the Utes.

After a time he crept back down to his campsite. All his belongings were gone. His livestock was gone, only cold ashes remained where the Indians had burned whatever they'd not wanted to take.

George Osteen faced a walk of at least seventy-five miles to the south to reach any kind of help. The Utes could be back at any given moment. He was badly wounded, hurting, and had no food.

Osteen passed out. He finally awakened to hunger, hurt, and nausea. His wounds were already inflamed. He went through a nightmare time after that, barely aware of his surroundings.

Sometime during this ordeal George cut strips from dead Indians, and fed himself. It was an act that haunted him the rest of his days.

Osteen at last reached Farmington, in a terrible, wasted condition. Kit Carson was county sheriff there at that time, and he saw to it Osteen was cared for. George rested three months there in Farmington and still was barely able to get around.

He went to Albuquerque for the rest of the year, gradually regaining his strength. He got with a man named Jean Oliver, whom he'd known in earlier years. They made plans to return to Ute Mountain. All we can say is, George Osteen was one tough, determined man!

In the summer of 1893 Osteen and Oliver attempted to return to Ute Mountain, but there were too many renegade Utes in that region. They could do little else than turn back. It was on this trip, however, that Osteen recovered the eight bars he'd buried by that small stream.

Osteen hired out, checking ore potentials for various people, over the years. It is not strange he could never forget about the cave on Ute Mountain and the rick of gold ingots he saw there.

In 1935 George and a young man, Givings Hjlmar, attempted to return to Ute Mountain. The renegade Utes had been put down, most of them by then dead and gone. Now, however, Osteen and Hjlmar were stopped by Indian police, and turned back from entering the Indian lands.

Osteen lived out his remaining years without making another attempt to recover the ingots or claim the mine. Nobody else has, either.

***

Some two miles north of Cortez, near the old Lewis Road, once marked by a pile of rocks, there is said to be a cache of gold.

***

Spanish miners are said to have had a rich gold placer in the Four Corners area. This dated back to 1776, to a discovery made during the Dominguez and Escalante explorations through the region. Stories of the richness of these placers continued, but never with any mention of precise directions and locations. The story expanded to include a silver mine on the hill above these placers.

Two cavalrymen, Merrick and Mitchell, in the 1870's found a cache of gold nuggets, and with it some silver, supposedly on a butte to the south of Cortez. Navajos warned them to stay out of the area and threatened them if they did not. The two cavalrymen had taken samples that assayed at the time $800 to the ton. Lots of money in the 1870's. Jim Jarvis, of Cortez, put money behind the two soldiers in 1879, organizing a mining party to work their find. Merrick and Mitchell were to get half of the resulting profits.

Fevered by the desire to get the project underway the two soldiers went back to the site to gather more samples.

When Merrick and Mitchell failed to return to Cortez men were sent out to look for them. Their bodies, filled with arrows, were found in a gulch. They had indeed picked up more samples, which were on their bodies, but had paid the ultimate price for doing so. Their discovery site was lost. The belief at the time was the Navajos had concealed the mine entrance.

In 1915 a western congressman, James O'Rourke, became intrigued with the story of the gold the two soldiers found. He organized a party to search for it. His group found a two hundred pound mass of silver matte, which is crudely smelted silver, buried beneath a pile of stones. With this were also a number of gold nuggets. Very angry Navajos found the group digging in their lands, and chased them out of the area. The group, with only a few nuggets in their pockets to show for their efforts, were glad enough to escape with their lives. They decided not to go back.

Since then the rich gold and silver discovery remains lost.

One source claims some records exist in a monastery near Santa Fe showing the Josephine Mine was discovered and worked as early as 1560 to 1585. The mine is supposed to be not too far from Dolores. Indeed, there is evidence of Spanish workings in that area.

Then there are those who believe the Josephine Mine to be closer to Cortez. The fact is, nobody is at all sure exactly where that rich old gold mine may be.

***

The Lost Butterfly mine is near Hesperus Peak.

***

-142-

MONTROSE COUNTY

Take your time. We've got all evening, so make yourself comfortable. I'll have another cup of coffee, anyone else want one?

"Indian" Henry Huff was a wealthy rancher and miner. His isolated cabin was on a branch of Corral Draw in Bull Canyon, some eighty hard miles from Telluride. It was well known the man had put down more than one cache of gold and silver coins as well as gold dust and nuggets. Simply put the man was a hermit and a miser. He made money, he did not spend it.

The man led a lonely life. Bull Canyon in earlier days was in about as lonesome and desolate an area as there is. Some would say it still is. Henry's only real friend was Carl Akers. He never got along with anybody else, nor seemed to want to.

He got into an argument with one John Keski in 1917 and was shot. It was at three o'clock in the morning, in John Keski's cabin, on May 11, 1917. It is not clear exactly why Henry Huff was there in the first place. In the second place it's hard to understand exactly why they were arguing so late into the night, or why Keski became angry enough to shoot Huff. All those reasons are now buried and gone.

Just before this happened he was known to have added $5,500 in hard money to his hoards. He had sold a large number of cattle shortly before he was shot. It is also known that he had a substantial quantity of gold dust, proceeds of the sale of several mining claims.

To Mrs. Keski, as he bled his life away, Huff verbally willed all he had to his friend, Carl Akers. At that time, however, the state of Colorado no longer honored such wills. Colorado authorities laid claim to whatever Henry Huff had owned.

His old cabin site or almost anywhere up and down Bull Canyon could have served as Huff's hidey-holes. The area was looked over, dug up, and all but plowed in a vain effort to find his money. Representatives of the state did this openly, Carl Akers and others did it more discreetly. None of it is known to have been found.

***

Sun-blackened dimes were found on the sheer north rim of the Black Canyon. This is high above the Gunnison River about midway in a line from Montrose to Crawford. The area is dissected by rough washes abruptly falling off into the deep canyon. A deer hunter had accidentally discovered one scattered heap pile of coins, each dime of sharp quality but burned by the sun.

The story is that four wagons carrying kegs of dimes from the Denver mint to Phoenix never even arrived as expected to Montrose. It was thought the caravan had been attacked by Indians.

It was reported that wagon wheels were seen in the narrow, sheer side washes just below where that one pile of dimes was recovered. There seemed to be no practical way of getting close enough to find out. If so, those wagons, the remains of the drivers, and those broken kegs of dimes are lodged in some tight, high rock crevice at some vertical distance between the Gunnison River and the North Rim of the Black Canyon. That is just about as inaccessible a spot as a would-be treasure hunter would ever care to see.

Hard rock climbers?

OTERO COUNTY

It never ceases to amaze me how today's folks ignore county and state history. They call themselves treasure hunters, and have never been in the local libraries of the areas where they want to hunt. Since we can't talk to those old timers who did these interesting things, we ought to at least know all we can about what they were doing. People hear this or that character put down some money, they don't even bother to see what local and state newspapers had to say about the matter. They just grab their detector and go. Most of the time they go in the wrong direction, like as not, but they want to get there even though they're not exactly sure where it is they're going.

William Bent was returning to Bent's Fort from Fort Bridger in 1848. His children found gold nuggets somewhere along Crow Creek. The site could never be relocated when adults realized what the children had found.

***

A tale persists concerning a $50,000 wagon train cache located near La Junta.

***

$200,000 was once stolen from Bent's Fort. The loot was supposedly cached somewhere in the area.

***

One story keeps returning, that a cache is somewhere within the old fort site. Many relics have been found there but no caches, yet.

***

OURAY COUNTY

Treasure hunting is like a bad itch. You scratch, but the itch doesn't ever seem to go away. You scratch too hard, you get bloody. You put on some soothing medicine, the wounds heal, but then the itch comes back. So you start scratching again.

Somewhere along the precipitous course of Bear Creek there is said to be $90,000 in gold ore cached.

Also somewhere along Bear Creek is located the Lost Colorado Lode.

***

The Lost Owl Creek Mine is in the general Ouray area. One certain direction is UP.

***

It was probably in 1863 that two California prospectors discovered and worked a rich gold-bearing quartz ledge high up on the head waters of Oak Creek. They said they were located on the flats to the west of the creek.

Working quietly, they tried to stay out of sight, for they often saw Indians in the Uncompahgre Valley below them to the north. To their east was the Continental Divide.

They found the quartz ledge close beside a small creek. Efforts to work discretely slowed any accumulation of ore. To speed the process they built a fire against the ledge, then threw cold water onto the hot rocks to fracture them. This worked well the first time they did it. They were able to hand pick about a hundred pounds of visbly good ore from the broken rock. They smashed this fractured ore to powder, and washed out the gold.

The results were even better than they had hoped for. Their intentions at that time were to take what they had, go out for supplies, come back to winter over and work as they could on the rich ledge.

What they did not know for a time was that a hot coal or two from the fire they'd built lingered on. It eventually set some brush afire. An acrid smoke swirled high, and they knew it would soon attract the attention of the Indians they'd been seeing. They took what gold they had, glad to leave the hostile area, happy to not have to face a hard winter.

They never returned, and their workings have not been rediscovered.

Forty years later, in California, one of the men, grown old and dying, told the story to a young man caring for him. He gave the youngster an old map he'd drawn and carried over the years. He told him everything about the area he could remember.

That young man found no old workings, even though he search long and carefully. He did not recognize any of the landmarks the dying old man had given him.

Should you look high up on the upper Oak Creek flats perhaps you may do a little better. But beware! The Utes may not get you if you start a fire against some ledge, but Forest Service people sure will!

***

The story is known because J. T. Boyd happened to be staying at Ouray's St. Elmo Hotel during the winter of 1906. Boyd was a respected mine manager. One day during a snowstorm a Swede Boyd knew came to his room with a pack filled with very rich gold ore specimens. J. T. knew the man, having worked with him at the Camp Bird Mine. That fact and the sack full of rich ore immediately caught Boyd's full attention.

The Swede was excited, and the feeling was infectuous. There were chunks of Calaverite ore weighing between five and fifteen pounds nestled among the smaller bits and pieces. All the rock was shot through and through with visible gold. Boyd had never seen richer ore, and he had for a long time worked at the Camp Bird Mine. Boyd bought a few small pieces from the Swede at that time.

(Cy Cress, one of the author's good friends, had a piece of the Swede's ore. He bought it from Boyd's estate sale in Lake City. This author felt while examining this bit of ore some of the excitement Boyd and the Swede were feeling that snowy day in Ouray. Yellow, buttery gold was visible throughout the small specimen. The outcropping must have been sticking up from its matrix, for lichens were growing on two sides of the piece of ore. The Swede only had to knock off the rich ledge with some tool or another rock and stick it into his backpack.)

The Swede had his ore melted down, and he sold his results for $7,300. That was an immense pile of money in 1906. It would be today, too, because that same bundle of ore would conservatively be worth twenty times that amount. Probably much more than that, if sold to collectors.

The Swede's finding it had been one of those happenstance sort of things. He'd been caught in a blizzard while heading into Ouray for the winter from high on the mountains towards Lake City. It became so bad he could no longer see the trail, and one had better be able to always see where they are going in that precipitous area. While taking refuge beside an overhang he found a very rich ledge of gold. He knocked off as much as he could carry in his knapsack. When the storm abated he continued down the mountain to Ouray.

He could not find the ledge the next spring. He started out too early, and that probably threw him off. He looked for the ledge all summer. It was undoubtedly hard on the man to winter over. The next spring and summer was even more frustrating, and the Swede began to come apart. The poor fellow was at last hauled off to Pueblo where they tried to take care of insane people. He died there shortly afterwards.

Boyd took up the search in 1909. He found a small piece of the same kind of float in a stream in that area. He looked when he could for several years, but did not want to end up like the Swede. He eventually stopped looking.

Many others have searched, with no better results. It sounds easy. It is there somewhere along the trail coming down from Mineral Point to Ouray. It is a narrow strip of land one must search. The strip is not three miles long, impossible to be half a mile wide, but with hardly one actually flat place in the whole area. Go in a four wheel drive vehicle, if you must, and wear the best quality boots. Take a knapsack, if you wish, in case you find the ledge.

***

A prospector on his deathbed said he had buried $50,000 in gold bullion under one of the saloons in Red Mountain.

Another miner claimed to have cached five hundred pounds of gold nuggets in a well in Red Mountain.

PARK COUNTY

Quite a story, the Reynolds Gang saga. Many doubt the amounts of their robberies were as large as told and re-told, many believe whatever treasure actually got buried also was dug up, and a few poo-poo the whole thing. The last viewpoint is wrong, because much of the story has some good basis of fact. Sit down, there's more to Park County treasure than whatever the Reynolds gang did, even though it sometimes doesn't seem like it.

Dead Man's Gulch got its name when Indians slaughtered some of the first prospectors to enter South Park. It's too bad it wasn't a bunch of today's politicians! Seven of eight men and all fourteen of their horses were killed in the fight. A later group of prospectors found the scattered, bleached bones in the gulch, thus its name.

Two Germans were secretly working a good gold vein in the Dead man's Gulch area during 1863. This gulch is on Kenosha Hill not too far from Tarryall. The Germans were staying in Tarryall, and their activities were noticed. They were extremely tight-lipped. The Germans made it plain they did not want to be followed when they left each morning, and a number of times when they were being followed or they thought so, they would simply return to town and not work that day. Then, after a time, there was only one German.

When pressed for an explanation he said his partner had been crushed by a cave-in. He couldn't dig him out. Not seeming to be too broken up about it, he told somebody they had accumulated between six and seven thousand dollars worth of gold. He was going to take whatever gold they had, enough to return to Germany where he could live comfortably on such an amount. He did not divulge the location of their workings.

Many searched for the mine but in those years it was not located. In 1885, after Tarryall was abandoned, a rancher by the name of David Baker thought he found traces of an old mine in Dead Man's Gulch. There was a tumbled-in shaft. He and some friends sunk a shaft near the old one. They found only traces of gold and bits and pieces of equipment they thought the Germans left behind. They probably did not dig deeply enough to find the skeletal remains of the missing German partner. Nor did they discover ore with the amounts of gold known to have come from there, if it indeed was the right mine.

***

Spanish Caves are in the bluffs above Buckskin Joe. There are stories of either Spanish or outlaw treasure being hidden in those caves. There are arrastres still visible in the stream below Spanish Caves.

***

In 1965 some treasure hunters were working a mile to the west of Alma. They found many old bottles and a metal box containing ten pounds of gold amalgam.

***

There probably wouldn't have ever been much of a treasure tale without Jim Reynolds. Jim Reynolds could have been a pirate, he was swash-buckling enough for the part.

The Reynolds gang was a busy outfit in the early 1860's. They were scoundrels, but they are not known to have killed anybody. Possible cache sites for loot from their multiple robberies are scattered throughout Colorado. Bayou Salado, Canyon City, Current Creek, Deer Creek, Devil's Head Mountain, Fairplay, Geneva Creek, Georgia Pass, Handcart Gulch, Kenosha Pass, Shafer's Crossing, the South Platte River, and Webster Pass all are possible cache locations. Many stories and variations of stories abound concerning Reynolds gang caches in each of these areas.

Any study of treasure in Colorado is forced to deal with stories of the infamous Jim Reynolds Gang. Undoubtedly credited with robberies they did not even do, thought to have cached loot they may or may not have cached, these outlaws did in fact performed robberies and buried some of their loot.

They actually started off their nefarious activities down in New Mexico, in a rather grand style. They lifted $63,000 from a stagecoach there.

In the early 1860's Jim Reynolds gang was a formidible group of twenty-two men. They had come north out of Texas, knew how to and were willing to use the guns they carried, and at least at first had a thin veneer of patriotism to the Confederate cause. They used that as enough of an excuse to steal anything they could from Northerners. That meant just about anyone they met in Colorado. They at first especially enjoyed the rich pickings offered by stagecoaches operating between the gold camps and Denver, but they did not confine their activities to stagecoaches.

At first the large band of thieves got along fairly well under Jim Reynold's leadership. By 1864, however, their brief unity had crumbled. The band had dwindled to Jim and John Reynolds along with seven others. The rest began to see that Jim Reynolds was keeping the biggest amount of everything the group appropriated. All in the name of the Confederate cause, of course. Doubt, mistrust, greed, jealousy, and some lead poisoning suffered during the course of robberies saw the others drop out of the gang one way or another.

It was about then, in 1864, when the Reynolds gang held up a stagecoach near at McLaughlin Station, two miles south of Hamilton. That's a ghost site near Como. They took an amount between $60,000 and $100,000, mostly in gold. Part of it was a good take from the mail pouches. The scoffers put the total haul as low as $5,000, but the mail contained probably that much by itself.

The gang afterwards holed up in Handcart Gulch, at the headwaters of the South Platte River. They are said to have wrapped their loot in buckskins, stuffed it into tin cans, and buried the cans.

They were on Upper Deer Creek, above Shafer's Crossing. They had as much as $100,000 in loot to bury, and did so near timberline on the flank of Mt. Logan at the headwaters of Deer or Elk Creek. Their main camp was on Deer Creek, but the cache site could easily have been four or five miles distant. $40,000 of this was in currency, carefully wrapped in silk oil cloth. There was $23,000 worth of gold dust.

The story goes they got word of a posse coming after them, and getting close. It was for that reason they made camp at Deer Creek, to forestall any attack and to hide their loot.

The posse was under the leadership of General David Cook, head of government detectives in Colorado, a hard, tough man. The posse was made up of Summit County miners, mad as hell over all the robberies of THEIR gold, nearly frothing at the mouth to get a few shots at one or all of the

Reynolds gang.

In spite of the gang's precautions, the posse managed to get close enough to their camp to open fire without any warning. One outlaw, Owen Singlterry, was shot dead at once, but the rest of the gang escaped into the woods. In their hasty retreat they left behind utensils, bedrolls, several guns, letters from the opened mail sack, some scattered currency, and a bundled amount of gold amalgam.

A few cynics suggest that one or more members of the posse may have retrieved the treasure, and turned in a few items to avoid any suspicion. It is possible but doubtful.

A Dr. Cooper, posse member, cut off Singleterry's head and displayed it on a stake in Alma to demonstrate the wages of sin.

Only eight gang members remained, and they were without most of their equipment and supplies. They hurriedly rode off in different directions.

Tom Holliman immediately became separated from the others. He found an old, vacant house about thirty miles from Canon City, and went to sleep. It was his luck, which turned out to be a good thing for Tom, that part of the posse came the same way. The posse, as the gang had done, split up and headed in different directions.

They captured Tom Holliman without trouble. Tom was meek enough. It is not said if he wet his pants, but he did faint dead away. When he awakened he sang like a canary, telling everything he knew. His captors took him to Fairplay for safekeeping.

Four other gang members found refuge at the Guiraud Ranch. The Guirauds were gone, there was no food in the house, and the desperate men decided to go into Fairplay where they could get what they needed. Before they arrived in Fairplay, however, they found a ranch. They took it over at gunpoint.

While two of them ate and stood guard the other two slept. Rested, and before any word could leak out, they left in the night.

They did not get too far. A detatchment of the First Colorado Cavalry, led by a Captain Shoup and accompanied by a talkative, helpful Tom Holliman, caught up with the now horseless gang. They captured most of them not far to the east of Canon City.

A Captain Kerber at the time was pursuing John Reynolds, John Andrews, and Jack Stowe. These three stayed well ahead of Kerber and his posse, and managed to get safely into the New Mexico mountains.

The captured gang members were taken to Denver, and not too well treated along the way. There was a feeling that Confederate sympathies for the gang members might cause trouble. They were quickly tried before a secret military commission for highway robbery. Not how it should have been done, by any miltary standards, as was not the restricting the records of what took place. It was ordered they be taken south to Fort Wise, outside Pueblo, for punishment, namely hanging.

The men were escorted by a company of the Third Colorado Cavalry headed by a Captain Cree. On the morning of the third day of their trip to Fort Wise the gang members were hauled from the coach, manacled together, and blindfolded. Then they were shot. Cree claimed the gang members were shot while attempting to escape.

Jim Reynolds refused to say a word about where he had hidden all the loot. One source says one gang member told of the cache being buried about three to four miles from the Deer Creek Camp. Whether he talked or not, he was shot along with the others.

Uncle Dick Wooten, old mountain man and scout, found the scene by happenstance a short time afterwards. The bird-pecked, skeletal remains of the men were lashed to a tree, there were bullet holes in their skulls. This wretched handling of the situation helped the Jim Reynolds legend live forever. Nothing the gang did matched their ignoble ending in perpetuating tales of their deeds and treasures.

Jack Stowe, badly wounded in the escape, died of his wounds somewhere in the New Mexico mountains, or so one version of the story goes. Some have Stowe and Andrews changing places and endings. One tale has the three of them eventually returning to Colorado and recovering the cache near the Spanish Peaks. It is more likely that descriptions of how John Andrews was killed in a barroom gun fight in Santa Fe, where he and John Reynolds had gone after Stowe's death, are closer to the truth.

John lived there in Santa Fe for a time. He headed back to Denver in 1871, with a friend named Albert Brown. The men could not resist raiding a Mexican ranch along the way. John Reynolds was badly wounded in the raid. Bleeding to death, he drew Albert a crude map and told him the details of the treasure buried near the head of Deer Creek.

"Go down Geneva Gulch a little ways and you'll find where one of our horses mired down and we had to leave it there. At the head of the gulch, you turn to the right and follow a mountain around a little farther. And just above the head of Deer Creek, you'll find an old prospector's shaft running back into the mountain at about timberline. It's back there in the hole, pard. We walled the hole up with stones and stuck a butcher knife into a tree about four feet from the ground, broke the handle off and left it pointing to the hole."

Not long after that fatal raid, Brown went to Geneva Gulch. He found the skeletal remains of a horse in the boggy spot. A forest fire, however, had recently burned off the timber. Brown could not find a trace of the right spot so of course he did not find the rocked- up hole. He ended up in Wyoming, a derilict drunkard.

Another version of the same tale places the cache in a cave not far upstream from Shafer's Crossing.

Still another version puts the cache only a few feet off the old Webster Pass road close to where it crossed Elk Creek.

There is reason to believe that Antone Glassman found this cache in 1870. He was living in the area at the time. He removed one can of gold dust and again carefully covered the rest of it. He had some business Denver, and died while he was there. Nobody has ever found the cache again since Glassman took the one can and went to Denver. Glassman's cabin was on the banks of Handcart Creek. Markings on trees across from his cabin were believed by many to point to the cache site.

A man called Tex Taylor came into the South Platte Valley about 1900, perhaps shortly later, claiming to be the nephew of one of the Reynolds gang members. He said this uncle had escaped and fled to live in California. Tex had with him a map to one of the gang's caches. The map and his uncle's tales were the sole reason for his coming to Colorado. He searched for a few years but never really found a clue.

His map showed that on one particular creek there was a rock barricade, put there by the outlaws to guard a steep trail before it came out into a small, hidden glade, where they had their camp. Not far from that was a brush corral to pen their animals. It also showed the grave of one of the gang members near the site, a knife symbol carved into a nearby tree. The man had been buried there after getting shot in a fight. These things were supposed to be close to the sealed shaft where the cache was located.

Tex looked for a long time, was never successful. The two things lacking in his directions were in which direction from these things around the camp and how far the cache site was.

Vernon Crowe, in either 1933 or 1937, located a knife stuck in a dead tree. Its point was broken off. In 1938 Crowe found time to do some looking. He located the ruins of a brush corral and a row of rocks that could once have been a barricade. Crowe continued to search and at last found a scarred tree. A treasure sign, he thought, and at last he found a grave. He dug up a fully dressed skeleton, boots still on.

Crowe searched the immediate area for years, but he could never find the backfilled hole. Therefore he certainly did not find the cache. Others have looked, most of them have found even less.

In 1973 a friend of the author, Gary Christopher, was reading through all the old Rocky Mountain News articles concerning the Reynolds gang. Lo and behold, up pops some very new old information. It had been there all the time, but obviously nobody else besides Gary must have noticed it. If they did they never brought it to the attention of the treasure field.

In 1906 the RMN ran an article about two prospectors, Sullivan Davis and Holmes Robbins, finding $18,000 in an abandoned mine shaft. Most of it was gold dust, but there was some paper money with it, all contained in three good-sized metal cans.

It turned out that Davis and Robbins had somehow obtained a copy of a map that led them to the old mine. How they got the map is unclear. Even with the map they had looked for the mine for about half a year before they found it.

It seems that Jim Bunnel, one of the survivors of the Reynolds Gang's last days, had a smaller share of the $63,000 the gang supposedly buried in the Deer Creek area. He buried his share in the old mine shaft somewhere in his escape. Bunnel was afraid to return to the area, so he drew a map that pinpointed his cache in the old mine shaft and sent it to a cousin, Frank Seymour, who lived in Fairplay.

Seymour never found the old shaft. Davis and Robbins somehow got a copy of the map, and they did find it.

An obvious question comes to mind. If Bunnel had a separate share, is it not possible there were several smaller caches, not just one large one?

***

A stagecoach was held up at the Ute Crossing, below Alma. The two outlaws got about $3,000 in gold bullion. A posse soon tracked the two thieves to the by then deserted and water-logged Dexter Mine. Both men were shot dead in a brief gun battle. The posse searched, but they could not find the missing gold bullion.

***

A man named Buzzard somewhere and somehow found a good many gold nuggets. One story is he found them in a ground hog burrow. He brought his recovery into Fairplay, bragged about his find, but would tell nobody where he found them.

A German fellow in Fairplay had a sixteen year old daughter. The girl was raped and murdered, and many thought it was Buzzard's doing. Buzzard was a ruthless, hateful braggart, and possibly a killer and rapist. It will never be known for sure. His body shortly thereafter was found, his widely shown nuggets were missing. Soon after these things happened the German went back to Germany, where it is said he lived most comfortably. Buzzard's secret groundhog hole location was never discovered.

***

Francis Brayler explored a deep crevice in South Park when he found a natural cave while hunting in 1946. Inside the crevice was a human skeleton, a .45 revolver, pots, pans, an 1886 Marlin rifle, and several 1880's gold coins.

***

Gold can still be found and recovered from just about any stretch of any stream throughout South Park. Some spots are better than others, of course.

***

A cache of Carson City minted coins was found by a Texas family exploring Tarryall in 1964.

***

An old miner worked his mine for years to the northwest of Wilkerson Pass. His cabin was near his mine. He was known to have buried several caches of gold in and around his cabin. He was killed and most of his caches have not been found.

One of his caches, some gold coins buried in the corner of his cabin, was recovered by treasure hunters since the increased use of metal detectors.

***

In the 1800's outlaws used a shack   nestled against the base of a rock pinnacle at the northern edge of the Higgens Ranch. The three Higgens boys didn't even know of the shack for a long time, not until Will was breaking sod at the north end of the valley, near the pinnacle, and by happenstance saw the structure. He could see someone had been living there and by the broken strongbox and some other trash he could easily guess the type of inhabitants. This old ranch is somewhat southwest of Lake George, southeast of Wilkerson Pass, high in the Saddle Mountains.

The group of outlaws tried to pull off one stagecoach robbery too many. All but one were shot dead in the attempt. The survivor was badly wounded, a shotgun blast having nearly taken off his arm. Bleeding heavily all the way back to the hideout he was nearly dead but somehow managed to limp and crawl to the Higgens ranch for possible help. He confided in one of the Higgens boys before he died about what he and his friends had been doing, that a number of caches were hidden around the shack and along the bluffs. The brothers buried the man's body down the valley from the barn.

Soon afterwards Charley Higgens found a shirt used as a bag, filled with coins and jewelry. It was enough to make them believe exactly what the dying outlaw had told them.

Some time after that, while Charley was digging a post hole near that old cabin he struck a bucket full of coins. Most of the coins were gold.

It was nothing like a full-time treasure hunt, because there was always work to be done. Most of the recoveries came while the work was going on. Bob Higgens, while digging up a tree stump in a pasture close by, found a cache of coins in the tree roots.

Still another small cache was recovered about a mile and a half from the cabin. It was the last one the brothers found, according to Will.

About 1970 a treasure hunter recovered an iron pot containing gold coins from where it had been fastened high in a ponderosa pine years before. This tree was located not too far away from the old cabin.

***

Confederate sympathizers held up the Fairplay stage at Como. $80,000 was taken. The following day a posse surrounded them on Tarryall Creek. The group was shot down to a man. The area was carefully searched, including the back trail to Como, but the $80,000 was not found.

PITKIN COUNTY

Most lost mines are really lost ledges, or lost ledges that had minimal if any work done on them. If a mine was worked out, then abandoned, it is not the same as the lost mines we talk about. A ledge containing thirty or fifty thousand dollar ore before the year 1900 is a treasure, as much or more so than a chest full of gold pieces.

In 1900 Widow Dorothy Faulk came to Norrie. She obtained a claim about a mile and a half south of town. The woman began to raise goats, trying to make something of a living, and became known as "the Goat Lady". Sometime about 1910 or a bit later a handyman she hired at times, Scott Sawyer, found a rich deposit of gold. It was scarcely a mile from the goat lady's cabin. The samples he took from the formation later assayed at more than $6,000 per ton. Sawyer died of a heart attack shortly thereafter, never revealing the precise location of his find. The Biglow Upthrust is thought by many to be the logical place to start looking. That is more or less a mile from the old cabin.

***

An unobtrusive man arrived in Leadville in either 1876, 1878 or 1879 with a pack loaded with extremely rich gold ore. The date depends on whose story one hears. He sold the ore to Birdell and Witherell for a substantial sum. Enough so he could comfortably and quietly winter over in Leadville, keeping out of peoples' way. He certainly did not say much to anyone about where he got the gold.

Early the following spring he quietly left Leadville, taking care not to be followed. Late that summer his body was found on Independence Pass by Frank Brown, who managed the Farwell properties at Independence. The body was exposed in the face of a thawing snow bank. It was plain to see he had been swept up and covered over by an avalanche.

As far as could be determined, the man had taken the gold from an area to the northeast of Independence Pass, at the head of Lost Man Gulch, a tributary of the Roaring Fork River. After his death various miners recalled seeing him doing some prospecting in Lost Gulch, which is a branch of the Roaring Fork. The area could not be too far from the ghost site of Independence. He certainly was not telling anybody the location, and the vicious snow slide silenced him forever before he got around to telling anyone.

The fellow's workings could be somewhere around Lake Creek, not far from where his body was found. There was gold mined up Lincoln Gulch, towards the now ghost site of Ruby.

***

In 1894, or possibly in 1899, a boy showed up in Aspen looking for work. He showed Owen Thom, feed merchant and lumber dealer in Aspen, a rock he'd picked up at the base of a cliff on the Roaring Fork River. He had only the one rock. The boy told Thom he had traveled light from Meeker to find a job, that he'd had a herd of horses but Indians stole them from him. The boy told Thom he found the specimen about ten miles up the Roaring Fork, that he had been heading for Independence but decided to return to Aspen. Being too late to go on he had to sleep that night near the base of a cliff. Thom gave him several ten dollar gold pieces to buy food and some new clothes, told him to return the following morning to go see about the outcropping the rock had come from.

Thom believed the rock would assay at $40,000 to the ton, which later proved to be an accurate guess, but the boy had left town by the following morning. With him went the location of where the ore had been found. It could have been a street-wise Eastern kid pulling a con-job on a Western merchant for a few ten dollar gold coins. Even so, plenty of folks have done considerable looking for the outcropping just in case the kid was telling the truth.

***

In 1885 "Old Man Hale", which is all he ever was known by, came with the 6,000 or so individuals to gather in Aspen hoping to strike it rich. With him was his son. By the time he got there Aspen Mountain, to the south of town, was pretty well claimed solid. Smuggler Mountain was on the north side of Aspen, and it was almost solidly claimed, too. Hale had few supplies, not much equipment, and no money to try to buy into a going proposition.

Hale was told if he went up Hunter Creek, a mile or more to the west of town and about a thousand feet higher, he would find it more open. Hale and his son did just that, and found a promising, yet unclaimed area. There was plenty of room and few people for almost five miles along Hunter Creek before it pinched out at Thimble Rock.

That fall Hale and his son came into Aspen with one or two mule loads of very good ore. It must have been rich ore, because they grubstaked themselves and at last had some good equipment and supplies. It was hardly noticed in those bustling days that he and his son headed right back up Hunter Creek.

In the spring they returned with another small but rich load of ore.

He said little, but did tell someone he and his son had constructed two solid cabins as well as working down to the fifty foot level of an incline.

The ore brought Hale and his son enough cash to make a trip back east to visit friends and family. It was not long after that word came back that Old Man Hale had died and his son did not intend to return.

This set of a search up Hunter Creek for the Hales' now-open workings. Nobody found the site and the brief enthusiasm soon died away.

Some years later, after the silver crash of 1893, young Hale returned to Aspen. He outfitted himself, and headed up Hunter Creek towards his father's claim. In little more than a week he was back in Aspen, discouraged, confused, and disgusted. He did not stay long in Aspen, and he never returned after he left.

A Forest Service ranger named Shoemaker may have seen the two cabins, but he was unable to find them again once he heard of their significance. Many have looked, at times, but thus far Old Man Hale's rich ore vein remains lost.

PROWERS COUNTY

Let's not dawdle, tonight! We need to hit the sack, because tomorrow is a big day. The one thing better than talking about treasure is hunting for treasure.

In 1828 a wagon train left Santa Fe. It was loaded with furs and the traders were carrying about $30,000 in silver coins. Indians began to harass the caravan, and the traders decided to bury the heavy coins on Choteau Island so they could make better time and an eventually escape from their tormentors. Only four or five made it back safely to Independence, Missouri. The others were killed or died of infected wounds and hunger. Those thirty thousand silver dollars have never been recovered.

Choteau's Island was very close to the Colorado/Kansas line. The location is far east of Bent's Fort, along the Arkansas River, recognized by those who used the Santa Fe Trail. It is fairly close to the site of old Fort Aubry, and near Hartman. There have been dramatic changes in the river channels over the years. It is hard to ascertain exactly where Choteau's Island was when that wagon train stopped there to cache their coins.

PUEBLO COUNTY

You think what you want, but I'm going to stick to what I know unless I get hold of important new information. If you think hunting a treasure is hard, just wait until you admit the cache you're hoping to find doesn't seem to be on this mountain, but it may be over on the next mountain. When that happens it's best to just go on to a different story.

There was a major train derailment at Eden in the early 1900's. A flash flood washed several cars off the Denver and Rio Grande line there at the station. Many people were severely injured, and a few were killed at the time. Not only were many personal valuables lost, thieves arrived before rescuers could get there. They broke into the express car, stealing all that had any value. This wash, north of Pueblo, still is worth carefully searching for valuables washed downstream and deposited elsewhere.

***

Apache Gulch has not produced much in the way of gold in modern times although a number of people have prospected the area. The Spaniards, however, are said to have produced some gold there. Old Arrastras, ancient tools, that sort of thing has been found up and down the gulch, which at least confirms the presence of Spanish workings.

One group of Spaniards supposedly did some heavy mining there and had some decent production. Indians slaughtered them, however, except for a twelve year old boy.

One local farmer claims to have found a crude gold ingot while doing some field work.

A few local would-be prospectors took this as enough evidence to warrant hunting for the surviving Spanish boy. They found him, grown old in Santa Fe, and he agreed to return to Apache Gulch with them. He looked with those who brought him back for a few days, but too many years had gone by for the old man to remember much of anything. The old man's ordeals must have toughened him, for he lived past the age of a hundred years.

Many people scoff at there ever being any great amount of gold in

Apache Gulch, or the stories about Spanish workings there. One local miner, however, claims he handled some ore from the area that assayed at $58,000 to the ton. If so, and they found a hot spot with such ore, it is no wonder the Spaniards were able to cast some crude gold ingots.

Perhaps it is not all gone.

**

There is a tale of an Aztec cache located somewhere along the St. Charles River.

Thirty-five miles south of Pueblo, in Apache Canyon, there is said to be a coin cache. This is almost due west of Apache City, at the base of the Greenhorn Mountains. A band of Apaches attacked a wagon train there, and one of the merchants had time to bury his money. It was not then nor later recovered.

**

A rich lode of gold ore was discovered in the Greenhorn Mountains, but its precise location has been lost. The way the story goes, a long-time Pueblo prospector thought he'd finally hit it big in the Greenhorn Mountain area. He loaded a wagon as full as he could get it and took it by an assayer's office in Pueblo to find out the value of the ore. The assayer told him the ore was without value.

Disappointed, dreams of riches shattered, the prospector dumped his wagon load of ore onto a vacant area at the edge of Pueblo. He packed up his belongings and headed off to who knows where, hopefully where he might find some better ore. He was never heard of or seen again.

Within days of these happenings a different man spotted the dumped wagon load of ore. He took a few samples and had them assayed. The assayer told him it was some of the richest gold ore he had ever seen. He pieced the story of what happened together, but nobody knew where the dejected prospector had gone. The source of the good gold ore was unknown. It's there, somewhere in the Greenhorn Mountains, but thus far nobody has found it.

RIO BLANCO COUNTY

The town of Meeker sits atop the site of an army post active from 1880 to 1883. There were 1,500 soldiers stationed there to insure peace after the Ute War was over. That corner of Colorado fairly reeks with treasure leads.

In 1879 Ute Indians raided the Indian Agency at White River. N. C. Meeker and nine employees were killed in the raid. It is believed that Meeker had some U. S. funds buried at the agency. If there actually was a cache it has never been reported as recovered.

RIO GRANDE COUNTY

I went to school in the San Luis Valley, first through fifth grades. Lived northeast of Monte Vista, for a time, up near La Garita for a while, and for a few years just to the southwest of Center. I was more interested in keeping warm during the winters, then, than I was in finding treasure.

There was an old man named Phillips show up in Del Norte every few months during the 1870's. He came into town to buy tools, beans, bacon and other foodstuffs, and various simple, typical mining equipment. The old man paid for everything he bought with gold dust, and he always seemed to have plenty of it.

He was a careful, crafty old man. For about fifteen years the wiley old fox twarted every effort to follow him, avoided every question put to him about where he was working. All through those years he paid for all he bought with gold dust and was trap-tight-lipped about where it came from.

Sometime in the 1880's the old man came into town, this time obviously ill. He had a raging fever, was shaking, and almost completely out of his mind. Some thoughtful souls put him to bed and attempted to take care of him, but the old fellow did not respond. He slipped into a coma from which he never recovered, never once saying anything anybody could understand about his mine. His death of course cemented the growth of many in the mining circles desire to search for the Lost Phillips Lode, and many did so for years.

All that was really known, since he never had been successfully followed, was that he always headed southwest from Del Norte.

A few announced they found it, but for a good long while all such claims were proved to be wrong.

Some think the Phillips claim may have been found in 1902. Not in Rio Grande County, mind you, but over in Mineral county in the area between Treasure Mountain and Summitville. There's even more people who don't think that the lode found that year was the Phillips Lode. It may or may not have been, but the rest of the story is told with the other tales of Mineral County.

ROUTT COUNTY

Pass me another of those biscuits. I can't start talking treasure without having at least one more! That Dutch oven is quite an invention, and it sure got plenty of use throughout these Colorado Rockies. Help yourself, but don't take that last biscuit!

In 1866 four French prospectors were prospecting near the head waters of Elk Creek, to the east of Hahn's Peak. They located a rich placer deposit up close to the divide. They camped on a small creek, a tributary to Bear Creek, and one man did some panning. He found colors. Following a dry side gulch, uphill from their camp, they came upon a rock rim at the head of the dry gulch. Digging into that produced some gold- rich gravel.

They were given no more time, for a band of Utes, led by feisty Chief Colorow, took them prisoners. They were lucky the Indians did not immediately kill them, but only took their animals and all their supplies. Colorow and his band, seeming to find the situation more humorous than did his captives, marched them to the Continental Divide. There he showed them which direction was east and let them know should they wanted to keep their hair they'd best not return.

It's easy to see how the group had no time or inclination to do any placering.

The Frenchmen made it safely to Laramie. While they were there, two of the men were killed in a gambling argument. The remaining two went south to Denver. Not long after they got there the third man came down with some kind of sickness and died.

The surviving Frenchman eventually wandered south into New Mexico. He was quite a talker, and eventually told enough people about his rich placer in northwest Colorado that he rounded up an expedition. He made it sound very simple, telling his new group the spot where their make-do camp was set up was about ten miles east of Hahn's Peak and at the headwaters of the Elk River. There was an old rifle cleaning rod leaning against the tree where they'd tied up a tarp.

The Frenchman led an enthused group in 1879 back to work the placer. In the intervening years, however, a forest fire or two set by Colorow and his braves had changed the looks of everything. Most of the Frenchman's landmarks had become ashes.

They searched hard enough, they just could not find the old campsite, let alone the right dry gully with that particular rim rock placer. The placer was not then nor later relocated. Every one gave up the search but old "Pony" Whitmore, a prospector who got in on the venture. He looked regularly for it until he died. His gravestone is the third marker set up in the old Steamboat Springs graveyard.

**

The Lost Phantom Mine was discovered and lost during 1881. It is somewhere on Wild Mountain, near Steamboat Springs.

**

Some prospectors gave Jim Baker some specimens of rich gold float in 1850. They said they found it to the south of Hahn's Peak, but as they wanted to hurry on to California they did not look for the source of the float. They told Baker the site was near the head waters of the Little Snake and Elk Rivers. The float was up a hill from some broken wagon parts. Baker later found the wagon parts, but he nor anyone else has ever found more of that rich float, let alone its source vein structure. Maybe a rockslide covered it up, Baker suggested.

The area is somewhere between Steam boat Springs and Hahn's Peak. It was another good treasure story Jim Baker heard. He is known to have gotten more stories than he ever got gold.

**

A number of silver dollars and rolls of buffalo nickels were recovered from the mud after a bulldozer leveled a tract of land in Oak Creek to put in a new trailer park. One of the author's friends recovered many of these about 1971.

**

In 1867 George A. Jackson and a prospector friend located a rich gold deposit just off Walton Creek. They had been seeing good colors in Buffalo Park, but there not only was not enough water to do any panning, there were all sorts of Indian signs. They did not want to be out there in open sight. Keeping to high ground they began panning a small stream for several miles, and at last came to a bar glittering with gold. This was southeast of Steamboat Springs, in the Middle Park area. George Jackson thought their canyon was located somewhere within four or five miles from Rabbit Ear Peak, which was visible from there.

Jackson and his friend hastened back to Georgetown, knowing full well they dared not work the rich strike by themselves because of it being located in Indian country. In Georgetown, in the spring of 1868, they easily got together a group of ten prospectors ready and willing to go into the wild area after good placering potential.

Jackson's group built a cabin, constructed a corral for their animals, and dug about a three hundred foot ditch to bring enough water to the placer bar. They whipsawed enough planks to build sluices. Then they worked their discovery, accumulated and buried about $10,000 worth of gold in buckskin bags somewhere in or near the cabin they built. During that time Jackson cut his name into a tree growing close to their cabin.

Twelve years before, in January of 1859, this is the same George Jackson who trudged all by himself up Clear Creek Canyon to the site of present day Idaho Springs and panned out enough gold to set off the big rush there. His Rabbit Ears area discovery is a different matter altogether.

In that spring of 1868, after the group had been placering for a good amount of time, they were attacked by Indians. Several men were killed in the fracas. Others escaped, but there was no time to recover their cached gold. The survivors other than Jackson decided not to return to the area. Most of them returned to Illinois, where they'd come from. The others, who knows elsewhere. Jackson was not about to give up that easily.

Jackson confided the story of what happened to a close friend. They made plans to go back to the cabin site and retrieve the stashed gold when spring weather permitted. Shortly after that, Jackson was called back to Missouri on family matters. His friend agreed to go get the cached gold and share with Jackson.

In June this friend of Jackson and another man returned to the Rabbit Ears area, confident of being able to recover the stashed gold. They found the cabin, they found Jackson's name carved into a tree trunk, they did not find the cached gold or its source. The man tried again and again, as late as 1912.

The man, and an old-time guide, did find some workings over on Harrison Creek, but that had nothing to do with the Jackson strike.

For many years other later searches were also not successful.

In 1947 some workings and ruins of an old cabin were discovered by Bill Keplinger and his father just off Highway 40, on Walton Creek. They had to go up through a very narrow, overgrown canyon before it opened up into a small clearing. It was thought the ruins had to be the twice-lost cabin of George Jackson's group, but no cache was found. Nor more placer gold, for that matter.

Perhaps one of Jackson's original group returned alone and retrieved the gold, maybe one of those Illinois men. Why not, that's exactly what Jackson hoped to do.

***

An old Swede located a rich gold lode not far from Hahn's Peak. He came wearily into Rawlins, Wyoming, and made the mistake of telling some people about his find. There are those who tried to butter up the old man, and since he'd worked for years out in the Comstock Lode, and was a Swede, they got to calling him Komstocker. When several men tried to follow him the next spring he gave them the slip, or at least gave most of them the slip. It was not long afterwards that his body was found along a trail near Dixon, Wyoming. None of his belongings were missing.

One good claim, with some old workings on it, was located a number of years later. Some thought it might have been the old Swede's, most did not think so. They think the Old Komstocker Lode is still out there to be found.

SAGUACHE COUNTY

Hey, fellows, don't argue which county a treasure is in. A good many times nobody can be sure which county it is in, because there's no way of being sure. In some cases it may even be over into the next state. Can't even know for sure which side of a certain mountain these things might be on, and very likely it's over on the next mountain.

Sit down, relax. There's always another treasure or two.

Somewhere in the Muddy Creek area there seems to be a disappearing cliff with some $5,000 (old gold prices) worth of gold-bearing quartz in it. It's on the southwest side of McClure Pass, going out of Pitkin County.

In 1890 a Carbondale prospector by the name of Joseph Johns was out deer hunting in that area. He discovered a small cliff, recently swept bare by a rock slide, that had some very promising quartz. Being a prospector more than he was a deer hunter, he knocked off as many pieces of the ore as he could carry, and staked a claim. He didn't pay much attention to other landmarks, because that cliff was the most prominent natural feature anywhere around there. He figured there was no possible way he could not come right back to the spot.

He had the ore assayed. $5,000 to the ton. He was soon geared up and headed back across McClure Pass. His cliff laced with gold-rich quartz would make him a wealthy man.

Johns got into the right area, or so he thought, but look as he would he could not locate that cliff. He criss-crossed the area. The first day and many days thereafter were increasingly futile and frustrating. He could not find the cliff.

Johns looked by himself for a couple or three years. Then he told B. B. Hills and W. L. Girdner about what he'd found, then lost. The three of them spent the next twenty years looking for John's lost cliff. They never found it. Johns made his last search for it in 1911, at the age of eighty.

***

There is a cave somewhere about thirty miles to the north of Creede. A freight line operator, Curt Garner, used the cave as a refuge in a blinding snowstorm. He took samples from a ledge inside the cave. The material assayed over $2,300 to the ton. He returned, the following spring, but could not relocate the cave.

***

Embargo Creek is in the Los Pinos Pass area. Two miners located a rich gold ore body in that area, worked it, and had begun to accumulate a good pile of ore. They were attacked by thieves on a trip from the mine, and murdered. It was clumsy work on the thieves' part. The location of the mine, their cache site, all was lost when they died.

***

Mark Biedell was a respected Colorado miner, entrepreneur, town builder, all-around Colorado citizen. He built a virtual fortress on the Saguache River in the early 1870's to better protect himself and his belongings against the active Ute Indian forays. One night he took into his walls a Frenchman and perhaps six Mexicans. Biedell was told of remarkable gold lode located at the head waters of Saguache Creek. The Mexican survey party, working on Maxwell Land Grant matters, had worked its way up Carnero Creek, then crossed over what they thought was Saguache Creek. At some point in that vicinity they discovered gold. They forgot about survey work for several weeks and dug into the rich lode. A band of Ute Indians attacked them, and the Mexicans barely had enough time in their headlong flight from pursuit to bury their gold somewhere along Carnero Creek.

They said they blazed a tree and heaped up three grave-like mounds of dirt to mark their cache. Their pursuers kept after them, following them as far as New Mexico.

It was 1880 before a Mexican showed up in the area with a soiled maps to look for the gold. Biedel accompanied him. They found what they thought were the three mounds of dirt, along Carnero Creek, as the original party had described. Look as they would, they could not find a blazed tree. The cache of gold was not found then, and nobody has claimed to have found it since.

In the 1890's there were some old workings found up Goose Creek, and there were some found up Cochetopa Creek. There was some suggestion this might have been the Mexican's workings. Most people did not think so, those old workings being well out of the correct area. Survey teams are not supposed to become that confused.

***

In the Crestones is the Lost Tenderfoot Mine.

***

On the west flanks of the Sangre de Cristos an area of rich gold float marks an almost legendary ledge of gold ore. Many are those in the mining years who looked hard for the source of that rich float.

Three men in 1880 found the source in some spare time prospecting. M. M. Warner was a successful Denver businessman. Dan De Foe was an attorney practicing in Aspen. They went prospecting when they could do so with a friend only remembered as Bert. They had often heard of the probability of a rich gold ledge rumored to be somewhere along the western flanks of the Sangre de Cristos.

On one such prospecting jaunt, well past the end of their vacation time, they were on their way back to base camp through the small cedar and pinon covered hills that make up the western base of the Sangre de Cristos. On one of those hills they found a very old prospect hole.

The hole had once been deeper. Brush and rocks and dirt had washed and fallen down into it for obviously a long time. Poking through the rubble they found what at first they thought was a low quality lead ore.

The visible vein structure looked good enough for them to check further, so they cleaned out some of the dirt and rocks from the hole. The other two men picked over the available ore, sorting out the better specimens, while De Foe wrote notes describing landmarks, charting directions, and that sort of thing. He was well aware of how easily something found can be lost without careful notation. They erected location notices, so if the ore proved to have some value, they would legally have a claim.

They left, already well overdue in getting back to their base camp and back to their workaday lives. Because of this the three men hurried. Somewhere in that hasty trip De Foe lost all the carefully-made notes he'd made, but the others told him it would be easy to return to the place if they ever needed to. When they got out of those low hills and back into the open San Luis Valley they discovered they were on Cottonwood Creek, two to three miles past their base camp.

A few weeks later Warner had some of his samples assayed. The results showed twenty ounces to the ton. Warner wrote to De Foe and told him to get the specimens he took assayed. When De Foe did so, one result was as high as forty-five ounces to the ton. This was extremely good ore, not the miserable stuff they had at first thought. Warner, on his way to Wisconsin, told De Foe to get their claim recorded.

De Foe rounded up Bert and they hurried down to the San Luis Valley to obtain the details needed to file their claim. It was the middle of the winter and there was by then three feet of snow or more covering all the subject area.

The men searched that spring, but search as they would they could not find the right hill with the test hole on it. They never did find it, and De Foe and his partners admitted as much about a dozen years later. Others have looked for it over the years, and they have fared no better.

***

In 1880 three prospectors got caught in a biting, blinding blizzard sweeping the length of the Sangre de Cristos. H. A. Melton, E. R. Oliver, and S. J. Harkman had been doing some prospecting but they were not prepared for such a storm. They were near the head of Dead Man's Creek, on the San Luis Valley side of the mountains. Several miles to the north of Dead Man's Camp they had taken refuge beneath a slight rock overhang. From this somewhat sheltered place they were thankful to spot a cave on the other side of the canyon. They fought the bitter winds to reach the mouth of the cave, in which they hoped to get out of the freezing blizzard.

In the overhang somewhat sheltering the entrance to the cave they found pithy pine knots with which to light torches. It would be too dark without them. The men decided to crawl into the narrow opening, to seek better shelter, even though they had to go on hands and knees and squeeze through in places.

They crawled and squeezed through about twelve or so feet, then the narrow opening widened into a chamber large enough for them to stand up. The place was damp, but another narrow passageway continued into the mountainside.

This they took, unable to stand up, and it led into a much larger chamber. Their torches did not begin to light up the place.

In this vaster cave they soon found a human skull. Within moments they discovered five other skeletons. Two of the men became rather frightened. Oliver, maybe somewhat more practical, goaded everyone into gathering enough wood to make a fire and prepare something to eat. They did not need to share with their new-found skeletal friends.

After they ate the men made new torches and did some exploring. Other than the skeletons there was nothing else of interest in the large chamber A small passageway led off the big chamber, however, into a smaller room.

Melton saw in this smaller room what he at first took to be some stones of similar size and shape. He tried to pick one up, and it was almost too heavy to lift. These were not stones, they were five crudely smelted gold ingots.

They took their five gold ingots when the storm eased, and made their way back to camp.

They later would say not a word about where they made their remarkable discovery to the other prospectors. They wanted to explore the caves further once the weather cleared up. It seemed very likely there could be more ingots in the cave. The winter storms could be waited out. They had made careful observations, knew exactly how to get back to the cave.

The men went to Silver Cliff to winter over, and made plans for the coming spring. In Silver Cliff they sold the five gold ingots for $900 each. News of that sale swept rapidly through Silver Cliff and throughout the mining West! Melton and his friends would not say a word about where they got the ingots.

Ah, the best laid plans of man. When the three men, taking precautions not to be followed, returned to the area in the late spring, most of the deeper snows at last gone, they could not find the entrance to the cave. Perhaps it had been covered by a landslide. Perhaps, somehow, they did not go back to the right gulch. Whatever the reason, they never again found their cave of skulls and gold. Neither has anybody else.

***

The Turkey Creek Lost Mine is somewhere in the Crestones.

***

In the 1930's a crafty thief stole a great many gold ingots near Bonanza and cached them somewhere in the area. His craftiness did not keep him from being arrested for the crime and sentenced to prison.

The cache probably was hidden somewhere in the shaft of an old mine near Saguache. As the man who put it there was convicted of murder and sentenced to life in prison he was unable to recover the ingots. It has been looked for, but the cache has never been found.

***

George Skinner's brother had a cabin near timberline on Horn's Peak. There is some chance it might have been on the Saguache County side of the mountain. In a letter found after his death in the cabin he spoke of finding an extremely rich gold mine in the immediate vicinity. His body was found at the base of a cliff. Among the scattered remains was a quantity of rich gold ore samples. The lode from which he got it has never yet been found. (See story in Custer County.)

SAN JUAN COUNTY

Yes, one wonders how those old prospectors ever got much done, working as they did at elevations of nine, ten, eleven thousand feet and more. It's hard enough for us to sit here, drink coffee, and still have enough energy to put more wood on the fire. Can you even imagine the hard work it was to pound drill steel with a four pound sledge into an ore seam for hours at a time?

Somewhere along Bear Creek is cached $185,000 in silver ore.

***

Sasario Silva found a high grade gold vein at the head of Lime Creek in 1909. This was high above Silverton. The location of the site became lost and in spite of many searches has not been relocated.

***

Late in the summer of 1932 two brothers, Sul and Charley Baker, set out to find an abandoned mine near the headwaters of Lime Creek. An old prospector named Flatus, dead several years before this time, had developed a tunnel on a seam of ore. The brothers thought the ore from that tunnel might get get them through those tough years. They wanted to find Flatus' old mine, and if the ore was good enough to work, put their claim on it. Nobody else had yet done so.

The Baker brothers were sheep men, but the sheep business was losing, not making any money those days.

They parked their old pickup off the Million Dollar Highway at the Coal Creek Campground and headed up the steep canyon. From the campground there at the highway, Coal Creek tumbles on down into Lime Creek. The Flatus cabin and tunnel were supposed to be located up the steep canyon from there. They carried no lunch. The only tool they had, since the only thing they wanted to do was find that tunnel and take some samples, was a small prospector's hand pick.

The Bakers went as far up Coal Creek as the point where two branches come together. The main branch comes down from Red Basin,

around a timbered ridge and joins the lesser branch that comes down from the basin nestled at the foot of Engineer Mountain.

In a triangular grassy bench, just above where it fell off steeply into the creek, Sul sat down to rest and smoke while Charley explored up through the timbered ridge.

Downsope from where Sull sat, the grass cover had slipped. Bedrock lay exposed in various places on the steep incline down to the creek.

In one such exposed section of bedrock Sul noticed a seam. It was maybe eight inches wide. The seam ran straight, and was composed of a far different material in both texture and color than the rock around it. It also stood up two or three inches above the surrounding bedrock.

It was a different enough formation to catch Sull's attention. He used the hand pick to knock of several pieces of the protrusion. The rock was hard, but brittle. It broke off from the protruding ledge easily, leaving sharp cleavages. The material had a rusty brown color and there were bright metal particals visible throughout it. Farsighted, Sul could see this even though he did not have along his reading glasses. Some of the pieces were as large and thick as a man's hand, wide on one side, tapered to a sharp edge at the other.

He continued to break off pieces until Charley returned from his explorations. They both were hungry and wanted to get back to the pickup, but Sul stuck a few of the better looking pieces into his pockets.

While fixing their meal once they got back to the pickup Sul dropped one of the pieces of rock into the fire. He knew that if those metallic spots were gold the fire would bubble them out. By the time they finished eating, however, it was late and it was a good drive back down to Durango. Sul forgot about his rock in their hurry to leave.

Right after that jaunt the two brothers got a job building a house. Any free time was spent with caring for the sheep they still owned. The Flatus tunnel idea was put aside, the specimens Sul broke off the ledge were forgotten, and there was seemingly endless work to worry about.

When the work ended, in January of 1933, Sull found his specimens. They were in a coat pocket, in the coat he'd hung up after the last August trip up Coal Creek. With his glasses on he became sure those metallic speckles were gold.

The brothers showed the rocks to a mining friend, who became excited at what he saw. He told them fifty pounds of that kind of material would get them out of their money troubles. Sul responded by telling his old friend he'd probably knocked fifty pounds off the ledge. these were only the ones he brought home.

The long time mining man told the brothers many rich pieces of float had been picked up over the years along the steep incline up Coal Creek. Many men had fruitlessly sought the source of the float. Perhaps Sul had unwittingly taken the pieces from the source so many others had tried to find.

The friend had the ore assayed, and the results came back at $40,000 to the ton. The following March of course the price of gold was increased, and a ton then was worth 75% more, or $73,000 to the ton.

These three men could not hardly wait for spring to come so they could go back up Coal Creek Canyon to the little flat near its headwaters. But the snows were extra heavy that winter, and the snowbanks lingered longer than usual. The fellows were chomping at the bit to go, but they had to wait for several extra weeks longer than they hoped.

When they at last reached the Coal Creek campground they found the rock Sul had thrown into the hot coals. Gold was bubbled out all over it.

They returned to the spot high up the canyon, and they were certain it was the exact spot. The ledge was not to be found. The snows obviously had shifted the grass overburden down across the area where that ledge had been exposed the summer before.

They poked, they did some digging. It had to be there in an area no wider than thirty or forty feet, and that not much more than a football field long. But it now was covered with a grassy overburden of ten inches to ten feet. They never again found their ledge. Others have looked, and had no better results.

***

Raw diamonds have been found in San Juan County.

***

172 silver dollars were found stashed in an old miner's shack in Gladstone in 1975. The townsite is eight miles north of Silverton on Cement Creek.

***

A detector user found a five pound chunk of melted silver coins in the ashes of a former Silverton house.

***

Edward Ennis was a wealthy New Yorker. Income from his million dollar inheritance allowed him to do more or less what he wanted to do. This million dollars capital was soundly in place, creating a splendid income, but Ennis decided he could enlarge his wealth by going into mining. As he was also a spiritualist, bored with the big city life, he became convinced that spiritualism would lead him to vast new riches.

He paid $50,000 in early 1870's dollars to a spiritualist for advice. Ennis was told that in southwestern Colorado, he would find near the continental divide "a lake of silver".

Ennis was promptly on a train to Pueblo. He purchased all the gear needed to go into mining, and went into the San Juans as the spiritualist advised.

He found just the spot. He paid $30,000 for a number of claims high in the mountains to the northeast of Silverton. Hardly before he could hire miners and begin mining he started an amazing building program, permanent structures of the finest construction, no worry about expenses. The shaft was hardly begun when he had work started on a palatial home for himself.

He named the mine the Highland Mary and promised to create outstanding mining achievements.

It all sounded good, and at first it looked good. Superb, not just good, for they struck some $7,500 ore not long into the project. A shipment of that kind of ore was sent to Pueblo in 1876. He went with the ore to Pueblo, sent back word to shut down operations until he returned.

Ennis felt compelled to talk it all over with his spiritualist. He went back to New York. Sure enough, the next spring he returned to the Highland Mary with more money and plenty of advice from the spiritualist.

Work was halted in the area already blocked out, which had produced the rich ore. It was not as rich as what they would find less than 2,000 feet into the mountain. There, had advised the spiritualist, lay the lake of silver.

So $7,500 per ton silver in hand was ignored. A tunnel towards the yet unseen lake of silver was begun. Each night Ennis communed with his spiritualist in his dreams. Almost daily the direction of the tunnel was changed. It soon became the most twisted tunnel in all the Rockies, and in a number of places cut through and bypassed good ore. After all, the goal was to reach that lake of silver.

This continued until 1895. The tunnel was by then a thousand sinuous feet in length. But that's when the project ground to a halt. One of the companies Ennis was getting his income from failed. No more income to pay for erratic tunnel drilling. The million dollars Ennis had already spent on fancy buildings and wandering tunnels suddenly meant nothing.

Ennis tried to raise more money but his spiritualistic approach frightened away any possible investors. The courts gave him a year to get his mining empire back on a sound financial footing. He could not do it, for even with rich known ore already blocked out nobody would help him. Ennis was forced to sell his Highland Mary property for pennies on the dollar to satisfy outstanding debts.

New owners took out the ore in sight, and did well financially from the start. To rub salt in the wound, at about some six hundred feet past where Ennis was forced to stop, a body of rich ore that could be described as a lake of silver was encountered.

The Highland Mary became one of the best money makers in the state of Colorado.

Ennis died broke, perhaps communing with his spiritualist adviser throughout his last miserable days in an insane asylum.

***

In the early 1890's a man named Tom Estes prospected throughout southwestern Colorado. His efforts at last were concentrated around the West Needles. He was friends with one Doff Lusk, a cattle man, even though Doff had turned him down when he once asked Doff for a grubstake. Tom stopped by Doff's cattle camp high on Cascade Creek one evening late in the Fall of 1893.

Being Doff's friend, and perhaps wanting to rub in the fact that Doff could have had an interest in what he was showed that evening had he only come up earlier with some grubstake money, Estes opened the two sacks he took off his burros. The ore was full of visible gold, very rich material.

Although Lusk, or his two young nephews helping with work around the cow camp that season, knew little about minerals or mining, they could see the gold in Estes' two heavy sacks of ore. Estes was free in showing his rich haul, not really paying attention to the wide- eyed boys taking in the scene. Harry and Dell McWilliams were to remember and talk about that evening and what they saw and heard for the rest of their lives.

Estes was not so free in telling anything about where he got it, although he did say he got it out of an eight inch seam he'd discovered on the south facing slopes of the West Needles Mountains. That's about as much information as would be hearing about a satchell full of money hidden under a New York East Side trash can.

Also, when asked about the ore's value, he said he thought it would bring him about a thousand dollars. Lusk and the boys protested, saying there was not more than fifty pounds in both sacks put together. Estes shrugged, and informed them he'd let them know how much he got.

Estes did mention, later that night, one could probably see the workings from the cow camp, if they had really good eyesight and knew just where to look. He also stated how carefully and well he had concealed those workings whenever he left.

Lusk told his nephews, after Estes was gone, and they remarked they would like to follow him back to wherever he got the ore, that they would do no such thing. Trust and confidence was a precious, priceless commodity, and was not to be ignored. The message was heard by the two boys, but somehow it did not soak in.

The following June Estes again came by the cow camp. He had a good supply of tools and equipment, foodstuffs, everything to last a full summer season. He was going back for some more ore. Not a lot, just enough to keep himself in good shape. He told Lusk it was safer where it was, unmined. He intended to only take out as much as he needed in any one season.

Before he left he told the boys he'd sold that almost fifty pounds of ore for $1,070.

That night they saw a pinpoint of light high on the West Needles. The boys made up their minds, in spite of their uncle's telling them to not even think about it, to find out exactly where the light was coming from.

It was only the middle of August when Estes came off the mountain and stopped by the cow camp to talk with Lusk. Much earlier than the previous year. Nevertheless, he had with him this time seven full sacks of ore.

There was time to talk with Lusk that evening, and Estes told him a good deal of what he'd been doing. It had only taken him two weeks to get the seven full sacks of ore. Most of the time on the mountain had been taken up by timbering and carefully covering the entrance to his tunnel. He also filled in and then covered up a nearby shaft he dug several years prior to finding his rich seam. Nearby, among some huge rocks, he constructed a forge. He did not build a blacksmith shop, he decided not to construct a cabin. Those things would call attention to his location. He had started a footpath from his out-of-sight camping place to the workings.

This time, after Estes left, the two nephews privately decided to follow Estes' tracks back to his workings. They had no trouble doing so, for the only way to get to their uncle's cow camp from the West Needles was to go down into Purgatory Canyon from wherever he needed to come down, and come back out of the canyon on an often used trail. Tracking was no trouble on the trail, not until they got into rocky terrain on the north side of Purgatory Canyon. There they lost the old man's tracks. That was fine, for the only place he could have been was up on those West Needles somewhere. They would just follow him when he came back the next spring.

Estes did not come back early the next summer. It was into the middle of the summer before Estes showed up. Harry was in camp, but Lusk and Dell were away. When Estes left camp the following morning, Harry waited a while, then followed.

This was fine, the old man's tracks were obvious, and Harry was well up on the north side of Purgatory Canyon before the old man stepped out from behind some rocks and accosted him. He had plainly been waiting for the boy. He had his rifle held in a menacing manner. He told the youth how angry he was, and that he had a mind to shoot him. He wanted him headed back the way he came. Estes minced no words in letting Harry know his life was in danger if he ever tried to follow him anywhere again.

Estes came back by the cow camp in only two weeks. He did not stay the night there, as had been his custom. In spite of being there such a short time he had five sacks of ore on his pack animals. Somehow he did not seem to be quite himself. He grumbled about having forgotten his Dutch oven back at camp, even though he'd intended to bring it down with him.

An acquaintance, Sim Hendrixson, rode out of the cow camp with Estes. Sim was a cow puncher during the winters, a prospector during the summer months. His excuse for going along was the desire of having company, but once on the trail Sim soon asked Estes for a loan. Estes agreed, but told Sim he'd have to wait until the ore was sold.

Hendrixson later said Estes had received $2,800 for the five sacks of ore. He loaned Sim $100 of it before he put the rest of it into his pocket.

Estes never took more ore from his workings. That winter he died of pneumonia. He left behind no notes, no maps, and by the time he realized he was dying he had become too incoherent for anyone to make sense of what he tried to tell them. He did seem very much want to tell of his site, but it was just rambling gibberish. Those who heeded his last words have looked over the southwestern fourth of the entire San Juans.

Lusk's nephews did not learn of Estes' death for several years, for they had not come back to their uncle's cow camp the following summer. When they did hear, and got the time, they looked hard for his rich workings. They found his Dutch oven. They found a partially filled shaft, once covered over but now exposed. They found Estes' permanent camp.

Sim Hendrixson looked, too. He found the location of the forge.

Nobody found Estes' tools. The tunnel was too well hidden, and that still has not been found. Probably Estes left his tools and anything else he wanted to keep safe inside the tunnel.

They certainly have been safe!

***

In 1895 Levi Carson brought his burros quietly into Silverton. There were four full sacks of gold ore on the animals. For the two hundred or so pounds in those four sacks he was paid $2,800. On that basis it was $28,000 per ton ore. The assayer at the smelter ran a second test to check the first. He could not believe such results. He then ran a third test.

The owners of the smelter were waiting for Levi when he came back later the same day to get paid for his ore. They asked all sorts of questions. Where did the ore come from, which district? Did Levi need a grubstake? Could they send an engineer with some helpers back to the site so the entire area could be staked out the right way, with Levi's interest taken care of, of course? Could they buy his claim?

Levi clammed up. His main answer was NO. He wanted no grubstake, he wanted no help, he wanted no partners, he sure as hell did not want to sell his rich claim. He did not want anybody to even know where he was working. He intended to work it by himself, take out only what he needed to be comfortable. He was an old man, and his rich strike would now take care of him. No, No, No, to all their questions.

With that kind of ore the story of a rich new strike went around Silverton like a flash of lightning. Before Levi Carson hardly had time to count his money and leave the smelter, owners standing in the doorway wistfully watching him leave, word of his ore had spread throughout Silverton. It was a different type of ore than what came from the mines in the immediate area. It was a brownish, oxidized quartz ore, with a sugary texture. Small beads and nodules of yellow free gold were visible all through it. It was the kind of ore dreamed of by men in places like Silverton. Every easy buck artist in town wanted to get next to Levi Carson.

The problem was, even though Carson liked to drink, he seemed to be immune to flattery. The old man did not enjoy the attention, and no matter how drunk he got on free drinks, old Levi knew how to keep his mouth shut. Not a word did he utter about the location of his rich strike. He enjoyed showing the specimens he'd held out of the four sacks. Also the smelter was free in showing a few finer specimens they held back from the smelter to anyone who wanted to look at them. But that was as far as it went. Levi told anyone who persisted the same things he told the smelter people. NO, NO, NO.

That certainly was a strong wind blowing away the air castles the hangers-on tried to build. Carson just slurped up the free drinks, shed the questions like water from a duck's back, and remained silent. Nobody even knew from which direction he'd come into Silverton, let alone had any idea of where he'd found and dug out the ore.

It soon became obvious the old man was in no hurry to leave. After a few days he was in a comfortable stage of intoxication, even though that failed to start him talking. He had plenty of money, when the free drinks didn't come around often enough.

Somewhere in between all those drinks Levi bought enough food and other supplies to get him through the winter. One thing he made sure to buy was a very large jug full of whiskey. These actions were noted by the hangers-on, and a few of them made up their minds to follow the old man back to his workings. It never occurred to them that Levi had no intentions of going back to his workings again that season.

One evening Levi had a wagon haul all his goods down to the south end of town. Here, on meadowland used as the town's ball park, his burros were tethered out to pasture.

Before dawn the burros were loaded and Levi Carson leisurely followed the old toll road winding around Mt. Snowden towards Big Molas Lake. The hangers-on set on following him watched his every move from a distance.

In all the long day the wiley old prospector covered only six miles. First, he departed from the long grade close to the old John Herr cabin. Off he went into the almost flat land just past the old cabin. The western fourth of this flat nearest to where it falls off into the Animas Canyon is an open meadowland, ending near Big Molas Lake. The other three fourths of the flat area was then covered with a dense stand of great spruce trees that were not destroyed in the huge Lime Creek Burn of 1878-79. This stand of spruce extended from where he left the toll road to a point south of Big Molas Lake. In this spruce forest he slowly zigged and zagged most of the day away. He circled back at times, often stopped for a while, never once seeming to be in a hurry.

That night he camped on a secluded little bench south of Molas Lake, towards Snowflake Creek. He'd traveled no more than six miles from Silverton. He chose a well-hidden spot, and his followers almost walked into his camp before seeing it. They hastily turned and hurried away, almost comic in trying not to be seen.

Levi's actions were as puzzling during the following day. Carson headed straight into the wide open valley containing Snowflake Creek. He could be seen at a distance from almost any direction. It was not the way a man trying to hide his route should act. He poked along directly across this open valley, then leisurely up onto the divide between Snowflake Creek and East Lime Creek.

A wide section of this divide was covered with a tangled mess of fallen logs, difficult terrain to cross, a harsh legacy of the Lime Creek Burn. Carson went through this tangle without seeming to have many problems.

Once safely across that he dawdled along down the banks of East Lime Creek, all meadow and easy to traverse. At a point along the creek he came to where it crossed the toll road he'd left the day before.

To the confusion of his followers the man simply led his burros onto the toll road and trekked casually down its long grade down to Lime Creek.

There the road turns sharply down the Lime Creek valley and runs beside the stream. Huge rocks at this point hid from the road a willow-covered bench above the creek. Onto this well concealed bench went Carson and his burros. He tied them up, well away from each other, then waited.

Levi Carson totally surprised his would-be followers. In their efforts to discover which way he'd gone after they lost sight of the old man they almost bumped into his burros tied there in the willows. That startled them, but it must have been a moment of surprised terror when the old man stepped out from behind the rocks. He showed no weapon, but he let them know he just about blew their heads off several times since leaving Silverton. He assured them he might still do just that, and that if they ever followed him again, he would do it. It was not a pleasant conversation. The conversation was all one-sided. He watched them until they disappeared back up that steep grade.

Levi had not been going back to his workings. He was headed to somewhere near Mancos, where he wintered over.

The old man did not come into Silverton the following spring. There were those who hoped he would, and watched for him. They had to wait until fall, then one day just as he had done the season before, here was Levi Carson and his burros. Nobody had seen him arrive. Again the burros carried sacks of rich gold ore.

It was the same thing the same way as had taken place the year before. All sorts of efforts were made to learn something from the old prospector. He again became pleasantly intoxicated. He again told nobody anything, let nobody get very close to him, refused any advice or offers of help.

Again one man tried to follow him out of town. This time Carson did have a weapon in hand when he accosted his follower in the tangled old burn area of the Big Lime Creek watershed. Prior to confrontation the man saw

Carson was headed towards the West Needles.

Old Levi was angry. He had probably not been aware of his more careful follower, or at least had not been aware of him early on. He reacted harshly, terrifying the man with threats of death. Before the fellow got back across the area of fallen logs Carson fired several shots in his direction. The man later showed a bullet hole in his hat to some people, and said Carson called to him he'd not miss if he ever followed him again.

The area this incident took place is atop the divide between Animas Canyon and Lime Creek. It is interesting to note that this divide extends down from the West Needles, and runs exactly in the direction Carson was traveling when he accosted his follower.

Levi came down that summer earlier than he had the years before. He had four sacks of ore, but this time they were not as full. He again got good money, just not quite as much of it. He also at this time was seen coming slowly down through the tangled logs on the slopes of the West Needles south of Big Molas Lake by Milt Holiday and Shorty Swink, two cattle men. They knew Levi Carson and did not at time think too much about the sighting. After all, that's what prospectors do, go up and down mountains.

Levi again got pleasantly intoxicated. This time he announced he was going out of the mountains, was not going to do any more mining that year, and anyone who wanted to follow him should feel free to do so. This time it is not known if a single soul followed him.

The next autumn Levi Carson again showed up in Silverton. He brought even less ore this time than he'd brought the year before. He looked older and weaker, and complained of not feeling well all that summer. He told several men he'd only worked a few days this summer. He got intoxicated, as usual, perhaps believing that was good medicine. He took a keg of "medicine" with him when he left Silverton two or three days later.

Late that same day two men found Levi Carson's body in a grassy stretch behind the old stage station at Big Molas Lake. He had suffered a fatal heart attack and tumbled off his burro.

A large amount of money was found on old Levi's body. He also had several extremely rich ore specimens. There were no notes, no maps, nothing to give any hint about the location of his workings.

It came out later that Levi had told a relative his workings were on the northern slope of the West Needles. That was no more than what had already been figured out by local pundits. He also told them the ore he was working had a large gold content but that he had done very little work yet on developing the seam. He'd not needed to do much work. The outcropping had been rich right on top, and the digging had been so minimal it had always been easy to conceal his efforts when he left. This site was above timberline and at a considerable distance from his camp.

His camp at the workings, he said, amounted to no more than a tarp thrown over some poles leaned up against an undercut rock ledge. There was no trail to the site. No pack animal could reach the place, which meant he had to carry tools, food, and everything else up there. He also had to carry down all the ore he accumulated.

These bits of information gradually added up, and when put together began to form a picture in the minds of prospectors, stockmen, and others who sometimes dreamed of finding Carson's lost lode. These individuals began to search the area past Big Molas Lake up into the West Needles.

First Levi's campsite was discovered in a small basin at timberline, located at the head of Twilight Creek. This was the old man's base camp there on the north base of the West Needles. It is to that spot he hauled all his supplies and equipment, storing it there until needed. There was excellent pasturage for his burros in the basin. He built a crude gate across the only way in or out of the basin to keep the animals from wandering.

This entire area was still a jumbled tangle of crisscrossed fallen timber caused by the big forest fire. That made any actual search difficult. Levi no longer annually bringing in another load of rich ore also made a difference, the story fading away more rapidly than one would think.

It was years after Levi Carson's death when the Million Dollar highway was built right through the Lime Creek country, giving simple access from either Durango or Silverton. Also a stockman's trail was hacked through the fallen timber area old Carson had to cross on his way to the head of Twilight Creek. These two things opened up the entire region to prospectors, cattle men, and ever increasing numbers of fishermen.

One man, John Edwards of Durango, was a prospector. He also had worked cattle and he loved to fish. After the new highway was built around Potato Mountain and down into the Lime Creek Canyon, John Edwards could not ignore the opportunities it offered him. There was some marvelous fishing. He knew the story of Carson's lost lode, and there on Twilight Creek he was looking right up at the West Needles.

In the early 1920's he camped in a beautiful spot along Lime Creek just below its juncture with Twilight Creek. If he was not fishing he went prospecting. Or maybe the other way around. Somehow cattle didn't enter the picture any more.

The first year he camped there, while fishing, John found along the banks of Twilight Creek a piece of float. It was good ore very much the same as that sold by Levi Carson years before in Silverton. After that for a long time he did more prospecting up Twilight Creek than he did fishing.

Had John Edwards been even less of a fisherman, or less reluctant to go clear to the head of Twilight Creek, he perhaps was a good enough of a prospector that he might have found Carson's lost lode. The problem was, it was a long, hard way up to the head of the creek from his campsite. The trip could not be made afoot in one day and still come back to camp before nightfall.

He found some old dynamite and some drill steel on a ledge about as far up Twilight Creek as he ever went. He searched, but there was no evidence of the lost ledge. John was still well below the area of the rich outcropping. John Edwards began to lose interest in prospecting.

Others also found the same kind of rich float on Twilight Creek. Edwards probably got closer than anyone else, and he simply stopped too far downhill.

Mike Powell, a rancher from the Durango area, in 1928 found a chunk of this float as big as a fist. He found it much farther down, near the mouth of Twilight Creek. He was not familiar with the Levi Carson story, however, and looked no farther.

It was Juan Quintana, a sheepherder come up from Mexico, who actually found Carson's lost lode. He was a man suited for the lonesome life of herding sheep, and he was in charge of a big herd in the West Needles area when he found Carson's workings. He enjoyed roaming the slopes during the summer months, once his flock was secure at pasturage. There were days there the man had few actual responsibilities. Juan was too crabby to enjoy human companionship, had no family, and never had many close friends through all his life.

He was working for J. J. McCormick in 1922, whose sheep allotment took in the Twilight Creek drainage area. In short, the north slopes of the West Needles. "Jack" McCormick set up the main camp in the very basin at the head of Twilight Creek once used as base camp by Levi Carson. Quintana was a grouch, but McCormick never remained long at camp, having more than enough to do elsewhere. He would return after a number of days to check on things and bring some supplies. So Juan liked the way things went because

McCormick left him to himself, Jack liked the way things went because Juan was a good sheepherder, and probably even the sheep were satisfied.

This camp was nestled at the base of the West Needles. Straight south of this basin Twilight Peak presented a jagged vista of bluffs, ridges, ravines rising for another few thousand feet to the top of the mountain. The terrain intrigued Quintana and he relished being able to explore it.

Within days of his arrival Juan found Levi Carson's workings. Scattered tin cans, poles leaning against an overhung ledge, a gold-rich ledge of ore that had some minimal work done on it in the past, and the ruins of an old fire pit.

Juan knew nothing of mines, did not care to know. He was doing what he wanted to be doing. The man had worked in a mine one summer near Telluride. That had convinced him he wanted no more of that sort of thing. He did know enough, and was interested enough to take some samples of ore from the ledge. He also picked up an extremely good piece of ore that had been broken off by whoever worked the spot. Some pieces he threw down before he left, but a number of the specimens he put into his pockets.

Jack McCormick found the samples in camp several days later while Juan was out with the sheep. He at once recognized how rich the ore was.

Perhaps if McCormick had been less eager and pushy in trying to find out where Juan had found the samples he might have done so. He kept after the sheepherder, though, with more intensity than the Mexican liked. The more Jack asked the more Juan clammed up. He told him nothing. Juan probably was afraid this hot-tempered Irishman might kill him, once he learned what he wanted to know, just to cover up where he got such valuable information.

Because McCormick so persistently kept after him, Juan did at last reluctantly show McCormich the poorest specimen he had. Because McCormick quickly stuffed the piece of ore into his own pocket instead of handing it back, Juan got up early the next morning and buried the rest of his specimens under the roots of a big spruce tree.

When Jack left camp the next day, Juan went back up to the workings. He was not going to be coerced into telling his pushy boss anything, nor would he ever show him the spot. He covered up the seam with rocks and dirt. He threw the poles leaning up against the overhanging ledge down the mountainside. He also tossed the tin cans as far downslope as he could. He covered up everything, ashpit, workings, anything else that might show somebody was ever there.

All Juan would ever tell his boss after that was the spot was somewhere in the vicinity of the basin in which they had their sheep camp. No help at all, for that could have been anywhere in an incredibly rugged, forty square miles of high-mountain terrain.

It was not long after this that Juan Quintana quit working for Jack McCormick. The man would give him no rest from his constant questions, and that was not Quintana's idea of a sheepherder's job.

It was in October of 1932 when Quintana at last went to work for a man he soon admired and liked. The previous ten years had not been too kind to Juan, and he was getting older. Nobody seemed to be having it easy during those depression years. His boss was barely scraping by. As Juan became more familiar with the man, who stayed in camp and helped with the endless tasks instead of going off as had McCormick and most other bosses, Quintana started to open up. He began to talk of what he'd found ten years before on Twilight Peak. Over evening campfires the story gradually emerged. In the end, Quintana made plans to show his new boss the spot come the following spring.

That winter Quintana came down with pneumonia and died.

His boss looked for what Quintana told him about. He found the big spruce and dug up the specimens Juan had hidden from McCormick. He certainly could have used some more of the rich gold ore. But the sheep needed to be herded, and there was always work to be done. He had no time to tramp the heights above that basin. Juan's directions were too vague, for he'd described every rock, every ravine, everything. Too much de- scription, actually.

Others have looked, but there always seems to be good reasons not to climb up that northern slope of Twilight Peak. That's where the lost ledge is, and one observation is worth making. Quintana did not destroy or bury those poles and tin cans, he threw them down the slope. Is that not some help? Levi's rich gold seam is still right where he and Quintana left it.

This is about where Levi Carson would have looked back and seen the men trying to follow him from Silverton to his rich ledge.

This was a little place called Middleton, downhill from Eureka, up the valley from Silverton. The Highland Mary is to the southeast of this site, far up the visible slopes in this picture. Jim Baker's group found placer gold not far north of this spot.

The author is on the trail of a Barber half dollar in the Red Mountain City townsite. It was a nice 1884 coin. The son of a friend was willing to give advice but didn't care much about any digging.

SAN MIGUEL COUNTY

I'm not real sure many people are prepared to find a treasure, especially a big one. I mean people who've considered themselves treasure hunters for years. The first thing too many people feel like doing, so they go ahead and do it, is let the world know all about what a marvelous thing they've done. If they do that, then they also probably do a whole list of other stupid things. It is not long before lawyers, police officers, deadbeats, long-lost relation, a few federal agents, and others of all sorts start introducing themselves. It is not long and these lucky but foolish people wish they had never found that treasure.

In the Slick Rock area of San Miguel County is thought to be one of Montezuma's caches of gold and silver.

***

Somewhere near Telluride Henry Huff is believed to have cached $150,000 in gold coins.

***

A searcher located a fine ten dollar gold piece in one of the foundations of old San Miguel City. This rip- snorting old town site is now actually one of modern Telluride's suburbs.

SEDGWICK COUNTY

The Italian Caves are near Julesburg. There are a number of tales of caches in or around these caves. Two names, Jules Beni and Jack Slade, pop up when those stories are told.

In 1904 a hog farmer named Stephen Mehlhorn died. He had been a money- hungry man, raising hogs on the South Platte River Bottoms to the west of Julesburg for many years. He converted his considerable profits throughout those years to gold coins. These he cached on his farm, not trusting banks. Not trusting family and friends much more than he did banks, he at times moved the caches from one spot to another.

One of Mehlhorn's sons found the cache. He reburied it somewhere else. He would not tell his father where. The son was killed in an accident without ever divulging the new cache site. Melhorn looked for years for his gold coins, never found them.

Mehlhorn was an excellent bookkeeper. His records state the cache contained 732 double eagles, 519 eagles, 214 half eagles, and 980 $3.00 gold pieces. There was a face value total of $23,840. Remember, those coins were all dated well before 1904, the date of Mehlhorn's death. The cache remains wherever the hog farmer's son hid it.

***

Stories of caches of robbers' loot in the Julesburg area. There are three ghost sites of Julesburg other than the current town. Old Julesburg, New Julesburg, and Weir were all within a few mile radius of the current townsite, but were for various reasons abandoned.

Jules Beni was one such robber. The man ran a trading post near Julesburg, but was a highway robber in reality. He used the trading post as a cover. He worked with Indians, having them do the dirty, bloody work, telling them about this lone traveler with cash, that wagonload of valuable goods, the stagecoach with wealthy passengers. That way, when a stage or wagon was robbed, after it had stopped at his trading post, he could be shouting with other angry citizens, bemoaning the savage cruelty of the Indians.

Much of his loot, in the form of gold and silver coins, according to local stories, he buried in the Italian Caves.

For some reason, although it seems to show poor business sense to us, the Leavenworth and Pikes Peak stage lines chose Beni's Trading Post as a stage stop. Even worse business savvy, it seems to us, one Jack Slade was chosen to serve as division chief of the stage line in that area.

The actual reasons are not clear, but Beni and Slade quickly got into a quarrel. Doubtful stories are that it was over a girl, or that Beni thought Slade was robbing money from the stage line. It is more likely that Slade found Beni and his Indians to be too much competition with his own band of thieves.

Slade knew how to use a bullwhip. He was proficient with one, and demonstrated his talents to Jules Beni by taking off both Beni's ears from a few yard's distance. Beni did not like that even a little bit, and threatened to kill Slade.

Slade did not wait to see if it was just a threat. Only days later Beni's body was found, shot through and through. Beni never revealed to anyone the sites of his caches. Slade made it out of Colorado soon afterwards, not too far ahead of a posse. He shot a man in Wyoming. A vigilante's rope ended his bad-actor ways in Virginia City, Montana.

There have been several caches recovered in recent years in this area. It is not known if any of the stashes were Beni's, or those of some other robber. There are also tales of Jack Slade putting down a cache or two in that immediate area.

SUMMIT COUNTY

A number of stories concern a marvelous "golden ledge" in the Gore Range. Different people have found such a thing at different times, and lost it. There is a strong possibility there is only one such ledge, and Utes, trappers, prospectors, and deer hunters have all found the same thing at different times, taken bits and pieces from it, and for good reasons have been unable to return.

The tales are worth retelling! Sit down, but first one of you put the coffee pot on the fire, would someone throw on another log or two?

The Utes, before 1850, had a source of gold somewhere in the Gore Range. A respected pioneer in Middle Park told of trading one pound of sugar for two pounds of gold with the Indians. Others claimed to have had similar experiences. After all, the Indians seemed able to get gold, but tobacco, whiskey, sugar, and those white man things were more precious to them than gold. But they were anything but stupid. They closely guarded their knowledge from the intruding white men, and the site has never been located. It was not located in the early days and it still has not been located.

General Bela M. Hughes was seeking a shortcut route through the Rockies to Salt Lake City. His explorations took him into the Gore Range. A young man named Lem Pollard was with the party. While in the Gore Range Pollard found "a piece of pretty rock" while he was hunting.

It was years later he had the rock assayed because they saw his rock and told him it was gold ore. It was very rich in gold. He returned to the area but could not find the site again. He became a clerk in Grand County, and looked for his pretty rock every chance he got. Lem couldn't find it, but then neither has anyone else.

A trapper named Hill was working in the area of the Gore Range in the 1870's when he came down with "mountain fever". Nobody at the time had figured it all out about wood ticks and Rocky Mountain spotted fever, but Hill was feverish and very sick when he made it down from the mountains. He had little time, but managed to tell friends his story.

He had camped along the head waters of Morrison Creek. Close by he found a great outcropping of ore rich in free gold. Hill did his best to tell his friends the details of the location, but he was feverish and rambling.

Specimens found in Hill's packs assayed between $15,000 to $20,000 to the ton. 1870's gold prices.

After Hill's death his friends fruitlessly looked for the ledge. The directions had not been clear enough. In 1879 a forest fire burned over the area, destroying most of the landmarks mentioned by Hill. Other searches for the rich outcropping have also proven to be futile over the years.

Somewhere in the Gore Range is the outcropping that became known as the Lost George Franz Gold Mine. George Franz of Clark told the story towards the end of the 1930's. He had prospected all through northern Colorado for fifty years, but he had known of the "Golden Ledge" of the Gore Range even before coming to Colorado in the 1870's. Franz first read about it in the San Francisco Examiner.

The newspaper story told of a man who left Georgetown to go to Salt Lake City. His first night out of Georgetown he had camped under the shelter of an overhanging ledge. Light from his campfire made the ledge sparkle.

This aroused his curiosity, and the next morning he discovered the material in the overhanging ledge contained gold. He broke off numerous samples and continued his trek to Salt Lake City.

Once there he had assays run on the samples. The results showed some $10,000 to the ton values. He had to go on to San Francisco, on business, but then was determined to return to claim the ledge.

While in San Francisco the man suffered a stroke. There was no way he could follow through on his plans to return to Colorado. He told friends of his find and drew them a detailed map.

The friends later went to Colorado to search, but found that fires set in 1879 by Colorow and his Ute braves had destroyed most of the landmarks noted on their friend's map. One of the landmarks had been the cabin of Charlie Nieman, once sheriff of Hahn's Peak. The cabin was only ashes mixed in with the ashes of most of the forest along the Gore Range. Having no idea where the gold-rich ledge could be, they left.

Also in the Gore Range, somewhere, exists the Lost John La Foe Gold Mine, really another ledge found then lost. John La Foe told the story out in the gold country of Nevada.

He and some friends had left Cripple Creek around the turn of the century to seek their fortunes elsewhere. Wile camping in the Gore Range, on their way to Nevada, they found an outcropping of good free gold. It was in the fall, however, and it began to snow even before they could get a camp set up, let alone do any digging.

They went on to Nevada, and did very well there. There was no need to come back to Colorado. They remembered good friends in Colorado, and sent them a detailed map of the site. The friends looked long and hard for the ledge, but never seemed to be able to find it.

Still elsewhere in the Gore Range the Lost Frying Pan Gold Mine awaits rediscovery. Many have searched for this one, a many-years prospector who is one of those who looked for it, W. A. Scott is the one who made the tale public knowledge.

In aftermath of the silver panic of 1893, Scott and a man called "Gold Pan" Jake, who was the first man to wash some gold out of California Gulch in 1860, began to hunt for a good gold prospect. Silver was at the time not worth looking for. Not going anywhere in particular, they camped one night on the Eagle River where Wolcott is today.

A stranger came into camp not long after they had eaten. He introduced himself and sat down to talk. He told them of a man in 1876 bringing two burros into Breckenridge, each loaded with two sacks of gold ore worth several thousands of dollars. It was enough to stir some real excitement in Breckenridge, a place that was used to seeing good gold.

Many wanted to buy into his discovery. He was tight-lipped, however, and would only say he'd found the spot over towards Rabbit Ears. He was going home for the winter, and would be back the following spring. He'd talk to people then.

A number of men were ready the following spring, but the man never showed up. There were many who headed off towards Rabbit Ears to look for it. Thus far none of them had located it.

Gold Pan Jake and Scott decided they would join those who were looking for it. It seemed to be better than wandering with no goal in mind.

Soon enough they were just over the crest of the range onto the headwaters of the Muddy, not far from Rabbit Ears. They one day made camp on Grizzly Creek, just west of the crest. They promptly saw evidence of old placer workings, a fallen cabin, and a rotted sluice box. Near these things the panned a little bit of color.

The day after that they found where the stream back had fallen away, exposing some piled-up ore. That led them to where some earlier work had been done. Soon enough they had exposed an eighteen inch vein of rotted quartz.

They pounded some up, panned it, and found only a small amount of black sand. No gold at all. They were both disgusted and disappointed.

The following day Jake would not even work, but Scott prospected the immediate area carefully. When he had no better luck, he returned to camp, where he found Jake talking to a stranger who'd come into camp. This man told them their specimens looked good.

They informed him there was no gold in the quartz. It was oxidized ore and any free gold would have shown up. He wanted to know if they had roasted the ore. No, they'd never thought of doing that, never heard of it before. It's tellurium, he told them, and that does n't free up the gold in it. It looks oxidized, but it isn't, there can be all sorts of gold in the rock, but it needs to be roasted. Crush it, soak it in diluted sulphuric acid, put it on a hot fire, continue to dampen it, and add salt.

They had no sulphuric acid, but roasted it anyway. They gave up, after a time, because all they got was an extra clean frying pan. No gold. What they did not realize until long afterwards is without being properly processed the tellurium and the gold in it had simply burned up, vaporized. Their gold burned up and drifted away.

They left the spot years before they figured this out.

In 1896 Horace Pullen was hunting deer high in the Gore Range. Pullen had come to Colorado from Council Bluffs, Iowa. He wounded an animal, followed it, eventually discovered he'd gotten himself lost. While trying to discover where he was he came across an exposed ledge of "peculiar-looking" rock. He broke off and took some samples with him. At some time later he had the material tested, the results came back at over $17,000 to the ton. Old prices, not today's.

Pullen was never able to relocate the ledge again. He was lost when he found the ledge, and Pullen really had little idea of where the ledge was. Nor have others found it. Maybe one is required to go deer hunting in the area, and get a bit lost.

One group of miners found a good placer area in the Gore Range. They very much wanted to work it, but cold weather and heavy snow drove them from the area. That winter they found other profitable ventures, they did not return to look for their placer.

Near Piney Lake, in the Gore Range, is the Lost Sir George Gore Gold Mine. Sir George Gore, wealthy Irish nobleman, brought a hunting party of about fifty into that area (and elsewhere, to be sure) in the mid-1850's. Secretaries, men to care for the horses and dogs, cooks, stewards, and other such help.

Louis Dapron was the foreman of the two year expedition. One day he reported to Sir George that a member of the party had found gold nearby the camp.

Gore became irate and had Dapron break camp. Gore was on a pleasure trip, out to hunt wild beasts, not there to grub for gold. The party moved on.

Dapron later returned to the area, not minding the thought of grubbing a bit for gold. Unfortunately he could not find the site.

***

Somewhere in the Jaques Mountains of the Gore Range is a lode of silver ore.

***

Heeney doesn't amount to much anymore, even if you can find it. It is a fine starting place if you want to look for Hill's Lost Silver Mine, because those old workings are somewhere in that area.

***

Two Missouri prospectors worked a ledge of good gold ore in the Breckenridge area in the late 1850's. They were most secretive and somehow kept their location private information. After all, they were extra big, husky men, red-bearded, and were not the sort to question too much. Not only huge and tough, they also carried big knives and guns.

These fellows seemed to sleep days, sneak away at night, and always bring back packs full of white clay, stuff called gouge. They always took care they were not followed.

One Jim Jorgenson, more foolhardy, perhaps sneakier, and more courageous than were others curious about the source of this white, gold-rich material, did manage to trail them onto the top of Big Baldy. He left it alone, then, confident any deposit of white clay on Big Baldy would be easy to find when and if the big men left.

The Missouri men left when the Civil War broke out. They never returned to Colorado, very likely met the same fate as did many others during the next four bloody years.

When he was sure the big men were gone Jorgenson led a party of searchers atop Big Baldy. They found no deposit of gold-rich white gouge. Neither has anyone else. George Bancroft, mining era historian, suggested in

1914 the two Missouri fellows could well have been mining other peoples' day-time mines at night.

If not, perhaps the Missouri men knew they were being followed and led Jorgenson on a wild goose chase. If so, on another hill there still may be a deposit of white clay, rich with gold awaiting someone to find it.

**

The Lost Bear Mountain Gold Mine is not too far from Brecken-ridge. Any distance in those rough mountains makes for a long and difficult search.

**

An old miner called Trapper Sam had a cabin and mine located near timberline somewhere above Breckenridge in the early 1860's. He was called Trapper Sam because that is what he did. He also hand carved small wooden spades, a great many of them. His shovels, hollowed out like a frying pan, were unique. He was also working a high grade gold source, with always plenty of gold to pay for supplies and some entertainment when he came into Brecken-ridge. He carefully kept secret the whereabouts of where he was doing all this.

It was known he had cached much of his higher-grade ore in the im-mediate vicinity of his cabin and mine. He did not reveal any details of the lo-cation. He died without telling anybody anything and those who hoped to find his workings had no luck doing so.

After his death, in 1890's, the site was accidentally found by a pros-pector named Zeb. Zeb came across a fallen-down shack near timberline above Breckenridge. On some tailings outside a tunnel he saw three unusual-looking shovels, the scoops carved out of wood and looking much like frying pans. Inside the tunnel he found another such shovel. He then discovered some black, talc-like ore, ore such as he'd never seen before. Unusual. Zeb knocked off some specimens, then emptied his tobacco pouch, having nothing else to hold the ore. He took the best one of the four spades and headed back to Breckenridge.

Zeb evidently became somewhat disoriented. Lost, actually. Con-cerned mostly with getting safely back to Breckenridge he didn't pay enough attention to the route he took. He wandered for two days.

Not long after he finally got back to town an old timer saw the spade Zeb brought off the mountain and got very excited. The old man recognized it as having been a product of the by then almost legendary Trapper Sam. Zeb then hunted for the tobacco sack full of sample ore. The sack wasn't anywhere upon him. He evidently had lost it during his two days of wanderings.

Zeb and his old acquaintance could not again relocate the site. They tried, any number of times. The cabin probably is mostly gone now, and the tunnel entrance may be fallen in, but Trapper Sam's cache of gold ore and that black, unusual talc-like ore all is very likely still right there, wherever right there is.

***

Three or four miles southwest of Breckenridge is the flooded shafts of the Black Princess Mine. The Reynolds gang used this site as a hideout during their stagecoach robberies. In 1884 lawmen raided the old mine site. The gang must have been warned, for they fled just before the lawmen arrived.

Three months later, fifty miles to the west of Denver, the gang again held up a stagecoach. They were after a $100,000 gold shipment. In the resulting gun fight two of the three bandits were shot dead. The third man was wounded but managed to escape. The two dead men were identified as the owners of the Black Princess Mine.

Twenty-five years after this incident the surviving gang member returned to the area to retrieve the loot hidden in the Black Princess Mine. The gang had cached three boxes in the then water-filled shaft of the mine. Two of the boxes contained a total of $100,000, the third had almost $50,000. This old outlaw suffered a heart attack after reaching the area. One Shorty Wilcox found and cared for the old man, and the outlaw told Wilcox quite a tale before he died.

On the strength of what the dying man told him Shorty Wilcox purchased the old Black Princess mine in 1909. He actually recovered the smaller of the two chests, which contained $34,000 in gold coins.

Shorty did not return to the water- filled mine after that recovery. He had more than enough to go to Denver and live in comfort his last few years. Wilcox died in 1914.

There now is considerable doubt as to exactly which one is "the" Black Princess Mine. Several claims were filed under that title. That drowned shaft is said to have caved in 1925. If so, there is about $100,000, mostly in old gold coins under a vast, loose, mass of rocks all totally water-filled. Which does not hurt gold coins a bit.

***

The Lost Huntsman Mine is also somewhere near Breckenridge.

***

A "tenderfoot" found a rich gold ledge high above Breckenridge late one fall. A rock seemed to be hanging from a ledge in an unusual, impossible manner. He examined it and soon found the reason. A network of sharp, sparkling wire gold held the rock to the ledge. More of the wire gold was laced through and through the structure. He pried out about twenty pounds of almost pure gold and headed downslope to Breckenridge.

In 1900 a piece in the Denver Republican reviewed the local story, and the writer felt certain someone would surely find the location from the strength of the article alone. Nobody seems to have done so, yet.

To the east of his ledge the tenderfoot could see the Warrior's Mark Mine. Far below to the northwest Breckenridge was in plain sight. It was too late in the fall for the fellow to do much of anything but take those twenty pounds of samples. In fact he reached Breckenridge in a snow storm. The next spring he was unable to relocate the ledge.

Old time miners believed the tenderfoot was probably somewhere on Bare Mountain. A few say, maybe, but it could be on Red Mountain. Whatever mountain, it's now called The Lost Tenderfoot Mine. About twenty pounds of gold is all that ever was removed from it.

I understand this house is now gone. It stood just east of Lincoln, to the east of Breckenridge, and was close to Farncomb Hill. Farncomb Hill was often called the wirepatch, because of the magnificent wire gold produced there.

TELLER COUNTY

There's more than just a twinge of nostalgia in going over old treasure tales, but looking back plays tricks on us. We see the good things and don't recall all the bad ones. Some of us would like to head down to one of those saloons for an evening, but I'll just bet you'd rather go over the pass in a four wheel drive to get there than on the back of a mule. Once there you'd immediately know most of the fellows in there hadn't taken a bath since last August. The nickel beer would be warm, not everyone hits the spitoon, and plenty of guys there would rather fight than drink.

Just sitting here talking about those good old days actually has some advantages over being there.

That coffee's not ready? Who on earth is interested in treasure stories without a fresh cup of coffee, that's what I want to know.

The gold pouring from Teller County attracted thieves like a magnet. Jack Smith and his pack of thieves stopped a stage and robbed it of $16,000, all in $20 gold pieces. A posse was able to track them to their hideout near Cripple Creek. In a fierce gunfight Jack Smith and his crew were shot dead. The missing loot was not found then or later. It was surmised those gold pieces had been buried at some point between the point of holdup and the outlaw's hideout.

***

The Halleluja Mine had a worker named Jeffrey Ralph Hoover in the 1890's. He highgraded premium ore from the mine over an extended period of time and is known to have cached at least a good portion of it near to where he was killed. That was not far from Cripple Creek. The amazing fact here, Hoover was but one of thousands doing the same sort of thing to greater or lesser degrees. It is estimated that highgraders got as much or more gold as the mine operators did. It was done quietly, of course, encouraged by lax laws and tight-lipped gold buyers. Where one such cache is known about, there are

thousands more that can only be guessed about. Recoveries of large and small deposits of high grade ore out from around the old dumps scattered throughout the area underline a probability of many other such caches.

***

An old locked vault in the court house at Cripple Creek, almost forgotten about for fifty years, was opened and searched in 1974. Inside was a skeleton. There was a bullet hole in the skull. Several revolvers, still in excellent condition, were recovered. There were eleven canvas bags filled with high-grade gold ore, $15,000 worth in 1974. There have been some wild guesses as to what exactly happened there and how and why for fifty years that vault remained locked.

****

Sherman Crumley and his band of outlaws robbed a train in the late 1890's. They took a substantial haul of jewelry and coins. The group is thought to have cached their loot in the vicinity of their hideout near the Strong Mine.

****

After rainstorms, in and around Cripple Creek, good nuggets of turquoise and visible fine gold can be found in any open ground, such as empty lots, streets, and parking lots. Many good old coins were recovered only a few years ago when Cripple Creek tore up its steets before repaving them.

****

Pinnacle Park was an amusement facility, complete with a zoo, at Cameron. Cameron is northeast of Cripple Creek. In 1900 alone there were more than 9,000 people who paid one thin dime to enter Pinnacle Park. Barber dimes. There is heavily mineralized soil conditions in the area, and until recent VLF detectors with good ground balance, it was difficult to impossible for people to take advantage of the coinshooting possibilities here.

***

About 1900 one Zachary Hutton lived in Victor. He was a cobbler. He saved every privately-minted Lesher dollar he could get his hands on. He thought these were backed by the U. S. government. The man cached two salt pork tin cans filled with Lesher dollars before he died of pneumonia in 1902. The nu- mismatic value of these coins today, each undamaged specimen, is at least one thousand dollars.

****

It was reported that a small, velvet-lined box was recovered from a deserted two story house in Victor. In the box were five $20 gold pieces, a gold stickpin, and a heavy gold chain.

***

Highgrading ran rampant in the area. Victor had at least 20,000 inhabitants, Cripple Creek even more, and still more in all the smaller towns and hamlets crowded around the mines. There still are many probable caches of rich ore still to be recovered even though a number of such recoveries have already been made.

***

A train was robbed in the late 1890's about three miles to the south of Victor. Four men took five chests of bullion being sent out by Victor area mines. The train was stopped at a trestle spanning a deep wash. A posse was formed immediately, and they caught up with the thieves in about half an hour. The four men were killed. The five chests of gold were nowhere to be found. Either the chests were hurriedly concealed, perhaps in some nearby test pit, and a few rocks thrown in atop, or some accomplice had some mules ready and waiting to haul away the loot. Prospectors at the time and modern treasure hunters have looked long and hard for this one. Your author is among the list of the unsuccessful. As far as is known they have never been recovered.

WASHINGTON COUNTY

Those old farmsteads deserve more attention from treasure hunters than they get. It was a long way to the banks, years back, and most people didn't trust banks too much. There's many an egg and butter cache that for various reasons was never recovered. Not known about, either. We can only sit here around a campfire and wonder about how many we've walked by.

Near Last Chance some combine field hands in 1957 discovered a cache on the farm where they were harvesting wheat. A wheel of the combine broke through a thin crust of soil into a cavity. In attempting to get the wheel out of the hole they discovered the cache. There was a saddle, a pouch of imitation diamonds, a can containing some currency, and a good many Mexican coins. The condition of everything showed it had been cached for many years.

WELD COUNTY

If you come across some old trade tokens-you may have found more than you first thing. Those trade tokens are actually often more rare than coins, and a good many people collect them. If you are in an out of the way spot, find an old token with the name of an establishment, the name of the camp, and of course its value in trade, you may have made your year's best find.

Three caches of gold coins have been recovered near Greeley's airport over many years. There is reason to believe there could be more of the same.

***

A story is told of a $200,000 army cache of gold coins being buried about four miles from Greeley. The troops were supposed to have been transporting that sum from Fort Collins to Fort Morgan.

***

A Kimberlitic structure is said to extend from around Fort Collins to the west of Boulder. This structure is similar in nature to those in South Africa and the Murfreesboro area of Arkansas. Gem quality diamonds have been recovered in this possible new Colorado diamond field.

***

On the old trail to Fort Laramie from Fort Collins a rich ledge of lead/silver ore was found and lost. People have searched fruitlessly for years.

***

Jaques LaBorgeans arrived in Fort Collins in 1911. He came to search for a large cache of gold and nuggets hidden by his uncle. His uncle and a band of miners were returning from the California gold fields in 1857 with an accumulation of five years hard placering.

They camped northwest of Fort Collins, near La Port. This is a stretch of the Cache la Poudre, pleasant even today, but then even more so, and often used by mountain men for campsites.

The following morning, not long after they broke camp, they were attacked by a Sioux raiding party. The miners took cover at the base of a pronounced bluff, hastily burying their gold. Only LaBorgeans' uncle survived, and he was badly wounded. The man was saved only because a group of freighters happened to come by shortly after the fight. They transported him to Fort Leavenworth where he slowly recovered from a terrible head wound. When he could do so he returned to his home in Montreal. The man got better, but was too infirm to attempt any recovery of the gold. He carefully gave his nephew all the details he could remember.

Jaques LaBorgeans made a long hard search for his uncle's cache, but could never find it. Neither have others. Be careful, the story starts near La Porte, northwest of Fort Collins, so one might start searching there. The tragic end of those California miners was farther east, into Weld County. Somewhere, not far from Windsor, still may be cached a big pile of California gold.

***

Orlie Vickers sold a herd of cattle in 1882. He was carrying $24,330 in gold coins in an elk hide bag, taking it to a bank in Fort Collins, when he discovered that the Curry gang was hot on his trail. He had no doubts as to what they wanted. On a rock ledge at the base of Glacier Creek Falls Orlie threw his elk hide full of gold coins into the churning water, thinking he would return for them if he could elude the Curry gang.

He found a good spot and ambushed the gang. Orlie started shooting without warning, killing several of them, and driving the others away.

When Orlie attempted to retrieve the coins he discovered that the pool was drained by an underground chasm. His coins had been sucked out of sight. They are still there, if anyone can figure out how to get at them.

YUMA COUNTY

One last word, or two, and then I guess we'll have to put out the fire. We all have other things to do besides drinking coffee and swapping tales around a campfire. Maybe another time, another place, another fire.

Seventeen miles south of Wray is Beecher's Island. Soldiers, holding off attacking Indians there, buried their valuables.

ACKNOWLEDGMENTS

I would not even pretend to present this compilation of treasure tales as being solely the result of my personal efforts. Most of these stories have been around for years, told and retold in many places by many different people. I have put into them my own observations and conclusions, there are a few stories new to the total I've picked up over the years, there's a few additions to the tales others have discovered in recent years, but my greatest effort has been in attempting to fashion sensible stories from a multitude of often conflicting renditions of the same stories. I have to thank many people for their efforts to pass along these tales over the years, and in many cases I must beg their forgiveness for ignoring or disagreeing with no few of their conclusions.

I regret not getting to meet and speak with many of the older authors and tellers of these tales. Murriel Wolle was alive for a time after I moved to Boulder, and I was planning to meet and talk with her. I always seemed to be too busy, and much to my regret that great woman died without my ever meeting her. How I would have enjoyed and benefitted from meeting Cornelius! John Marshall and he have the honor and respect they richly deserve from the treasure hunting community and anyone interested in Colorado's golden histories. Perry Eberhart has long been somewhat of a hero to me, although I never met him. I did have the priveledge and honor of meeting Robert L. Brown. Although he did not directly affect this book, I have to mention Karl von Mueller as being instrumental in the spirit and direction of my writings. I enjoyed my conversations and correspondence with KvM. A few have told me I am the "new old man of treasure hunting", but I only admit to being newly old.

My thanks to Gary Christopher and Ike Osteen, for digging up some facts a few years back that had long been overlooked, and getting them into print.

I would like to mention any number of other people, but should I try to do so I would surely leave someone out who should not be left out. There is no possible way to credit everyone who did affect this book. Many passed away years ago, but their works certainly affected both myself and my writing.

I must make a very special acknowledgment to my wife, Mary Lee Carson. She first of all told me that I should have gotten started on this book at least ten years ago. Then, once I did get started, she gave me all sorts of back up help. She put up with my crabby, isolationist ways of doing things, and was largely instrumental in getting the monster ready to go to press. 1001 thanks would not be enough.

I considered footnoting the entries of the book, but rejected doing so. In many cases the footnotes would have exceeded the entry. I have entered into the bibliography each and every source that was used in the compilation of these pages.

I take full responsibility for my own observations. I have tried hard not to stray from the available information and in doing so create something erroneous for the sake of "being more interesting". I don't like that way of doing things, and have attempted not to be guilty of it. I am sure I have failed to get bits and pieces of information into this work that should be there, there undoubtedly are stories that got left out, but I hope the result is not too disappointing.

Thank you, all you tellers of Colorado treasure tales who came before me, who sat at other, earlier campfires spellbinding your listeners. I could never have perched here on my log, telling these tales, without your help!
H. Glenn Carson

BIBLIOGRAPHY

Apache Jim, APACHE JIM, pages 10- 15, 23-29, 1973.

Baggs, Mae Lacy, COLORADO, THE QUEEN JEWEL OF THE ROCKIES, The Page Company, 1918.

Baker, James H., editor, and Hafen, Le Roy, associate editor, HISTORY OF COLORADO, prepared by the State Historical and Natural History Society of Colorado, Linderman Co., Inc., 1927.

Bailey, Tom, TRUE WEST, Vol. 9, No. 2, 1961.

Bancroft, Caroline, COLORADO'S LOST GOLD MINES AND BURIED TREASURE, 1961.

Bancroft, George Jarvis, Lost Mine Legends and Western Stories and Material, an unpublished collections written in 1914 when Bancroft was Mining Page Editor of The Rocky Mountain News. Collection donated to Denver Public Library Western History Section by Caroline Bancroft.

Bancroft, George Jarvis, Rocky Mountain News, 1914.

Baskin, O. L., HISTORY OF THE ARKANSAS VALLEY, COLORADO, O. L. Baskin & Co., Historical Publishers, 1881.

Boren, Kerry Ross, TREASURE WORLD, Vol. 6, No. 3, 1972.

Botkin, B. A., TREASURY OF WESTERN FOLKLORE, edited by Botkin, Crown Publishers, Inc., 1951.

Brigham, Lillian Rice, HISTORICAL GUIDE TO COLORADO, W. H. Kistler Co., 1931.

Brigham, Lillian Rice, COLORADO TRAVELORE, Peerless Printing, 1938.

Brown, Robert L., AN EMPIRE OF SILVER, 1965.

Busher, Jimmie, LOST MINES AND TREASURES OF THE SOUTHWEST, Treasure Guide Publishing Co., 1975.

Cairns, Mary L., GRAND LAKE: THE PIONEERS, World Press, 1946.

Cairns, Mary L., THE OLDEN DAYS, World Press, 1954.

Campa, Arthur L., TREASURE OF THE SANGRE DE CRISTOS, 1963.

Carhart, Arthur H., COLORADO, Coward-Mc Cann, Inc., 1932.

Carson, H. Glenn, LOST LEDGES OF THE WEST, 1991.

Carson, Xanthus, TREASURE! BONANZAS WORTH A BILLION BUCKS.

CENTRAL CITY REGISTER-CALL, 1954.

Christopher, Gary W., TREASURE WORLD, Vol. 8, No. 11, 1974.

Cook, John W., HANDS UP, W. F. Robinson Printing Company, 1897.

Cook, D. J., DENVER POST, 1947.

Cook, D. J., ROCKY MOUNTAIN NEWS, 1949.

Crofutt, George A., GRIP-SACK GUIDE TO COLORADO, Denver, Alvord Co., 1881.

Davidson, Levette J., and Blake, Forrester, editors, ROCKY MOUNTAIN TALES, University of Oklahoma Press, 1947.

DENVER POST, EMPIRE MAGAZINE, 1957. Denver Times, 1899.

Dobie, Frank J., CORONADO'S CHILDREN, Southwest Press, 1930.

Duncan, S. Blackwell, TRUE TREASURE, Vol. 5, No. 10, 1971.

Dunning, Harold Marion, OVER HILL AND VALE, Johnson Publishing Co., 1956.

Eberhart, Perry, GUIDE TO COLORADO GHOST TOWNS AND MINING CAMPS, Sage Books, 1959.

Eberhart, Perry, TREASURE TALES OF THE ROCKIES, 1961.

Eichler, Geo. R., COLORADO PLACE NAMES, copyright, 1977.

Ellis, Amanda M., LEGENDS AND TALES OF THE ROCKIES, The Denton Printing Co., 1954.

Ellis, Amanada M., THE STRANGE UNCERTAIN YEARS, The Shoe String Press, Inc., 1950.

FAIRPLAY FLAME, 1880.

Ferguson, Robert G., LOST TREASURE: THE SEARCH FOR HIDDEN GOLD, Vantage Press, 1957.

Ferguson, Harvey, RIO GRANDE, Tudor Publishing Co., 1945.

Forbes, William B., TRUE WEST, Vol 8, No. 5, 1961

Fossett, Frank, COLORADO, ITS GOLD AND SILVER MINES, C. G. Crawford, 1880.

Griswold, Don and Jean, A CARBONATE CAMP CALLED LEADVILLE, University of Denver Press 1951.

GUNNISON COURIER, 1950.

Hafen, LeRoy and Ann, THE COLORADO STORY Old West Publishing Company, 1956.

Hafen, LeRoy, PIKES PEAK GOLD RUSH GUIDEBOOKS OF 1859, edited by Hafen, Arthur H. Clark Co., 1941.

Hallenbeck, Clive, LEGENDS OF THE SPANISH SOUTHWEST, The Aruthur H. Clark Co., 1938.

Hall, Frank, HISTORY OF THE STATE OF COLORADO, (4 volumes) Blakely Printing Company, 1889-1895.

Hedges, William Hawkins, PIKES PEAK...OR BUSTED, Branding Iron Press, 1954.

Hollon, Eugene, BEYOND THE CROSSED TIMBERS, Travels of Randolph B. Marcy 1812-1887, University of Oklahoma Press, 1949.

Horgan, Paul, GREAT RIVER, THE RIO GRANDE (two volumes), University of Oklahoma Press, 1954.

Inman, C. Henry, THE OLD SANTA FE TRAIL, The Story of a Great Highway, Crane & Co., 1916.

Jameson, W. C., BURIED TREASURES OF THE ROCKY MOUNTAIN WEST, 1993.

Johnston, William Cameron, AMERICAN TREASURE HUNTERS GUIDE, published by author, 1952.

Kelly, Charles, THE OUTLAW TRAIL, The Devin-Adair Co., 1959.

Ketchum, K. M., TRUE TREASURE, Vol. 8, No. 12, 1974.

Kildaire, Maurice, TREASURE WORLD, Vol. 6, No. 5, 1972.

Klink, Richard E., LAND OF ROOM ENOUGH AND TIME, 1953.

Latham, John H., editor, FAMOUS LOST MINES OF THE OLD WEST, pages 151- 152, copyright 1971.

Lavender, David, THE BIG DIVIDE, Doubleday and Co., Inc., 1948.

Lavender, David, ONE MAN'S WEST, Doubleday and Co., Inc., 1956.

LEADVILLE CHRONICLE, 1879.

Long, Margaret, SMOKY HILL TRAIL, W. H. Kistler Co, 1943.

Lovelace, Leland, LOST MINES AND HIDDEN TREASURE, Naylor Co., 1956.

Marshall, John B., and Corne- lius,Temple H., GOLDEN TREASURES OF THE SAN JUAN, copyright 1961.

Marshall, John B., and Cornelius, Temple H. TRUE WEST, Vol. 15, No. 3, 1968.

Montroy, Ila P., PIONEERS OF THE SAN JUAN COUNTY, Volume I, 1942.

Nasatir, A. P., BEFORE LEWIS & CLARK, edited by Nasatir, Published by the St. Louis Historical Documents Foundation, 1952.

Ormes, Robert M., GUIDE TO THE COLORADO MOUNTAINS, Sage Books, 1955.

Osteen, Ike, TRUE WEST, Vol. 16, No. 3, 1969.

Osteen, Ike, OLD WEST, Vol. 11, No. 5, 1975.

Pearl, Richard M., COLORADO GEM TRAILS, Sage Books, 1951.

Penfield, Thomas, DIRECTORY OF BURIED OR SUNKEN TREASURES AND LOST MINES OF THE UNITED STATES, True Treasure Publications, 1971.

Penfield, Thomas, LOST TREASURE TRAILS, Grosset and Dunlop Inc., 1954.

Perkin, Robert L., FIRST HUNDRED YEARS, Doubleday & Company, 1959.

Pike, Zebulon, ZEBULON PIKE'S ARKANSAW JOURNAL, edited by Stephen Harding Hart and Archer Butler Hulbert, 1932, published by the Stewart Commission of Colorado College and the Denver Public Library.

Porter, Clyde and Mae Reed, RUXTON OF THE ROCKIES, collected by the Porters, edited by LeRoy Hafen, University of Oklahoma Press, 1950.

Quiett, Glenn Chesney, PAY DIRT, D. Appleton-Century Co., 1936.

Rockwell, Wilson, SUNSET SLOPE, Big Mountain Press, 1956.

ROCKY MOUNTAIN NEWS, 1948.

ROCKY MOUNTAIN NEWS, 1955.

ROCKY MOUNTAIN NEWS, 1959.

Ruxton, George F., LIFE IN THE FAR WEST, edited by LeRoy Hafen, University of Ok-lahoma Press, 1951.

Sage, Rufus, LETTERS AND SCENES IN THE ROCKY MOUNTAINS (two volumes), edited by LeRoy Hafen, The Arthur H. Clark Co., 1956.

Sporleder, Louis B., HUAJATOLLA, COLORADO'S MYSTIC MOUNTAIN, Pueblo, 1916.

Sporleder, Louis B., ROMANCE OF SPANISH PEAKS, O'Brien Press, 1960.

Sprague, Marshall, MONEY MOUNTAIN, Little Brown & Co., 1953.

Stone, William Fiske, HISTORY OF COLORADO (four volumes), S. J. Clark Publishing Co., 1918.

SUMMIT COUNTY JOURNAL, Breckenridge, 1936.

Terry, Thomas P., UNITED STATES TREASURE ATLAS, VOLUME 2, pages 179-210, copyright 1985.

Thomas, Alfred Barnaby, AFTER CORONADO, SPANISH EXPLORATION NORTHEAST OF NEW MEXICO, 1696-1727, translated and edited by Thomas, University of Oklahoma Press, 1935.

Walrich, William, THE DENVER POST, Empire Magazine, 1950.

Watson, Editha L., ASPEN TIMES, 1935.

Watson, Editha L., CENTRAL CITY REGISTER-CALL, 1935.

Watson, Editha L., DOLORES STAR, 1935.

Watson, Editha L., FLAGLER NEWS, 1935.

Watson, Editha L., LEADVILLE HERALD DEMOCRAT, 1935.

Watson, Editha L., LIBERTY PRESS of Denver, 1935.

Watson, Editha L., Grand Junction DAILY SENTINAL, 1936.

Wellman, Paul Iselin, GLORY, GOD AND GOLD, a Narrative History, Doubleday & Co., Inc., 1954.

Willison, George, HERE THEY DUG GOLD, A. L. Burt Co., 1931.

Wolle, Muriel Sibell, STAMPEDE TO TIMBERLINE, published by author, Boulder, 1957.

Wolle, Muriel Sibell, TIMBERLINE TAILINGS, 1977.

GHOST TOWNS

Ghost towns are not listed within these pages. It is not because those places where people used to live are not interesting or very much worthwhile to treasure hunters, for they are! The simple problem of not having sufficient space demands the omission of ghost sites.

Don't ignore those now uninhabited spots. Ghost towns are not just dots on maps, they were where people lived, worked, and at times lost or hid their wealth. In Colorado there are approximately 4,000 ghost sites. Leanne Boyd and I put together a two volume set of the Atlas of Colorado Ghost Towns. There were two volumes, more than 350 pages, all sorts of maps and illustrations, and about 4,000 listings of actual sites. If you have any interest in treasure in Colorado you definitely should have and study these two books.

A listing of books dealing with the Colorado ghost towns is given here for your possible attention and use.

Boyd, Leanne C., and Carson, H. Glenn, ATLAS OF COLORADO GHOST TOWNS, Volume I, copyright 1984, 134 pages.
Boyd, Leanne C., and Carson, H. Glenn, ATLAS OF COLORADO GHOST TOWNS, Volume II, copyright 1985, 182 pages.

Carson, H. Glenn, HUNTING THE GHOST TOWNS, copyright 1977, 84 pages.
Brown, Robert L., GHOST TOWNS OF THE COLORADO ROCKIES, copyright 1968, 401 pages.
Brown, Robert L., COLORADO GHOST TOWNS PAST AND PRESENT, copyright 1972, 322 pages.
Brown, Rober L., JEEP TRAILS TO COLORADO GHOST TOWNS, copy right 1963, 245 pages.
Dallas, Sandra, COLORADO GHOST TOWNS AND MINING CAMPS, copyright 1985, 254 pages.
Eberhart, Perry, GUIDE TO COLORADO GHOST TOWNS AND MINING CAMPS, copyright 1959, 496 pages.

Shaffer, Ray, A GUIDE TO PLACES ON THE COLORADO PRAIRIE, copyright 1978, 386 pages.

Wolle, Muriel Sibell, STAMPEDE TO TIMBERLINE, copyright 1949, 583 pages.

Wolle, Muriel Sibell, TIMBERLINE TAILINGS, copyright 1977, 337 pages.

OTHER HELPFUL AND INTERESTING BOOKS
for Colorado treasure buffs

COINSHOOTING, HOW & WHERE TO DO IT, H. Glenn Carson, 1971.

COINSHOOTING II, H. Glenn Carson, 1982.

COINSHOOTING III, H. Glenn Carson, 1994.

A NEW GUIDE TO TREASURE HUNTING, H. Glenn Carson, 1992.

CACHE HUNTING, H. Glenn Carson, 1984.

CACHE HUNTING II, H. Glenn Carson, 1988.

HANDBOOK OF TREASURE SIGNS AND SYMBOLS, Mary Carson, 1980.

GOLD...ABC's OF PANNING, E. S. "Rocky" LeGaye, 1975.

THE EXTRACTION OF FREE GOLD, Al McGowen, 1973.

PRINCIPAL GOLD-PRODUCING DISTRICTS OF COLORADO, Geological Survey Professional Paper reprint.